W9-CDX-438

ARCHAEOLOGY

Herman Rooks

DISCARDED

KETER BOOKS

This book is compiled from material originally published
in the *Encyclopaedia Judaica*

Copyright ©1974, Keter Publishing House Jerusalem Ltd.
P.O.Box 7145, Jerusalem, Israel

Cat. No. 25074
ISBN 0 7065 1334 7

Printed in Israel

CONTENTS

CONTRIBUTORS

Prof. Michael Avi-Yonah: Professor of Archaeology and of the History of Art, the Hebrew University of Jerusalem

Prof. Yohanan Aharoni: Professor of Archaeology and of the Historical Geography of Palestine, Tel Aviv University

Dr. Moshe Dothan: Director of Excavations and Surveys and Deputy Director, Department of Antiquities and Museums, Jerusalem

Dr. Avraham Negev: Senior Lecturer in Classical Archaeology, the Hebrew University of Jerusalem

Joseph Braslavi (Braslavski) (deceased): Historian, Tel Aviv

Prof. Nachman Avigad: Professor of Archaeology, the Hebrew University of Jerusalem

Prof. Benjamin Mazar: former President and Professor of Archaeology and of Jewish History, the Hebrew University of Jerusalem

Prof. Yigael Yadin: Lieutenant General (Res.), Israel Defense Forces; Professor of Archaeology, the Hebrew University of Jerusalem

Dr. Joseph Naveh: Research Fellow in West-Semitic Epigraphy, the Hebrew University of Jerusalem; Jerusalem-District Archaeologist, Department of Antiquities, Jerusalem

Prof. Frederick Fyvie Bruce: Professor of Biblical Criticism and Exegesis, the University of Manchester, England

Mordkhai Neishtat: Journalist, Tel Aviv

CHRONOLOGICAL TABLE

DATE	ARCHAEOLOGICAL PERIOD	HISTORICAL PERIOD	
12,000–7500 B.C.E.	Mesolithic	Pre-History	Natufian Culture
7500–4000 B.C.E.	Neolithic	Pre-History	Yarmukian Culture
4000–3150 B.C.E.	Chalcolithic	Pre-History	Ghassulian Culture
3150–2850 B.C.E.	Early Bronze I		Bet Yerah Culture
2850–2650 B.C.E.	Early Bronze II		
2650–2350 B.C.E.	Early Bronze III	Early Canaanite	
2350–2200 B.C.E.	Early Bronze IV (III A)		
2200–2000 B.C.E.	Middle Bronze I		
2000–1750 B.C.E.	Middle Bronze II A	Middle Canaanite	
1750–1550 B.C.E.	Middle Bronze II B		Hyksos Period
1550–1400 B.C.E.	Late Bronze I		Egyptian Rule
1400–1300 B.C.E.	Late Bronze II A	Late Canaanite	El Amarna Period
1300–1200 B.C.E.	Late Bronze II B		
1200–1150 B.C.E.	Iron Age I A		Israelite Invasion
1150–1000 B.C.E.	Iron Age I B	Israelite I	Philistine Invasion
1000– 900 B.C.E.	Iron Age II A	Israelite II	
900– 800 B.C.E.	Iron Age II B		
800– 586 B.C.E.	Iron Age II C	Israelite III	
586– 332 B.C.E.	Persian		
332– 152 B.C.E.	Hellenistic I		
152– 37 B.C.E.	Hellenistic (Hasmonean) II		
37 B.C.E.–70 C.E.	Roman (Herodian) I		
70– 324 C.E.	Roman II, III		
324– 640 C.E.	Byzantine		
640–1099 C.E.	Early Arab		
1099–1291 C.E.	Crusader		
1291–1516 C.E.	Mamluk		

B.C.E.   Before Common Era (B.C.)

C.E.   Common Era (A.D.)

Archaeological sites in Ereẓ Israel.

→

1 THE ARCHAEOLOGY OF ISRAEL

Introduction. The term archaeology is derived from the two Greek words *archaios* ("ancient") and *logos* ("knowledge"). In its modern sense it has come to mean the study of the material remains of the past and is generally restricted to the study of artifacts dating up to the end of the Middle Ages. Although the discovery of written material is often the result of archaeological investigations, its study does not belong to archaeology proper; the disciplines of epigraphy, paleography, and numismatics are thus related to archaeology, but they can be regarded as comprising separate fields of research. The importance of archaeology obviously decreases as written sources become more plentiful. For the period before the invention of writing (throughout the whole of prehistory), archaeology is the sole source of information. The written record of the Bible, however, must also be supplemented by the study of material remains; mighty peoples such as the Sumerians and Hittites would be practically unknown but for archaeology. Its results have been decisive even for the later periods, as, for example, in regard to the existence of a Jewish figurative art.

Archaeological research has been naturally most instructive in all matters concerning the material side of life, such as the transition from food-gathering to agriculture, the beginnings of irrigation, the types of wheat and other products grown, etc. It has been also possible to follow the development of architecture, from the earliest fortifications at Jericho, by way of the Israelite four-room house, the Canaanite palaces and temples, and the revolutionary, introduction of Greek models in the Hellenistic period.

Methods. The main methods of acquiring knowledge of the material past are surveys and excavations. The survey (surface exploration) has been the principal archaeological method for exploring unknown and largely deserted areas in the ancient Orient. Explorers recorded in writing, or graphically, all visible or accessible ruins, without, however, excavating them. The Napoleonic survey of Egypt (1799), the surveys of Wood at Baalbek and Palmyra (1753, 1757), and the British survey of western Palestine (1871–77) are landmarks in this stage of archaeological research. The rising costs and complications of modern excavations have revived the systematic surface surveys and their results have become increasingly reliable, since the exact dates of pottery collected on the surface can now be established. The

General view of excavations at Tel Ashdod, showing workers uncovering Early Iron Age brick houses of the Philistine period.

principal method of archaeology is, however, excavation, i.e., the systematic removal of accumulated earth and debris covering ancient remains. The period when the excavator searched mainly for removable antiquities was followed first by the systematic excavation by trenches and then by the systematic removal of whole strata. This has now been superseded by the stratigraphic examination of sections of earth accumulated against the foundations of walls. The various phases of the history of a building, such as the foundation trenches and their fill, the midden accumulated against the face of the wall, robbers' trenches, and levels of destruction, are distinguished and dated by a careful examination of the pottery and other remains. In this way the history of each stratum can be determined. The dating of the strata is based on both absolute criteria (levels of destruction associated with known events, inscriptions, and coins) and the relative chronological dating of pottery sequences. Pottery vessels are easily broken, and though their sherds are valueless they are practically indestructible. As pottery styles change and develop through the ages, these sherds are the best indication of the chronology of a settlement. Other means of dating, such as the examination of carbon (C^{14}) contents and fluorine tests, are valid mainly for the long periods of pre- and proto-history.

Archaeology and the Origins of Israel. Up to the time of the Patriarchs (Middle Bronze Age, 2200–1550 B.C.E.), the ancestors of Israel shared in the general development of the human race in the ancient East, as is revealed by archaeological research. The general development includes the emergence of homo sapiens, the transition from food-gathering and hunting to agriculture and animal domestication, the creation of settlements, the beginnings of religious cults, the consolidation of political entities, and the crystallization of the cultures of Egypt and Mesopotamia which thereafter began to influence Canaan. According to the biblical account, the family of Abraham originated on the fringe of Sumerian society forming part of the western-Semitic groups which began to infiltrate into Sumer

3

Reconstructing a jar from pottery sherds.

in the 19th century B.C.E. As a nomadic group, these forefathers of Israel are not likely to have left material traces of their passage; Mesopotamian documents, however, illustrate some aspects of their story. Thus a document found at Nuzi parallels the biblical narrative of Jacob, his wives, and his maidservants. The archives of Mari furnish examples of biblical names and parallels to prophecy. The connection between the Habiru (written Hapiru) mentioned in these and other sources, and especially in the el-Amarna letters, and the Hebrews, is one of the most controversial questions raised by archaeology. The Habiru appear as a class of wanderers on the fringe of society, and occasionally as mercenaries or bandits. Their name is possibly connected with the root '*br* ("beyond"). Another problem raised by archaeology is the relationship between the early Hebrews and the Hyksos invasion of Egypt. The names of Hyksos rulers include many Semitic forms, such as Jacob-el. Whether a connection exists between the sojourn in Egypt and the Hyksos invasion has not yet been resolved. Egyptian art furnishes vivid representations of Semitic nomads entering Egypt (fresco painting in a 12th dynasty tomb at Bani Hasan (Beni Hasan)) and of Egyptian bondage (slaves, including an aged Semite at work making bricks for a temple, depicted on a fresco in the tomb of Rekhmire,[1] 18th dynasty). Archaeological sources yield a broad picture of the background of the patriarchal story, of the Canaanite cities and sanctuaries, and of the power vacuum at the time of the Exodus. The mention of the tribe of Asher in Egyptian documents, as well as the name "Israel" in the famous stele of Merneptah, raises the question of a possible Hebrew presence in Canaan before Joshua's conquest. The seizure of Shechem by the Habiru under Labaya can explain the biblical account of the peaceful occupation of the central hill country. Archaeology has also provided considerable important evidence on the development of the Semitic alphabetic script. The date of its origin (Middle Bronze Age) and its fairly wide diffusion in Canaan make more plausible an early use of written records, as is implied in the event of the Lawgiving. The discovery of the archives of Ugarit has thrown new light on Canaanite mythology and religious poetry, providing valid parallels with the epic poems, wisdom literature, and psalms included in the biblical canon.

[1] King of Egypt, reigned 1236–1223 B.C.E.

5

Philistine clay jug, 12th century B.C.E., found at **Tell Itun**, south of Hebron, decorated with typical bird and fish designs.

6   Anthropoid coffin lid from Beth-Shean, c. 12th century B.C.E.

→

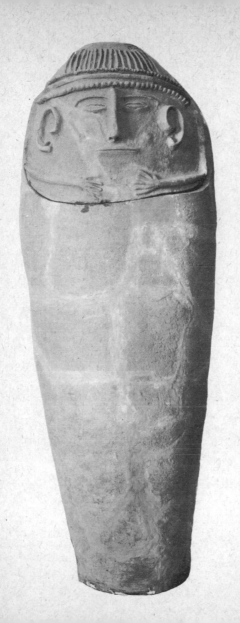

7

From Joshua's Conquest to the Babylonian Exile. It is with the emergence of the Israelites as a group of conquering tribes that material evidence of their history may be expected. The destruction of the Late Bronze Age cities of Lachish, Beth-El, Tell Beit Mirsim, and Hazor pinpoints Joshua's conquest in the mid-13th century B.C.E. In Jericho and Ai, however, no evidence corroborating the biblical account has thus far been found, and at Shechem the transition from the Canaanite to the Israelite period seems to have been peaceful. Furthermore, there is evidence of Israelite infiltration into the wooded parts of Galilee, while the Canaanites held the plains and their cities. The lower material standard of the Israelite dwellings and pottery points up the difference between the newcomers from the desert and the well-established Canaanites. The Philistine occupation has been evidenced by their characteristic pottery (derived ultimately from Mycenean prototypes) and the anthropoid clay coffins found at Beth-Shean and attributed to the Philistine garrison stationed there. The destruction and total abandonment of Shiloh mentioned by Jeremiah (7:12, 14) is fully confirmed by archaeological evidence, although the Book of Samuel passes over it in silence. Excavations at Jerusalem have shown that the Jebusite town extended much further east than previously believed and that its conquest by way of its water tunnel (the *zinnor* ("gutter") of II Samuel 5:8) was quite feasible. Many traces of Solomon's religious and administrative activity have survived, among them the temple at Arad with its threefold division, which recalls both the Temple of Jerusalem and Canaanite prototypes found at Hazor and at Tell Ta'īnāt (or Tainat, Syria), and the fortress gates at Hazor, Gezer, and Megiddo built by Solomon's architects according to a uniform plan. For the period of the Divided Monarchy, archaeology provides excellent proof of the might of the House of Omri: his palace and walls at Samaria and Hazor, the buildings and huge water tunnels of Ahab at Hazor and Megiddo, and the ivories from his "ivory house" (I Kings 22:39) which, incidentally, supply a visual image of the ornaments of the Temple. The written sources from the period of the monarchy (the ostraca from Tell Qasīle, Samaria, Arad, and Lachish) provide interesting sidelights on the political, religious, and military history of the period. The Siloam

Fourteen-line fragment of a letter written in ink on pottery in the reign of Josiah (639–609 B.C.E.). Found at Meẓad Ḥashavyahu near Yavneh-Yam, it is a peasant's complaint to the governor that his coat has been impounded by a creditor. The request for its return is in accordance with Mosaic law (Ex. 22:25–26, Deut. 24:10–13).

The "Black Obelisk" of Shalmaneser III of Assyria from Nimrud (c. ninth century B.C.E.). According to the cuneiform inscription, the second register from the top shows "Jehu, son of Omri" paying tribute to the king.

inscription[2] and the Siloam tunnel itself illustrate the waterworks of Hezekiah (II Chron. 32:30). The Judean fortresses and settlements in the Negev demonstrate the pioneering efforts of Uzziah and his successors there. The prophetic strictures against idolatry can be comprehended against the background of the numerous Astarte figurines

[2] An inscription in biblical Hebrew telling the story of the digging of the Siloam tunnel

found in excavated Israelite strata. The finds at Samaria fully bear out the biblical account of the Phoenician influence at the court of Ahab and Jezebel. The discoveries at Ramat Raḥel indicate its spread to Judah. Even such an obscure detail as the "horns of the altar" (I Kings 2:28) has now been clarified by archaeological finds. The destruction of the Arad temple and the gradual disappearance of idolatrous motifs from Judean seals are evidence of Josiah's reforms. The letter of a wronged peasant from Meẓad Ḥashavyahu (near Yavneh-Yam) shows how deeply the social laws of the Bible had penetrated during the reign of Josiah.

Painting on a pottery sherd from Ramat Raḥel, Jerusalem, of what is believed to be the seated figure of a king of Judah (c. 600 B.C.E.).

Finds made outside Israel have also greatly contributed to advancing knowledge of the biblical period. Thus the inscription of Mesha, king of Moab, supplies a hostile account of the events mentioned in II Kings 3. The "Black Obelisk" of Shalmanesser of Assyria contains the only extant image of a king of Israel (Jehu), apart from the painting on a sherd from Ramat Raḥel, which probably represents a king of Judah. The inscriptions of Shishak of Egypt and of Tiglath-Pileser III of Assyria add geographical substance to the biblical accounts of their conquests (I Kings 14:25; II Kings 15:29). The chronicles and reliefs of Sennacherib of Assyria present textual and visual evidence of his campaign against Hezekiah while Nebuchadnezzar's chronicle contains a record of the events of 597 B.C.E.

From the Return to Zion to the Fall of Jerusalem. The period of Persian domination, including the First Return to Zion, is as obscure in archaeology as it is in history. The principal material remains of this period include the walls built by Nehemiah in Jerusalem, the administrative center continuing at Ramat Raḥel, the evidence of Phoenician settlements at Tell Makmīsh near Tel Aviv and at Tell Magadim on the Carmel coast, and a settlement of Greek mercenaries at Athlit. The first signs of Greek penetration appear in this period: Attic pottery found along the coast and on the Gaza—Elath road and the YHD coins of the Judean authorities, which are an imitation of Attic drachmas. The Hellenistic and Roman periods which conclude the era of the Second Temple are marked by the conflict between the Jewish nation and contemporary world civilizations. The spread of Greek culture is illustrated by the Greek temple at Dora, the Hellenistic remains at Ashdod, the paintings of the Mareshah tombs, the temple at Beth-Shean, and the strong walls of Samaria. The Hasmoneans who turned back the tide of Hellenism have left few monuments aside from their coins. Part of the walls of Jerusalem date to their rule, as do three monumental tombs in the vicinity of the town. Their hellenizing opponents have left a magnificent monument of Greco-Oriental art in the unfinished temple at 'Irāq al-Amīr. Some of the most impressive monuments in the country have survived from the reign of Herod and his dynasty, such as the enclosure walls of the Temple esplanade. Recent excavations have uncovered the imposing height of the Herodian wall, its huge ashlars, and the broad streets and piazzas surrounding it. Other Herodian remains are the wall surrounding the Machpelah sanctuary at Hebron, the fortresses at Herodium and Masada, the palace at Jericho, the harbor and walls

Jason's Tomb in Jerusalem. This reconstructed Hasmonean burial chamber was erected during the reign of Alexander Yannai (beginning of first century C.E.). On the porch wall is one of the earliest representations of the seven-branched *menorah*.

of Caesarea, and the temple and walls of Samaria. The monumental sepulchers dating from this period present a vivid contrast of classicizing forms with oriental overtones; the spreading use of ossuaries indicates the prevalence of the Pharisaic belief in individual resurrection. The strict aniconism of Jewish art—to which even Herod subscribed as is evidenced by his palaces at Masada—is one of the most prominent features of this period. The Qumran "monastery" and the scrolls originating from it have visibly and legibly presented the Essene contribution to the religious development of this crucial period. The Pontius Pilate inscription from Caesarea is the only external evidence of this New Testament personage. Explorations of the Negev and southern Transjordan have yielded much information on the development of the Nabateans, in some senses parallel, and in others contrary to, that of the Jews. Their rock-hewn palaces and delicate eggshell pottery remain

The Dead Sea Scrolls. Column 5 of the War Scroll from Qumran
(c. first century C.E.).

A section of the Herodian enclosure wall (c. first century C.E.) of the Temple esplanade in Jerusalem, showing typical Herodian masonry.

Dedicatory inscription by Pontius Pilate, procurator of Judea, in honor of Tiberius Caesar (14 C.E.–37 C.E.). The inscription, found on a building in Caesarea, reads: *Tiberieum/...[Pon]tius/ Pilatus [Praef]ectus Iuda[ea]e.*

outstanding examples of the transformation of Hellenistic culture by an Oriental nation. Tangible remains, apart from coins, of the two armed struggles against the Romans—the war of the Zealots and that of Bar Kokhba[3]—include for the former, the burnt debris in the foundations of

16 [3] Leader of the revolt in Judea against Rome (132–135 C.E.)

"Seat of Moses," a stone *bimah* from the synagogue at
Chorazin, near the Sea of Galilee (second–third century C.E.).
The inscription reads: "Remembered be for good Judan b.
Ishmael who made this stoa and its staircase/As his reward
may he have a share with the righteous."

houses in the Old City of Jerusalem, an inscription in
Jerusalem mentioning Vespasian,[4] and the vestiges at
Masada with the pathetic evidence of the Zealots' last
stand, and for the latter, the caves in the Judean desert
where a wealth of everyday articles and written documents
have been discovered. This period of struggle with the
Greco-Roman world was witness to the development of a
rich Jewish Diaspora of which synagogue inscriptions in
particular have survived (at Schedia near Alexandria), and
possibly synagogue ruins (at Delos). The earliest known
synagogues in Erez Israel are those at Masada, Herodium,
and of Theodotus at Jerusalem, the last destined character-
istically for sojourners in the Holy City (Acts 6:9).

[4] Roman emperor 69–79 C.E.

The beginnings of the Gothic style are apparent in the Crusader church at Abu Ghosh outside Jerusalem.

After the Destruction of the Jewish Commonwealth. The change in the character of Jewish life after the loss of its territorial status was gradual. Large sections of the population still lived compactly in Galilee where, apart from specifically religious buildings, material evidence of their life has been found (e.g., at Chorazin). On the whole, however, Jewish archaeology from the third century becomes a denominational lore, influenced by its surroundings and other artistic trends. The Galilean synagogue of the early type (second to fourth century C.E.) and the necropolis at Bet She'arim show an astonishing development of Jewish figurative art, which continues in the mosaic pavements of the later-type synagogues (Hammath-Tiberias, Bet Alfa). From the mid-sixth century this figurative thematism becomes gradually restricted until the final victory of aniconism under Islam.

Remains of the later periods are standing in great numbers and some of them, such as the Church of the

Nativity in Bethlehem, are still devoted to their original purpose. Nevertheless, archaeological research has disclosed new facts about the Byzantine, Arab, and Crusader periods. Thus the earlier (Constantinian) Church of the Nativity as well as dozens of Byzantine churches from the fifth century onward (Shavei Zion, Evron, Masada, etc.) have been excavated. The excavations of the Umayyad[5] palaces at Khirbat al-Mafjar, north of Jericho, of Khirbat Minnim (al-Minya) on the shore of the Sea of Galilee, and, in Jerusalem at the Southern Wall, have revealed a new dimension of Moslem art — stucco sculptures of the Caliph, his warriors, dancers, and dwarfs, together with the beginnings of the typical Islamic arabesque decoration. Other excavations of the Islamic period have been the eighth-century cisterns at al-Ramleh (Khirbat al-'Unayziyya) in which the pointed arch was used for the first time, the caravanserai at Abu Ghosh, and the remains of the Arab city of Ramleh itself.

The crusaders were great builders, and their castles and forts still dot the countryside of Erez Israel. Excavations have shown the development of the crusader castle, beginning with the early type at Belvoir (Agrippina) with its square towers in an outer and inner wall. This castle was the work of the Hospitaler Order (1182). On the other hand, the later castle of Athlit (Chastiau Pelerins) built in 1218 reflects the experience acquired in the Orient in the meantime: the double wall is arranged in two tiers, with the rounded towers of the inner wall dominating the outer one; a fosse going down below sea level ensured that no mining operations by besiegers could be undertaken with success. The fortress of Montfort, built for the Teutonic Order in 1228, was also provided with a deep fosse, cutting off the spur on which it was built from the Galilean mountains. The excavations of the Crusader churches at Athlit, Abu Ghosh, and in the Kidron Valley east of Jerusalem revealed the beginnings of the Gothic style, which became dominant

[5] An Arab dynasty 660–750 c.e.

The tower at Ramleh, with its imitation Gothic belfry, was built between 1267 and 1318.

in Europe from the 13th century onward. The material culture of the crusaders appears as a mixture of elements imported from Europe (furniture, weapons, ornaments, and especially those in the churches, e.g., the capitals in the Nazareth church) with other objects of Muslim origin. The glazed pottery from the Crusader period, for example, reveals a combination of Byzantine and Islamic techniques.

History of Archaeological Research in Israel. The antiquities of the Holy Land attracted the attention of talmudic sages and Christian pilgrims from the second century on. Some of this interest can still be seen in the itineraries of the Middle Ages. In the 17th and 18th centuries Quaresmius and Reland summed up all the then existing knowledge, which was to a large extent traditional and unconnected with reality. In the 19th century, the great surveys of Guérin and the Palestine Exploration Fund were paralleled by the first excavations at Jerusalem, in particular the explorations of Warren (1867) around the Temple enclosure. Toward the end of the century, Frederick Bliss and R. A. S. Macalister continued to excavate at Jerusalem; they also made a rapid exploration of tells in the Shephelah (1894–1900). In 1890 Flinders Petrie excavated Tell al-Hasī, noting the succession of strata and distinguishing between the pottery of each period. In the first decade of the 20th century the great excavations at Gezer (1902–09) and Samaria (1908–11) marked the beginnings of the modern method of excavation, including the registration of all objects found and the distinction of strata. The explorations of Megiddo, Jericho, and Shechem, as well as the survey of the Galilean synagogues (1905), all belong to this first period of scientific study, which came to an end with World War I.

Under the British Mandate, large-scale excavations were undertaken by American archaeologists at Megiddo (1925–39), Beth-Shean (1921–33), and Tell Beit Mirsim (1926–32). The last-named site, with its meticulous excavation by William F. Albright, served to establish pottery sequence on a firm basis. The British excavations at Samaria (1931–35) developed the method of stratigraphical sections, while the work of Petrie and his school at Tell al-Fàra (Tell Sharuḥen) and Tell al-Ajjūl (1927–36), and of J. L. Starkey at Lachish (1932–38), added much to the knowledge of the Middle and Late Bronze Ages. Excavation was extended to fields outside the scope of biblical studies, such as the Nabatean and Byzantine cities in the Negev (H. Dunscombe Colt, 1934–38) and the Crusader fortress of Athlit (1930–35).

Jewish scholars of the Hebrew University and the Jewish Palestine Exploration Society (now the Israel Exploration Society) concentrated on the remains of the Second Temple period (Sukenik-Mayer from 1925 to 1927 on the Third Wall of Jerusalem), Jewish tombs (Slouschz in 1924 in Jerusalem, Maisler [Mazar] in the patriarchal necropolis at Bet She'arim, 1936–39), and synagogues (Sukenik at Bet Alfa and Ḥammat Gader). The Arab revolt, World War II, and the troubled times which ended with the Israel War of Independence suspended all archaeological activity. After 1948 Israel scholars were at first occupied with excavating sites which were in danger because of the rapid development of the country (Tell Qasīle, Jaffa, Bet Yeraḥ) but in the 1950s a series of large-scale planned excavations were undertaken at Hazor (1955–58, 1968), Ramat Raḥel (1959–62), Avedat (1958–60), Caesarea (1959–63), caves in the neighborhood of the Dead Sea (1960–61), Masada (1963–65), Arad (1962–65), Ashdod (1962–), and Dan (1966–). Some of these, e.g., Caesarea, Tel Ẓeror, Azor, and Beersheba, were undertaken by foreign expeditions (French, Italian, and Japanese). At the same time work was resumed in Jordan, especially at Jericho (1952–57), Shechem, Tell Dothan, various tells in the Jordan Valley, and Jerusalem. After the Six-Day War of 1967; Israel archaeologists commenced excavation around the Western and Southern walls of the Temple site (1968–) and in the Jewish quarter of the Old City of Jerusalem. A survey of the Golan Heights began in 1968, revealing intensive Jewish settlement during the first few centuries of the Common Era. Other excavations were carried out at Tell Dan in the north, at Tell Aphek (Rosh ha-Ayin) near Petaḥ Tikvah, at Beersheba, and at Shikmonah near Haifa. At Eshtemoa, south of Hebron, the ancient synagogue was excavated and restored. A prehistoric research was carried out in the Jordan Valley, south of the Sea of Galilee, on the Mount Carmel ridge and other places. In Sinai, archaeological explorations were carried out at different sites.

Archaeology is a matter of widespread interest. Excavations receive extensive press, radio, and television coverage, and lectures and conventions on the subject are widely attended. The Department of Antiquities and Museums in the Ministry of Education and Culture conducts country-wide surveys, protects ancient sites, arranges for the preservation and display of finds, and provides assistance for local and foreign archaeologists. The Israel Exploration Society not only conducts excavations and publishes the findings, but also does much to spread knowledge of the subject. In addition to the Israel Museum and the Rockefeller Museum in Jerusalem, a number of towns and villages maintain local collections, many of which display the discoveries of amateur archaeologists from the neighborhood.

Evaluation. The nature of archaeological evidence is such that it can be expected to provide only a background for the history of an ancient nation, such as the Jews, whose past has been recorded in a written document. This fact explains the relative importance of the fragments of written evidence discovered in excavations, despite their numerical insignificance. For topographical and chronological research, archaeology is vital; it is sufficient to recall that the first certain date in biblical history—the battle of Karkar in 853 B.C.E.—was established through archaeological findings. Archaeology has supplied a wider view of the biblical past, and has discovered trends in Jewish history which have disappeared from literature in the course of time. It is also a vital factor in the linking of Jewish national consciousness to the soil of Israel.

2 MAJOR ARCHAEOLOGICAL SITES

i ARAD. Arad is an important biblical city in the eastern Negev which controlled the main road to Edom and Elath.

In the Bible, "the Canaanite, the king of Arad, who dwelt in the South [Negev]" prevented the Israelite tribes from penetrating into Canaan directly from Kadesh-Barnea "by the way of Atharim" (Num. 21:1; 33:40) and he defeated them at neighboring Hormah (Num 14:44-45; Deut. 1:44). Another biblical tradition, however, recounts a second battle between the Israelites and the king of Arad near Hormah. This time the Canaanites were defeated and the victorious Israelites "utterly destroyed them and their cities." The name Hormah ("utter destruction") is derived from this event (Num. 21:2-3). In the list of defeated Canaanite kings in Joshua 12:14, which follows the latter tradition, the kings of Arad and Hormah appear side by side. It is further recorded in the Bible (Judg. 1:16) that "the children of the Kenite, Moses' father-in-law [the Septuagint reads "the children of Hobab the Kenite"] went up out of the city of palm-trees with the children of Judah into the wilderness of Judah, which is in the south [Negev] of Arad, and they went and dwelt with the people" (Heb. *ha-am;* but the Septuagint reads the "Amalekite"; cf. I Sam. 15:6). This account of the settlement of the important Kenite family in the vicinity of Arad acquired special significance after the modern discovery of the sanctuary at Arad. Pharaoh Shishak in listing cities conquered by him in Erez Israel (c 920 B.C.E.)

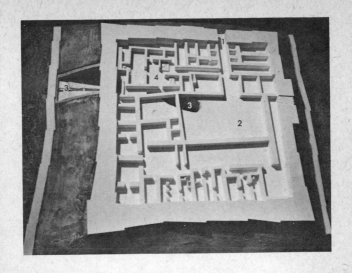

Model of the Israelite citadel of Arad (prepared by the Israel Museum): (1) Main gate. (2) Central courtyard. (3) Waterworks and cistern. (4) Temple complex.

records the capture of two places in the Negev bearing the name of Arad, these being "the fortresses of Arad Rabbat [Arad the Great] and Arad of the House of Yeroḥam." It seems, therefore, that in the days of Solomon there were two fortresses with the name Arad: a large, main city and a second named for the family of Yeroḥam (probably the biblical Jerahmeelites; and cf. "the South [Negev] of the Jerahmeelites" and "the cities of the Jerahmeelites" in I Samuel 27:10 and 30:29). Eder (Heb. עֶדֶר), which is mentioned as the second city in the Negev district of Judah (Josh. 15:21) is apparently a corruption of the name Arad. A village called Arad was still known to Eusebius in the fourth century C.E. (Onom. 14:2), 20 mi. from Hebron and four mi. from Malaatha (Moleatha), a description which fits Tell Arad, which is about 18½ mi. (30 km.) E.N.E. of Beersheba. On the Madaba Map, Arad is erroneously placed south of Beersheba.

Excavations conducted by Y. Aharoni and R. Amiran at Tell Arad from 1962 to 1967 uncovered a large city from the Early Bronze Age II (c. 2900–2700 B.C.E.) which was built over a scattered, unfortified settlement from the Late Chalcolithic period. The Early Bronze Age city was surrounded by a stone wall, 8½ ft. (2.50 m.) thick, which was strengthened at intervals by semicircular towers. It was a well-planned city which was divided into various quarters by narrow lanes. The houses were built according to a uniform architectural design and were of a typical "broad house" construction—a rectangular room with the entrance on one of the long sides. Of major importance was the discovery of imported pottery from Egypt as well as an

Excavations at Tell Arad: (1) Iron Age citadel, with Israelite occupational phases between eleventh and sixth centuries B.C.E. (2) Remains of settlements from the late Chalcolithic period (c. 3400–3200 B.C.E.) and the Early Bronze Age II (c. 2900–2700 B.C.E.).

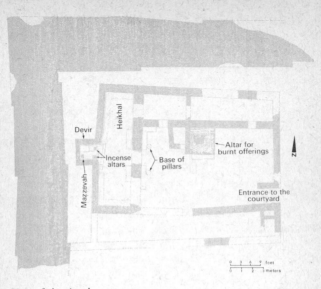

Plan of the Arad sanctuary.

Clay model of Early Bronze Age II "broad house" at Tell Arad.

abundance of decorated pottery which had previously been known mainly from first dynasty tombs in Egypt (Abydos ware). This pottery is of great chronological value and it proves that commercial ties between Egypt and Arad were already well-developed at that time.

The ancient town was destroyed not later than 2700 B.C.E. and the site remained deserted until some time in the 11th century B.C.E. when a small settlement rose. In the center of the village, a sacred precinct with a *bamah* ("high place") and altar was built. This was undoubtedly the Kenite sanctuary whose priests traced their sacerdotal heritage back to Moses (Judg. 1:16). In the tenth century B.C.E., probably during Solomon's reign, a strong citadel was built on the site which was in existence until close to the destruction of the First Temple. The citadel was destroyed six times during this period. It was followed by a succession of Persian, Hellenistic and Roman fortresses. The latest stratum at Arad dates to the beginning of the Arabic period.

The outstanding discovery at Arad was the temple which stood on the northwestern corner of the Israelite citadel. It is the first Israelite sanctuary to be uncovered in excavations. Its westward orientation, contents, and general layout in many ways recall Solomon's temple in Jerusalem but the temple shows an even more striking resemblance to the biblical description of the Tabernacle in the desert. The sanctuary consists of a main hall from which three steps lead up to the Holy of Holies, in the entrance of which were found two incense altars. In the center of the Holy of Holies were a small *bamah* and a *mazzevah* ("stone stele"). Along the eastern side of the hall was a large courtyard which was divided by a stone sill into an outer courtyard and an inner one (porch). Flanking the entrance to the hall were two stone slabs which apparently served as bases of pillars similar to the Jachin and Boaz in the Jerusalem temple (cf. II Chron. 3:17). In the outer courtyard stood an altar for burnt offerings, which was a square of five cubits, the exact measurement of the Tabernacle (Ex. 27:1; cf. II Chron.

The Holy of Holies in the Arad temple. Two incense altars stand at the entrance and opposite them is the *mazzevah*.

6:13), and built of earth and unhewn field stones (cf. Ex. 20:21–22). Among the various finds and ritual objects discovered in the temple, two ostraca (ink-inscribed sherds) are of interest. These bear the names of Pashhur and Meremoth—two priestly families known from the Bible. A third ostracon contains a list of family names including, among others, "the sons of Korah." The temple was built over the early Kenite high place at the same time as the first citadel, probably during the days of Solomon, and it was destroyed when the last Israelite citadel was erected in the days of Josiah. The destruction of the temple was certainly connected with Josiah's concentration of the religious ritual in Jerusalem which is described in II Kings 22.

In addition to the ostraca found in the temple, numerous others inscribed in Hebrew and Aramaic were also uncovered and these considerably enrich knowledge of ancient Hebrew epigraphy. One group belongs to the archives of "Eliashib, son of Eshyahu," who was a high-ranking official and perhaps the commander of the last Israelite citadel (c. 600 B.C.E.) Most of these contain orders to supply rations of wine and bread to travelers, including the "Kittim," who were apparently a group of mercenaries of Aegean origin. One of the letters mentions Beersheba and another contains reference to "the house of YHWH,"[6] apparently the Temple in Jerusalem. Another ostracon from the same period contains an order for the urgent dispatch of reinforcements from Arad to Ramat Negev ("Ramah of the South," Josh. 19:8; I Sam. 30:27) to head off a threatening Edomite attack. This is possibly a reference to the Edomite invasion during the time of Nebuchadnezzar, hinted at in II Kings 24:2 (reading Edom instead of Aram).

The generally accepted theory that Tell Arad is Arad of the Canaanite period has been refuted by excavation of the site since no traces of settlement from the Middle or Late Bronze Ages were found. Its identification with Israelite Arad, on the other hand, was confirmed, the name even found inscribed on two ostraca. There are two possible solutions to this problem: 1) In the Canaanite period, Arad was the name of a region and not of a specific city; 2) The site of Canaanite Arad is Tell el-Milḥ (present-day Malḥata) 7½ mi. (12 km.) southwest of Tell Arad where strong fortifications dating from the Hyksos period (Middle Bronze Age) have been discovered. This identification is substantiated by the inscription of Pharaoh Shishak

[6] i.e. God.

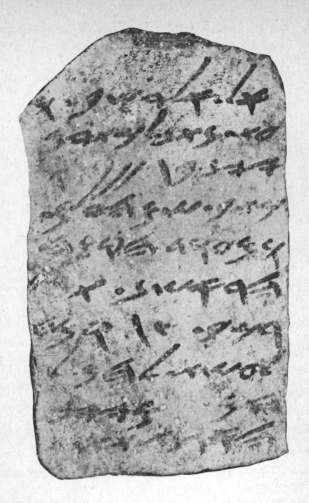

One of the numerous Ancient Hebrew ostraca from the "Eliashib archives."

according to which it can be assumed that "Arad of the House of Yeroḥam" is the early Arad which was settled by the Jerahmeelite family (cf. I Sam. 27:10; 30:29) and "Arad Rabbat" (Arad the Great) was the strong citadel established in the days of Solomon in the Negev of Judah on the site of the Kenite sacred precinct.

ii ASHDOD. Ashdod was a city in the southern coastal plain of Ereẓ Israel and situated about 3 mi. (4½ km.) from the sea. (The modern city is on the seashore.) In the Late Canaanite period ancient Ashdod served as an important harbor city as is shown by archaeological finds and references to its maritime trade in the archives of Ugarit. According to biblical tradition, it was a town of the ancient Anakim (lit. "giants"; Josh. 11:22). After its conquest by the Philistines, it became one of their five chief cities and they erected a temple dedicated to the god Dagon at Ashdod (Josh. 13:3; 15:46; I Sam. 5:1–7; Amos 1:8). Uzziah, king of Judah, breached the fortifications of the town and built in the area (II Chron. 26:6). In 734 B.C.E. the city capitulated to Tiglath-Pileser III of Assyria and in 712 B.C.E. Sargon crushed a rebellion led by Ashdod which then became the capital of an Assyrian province (cf. Isa. 20:1). Although the city was situated on the *via maris,* the trade route near the sea, it was not directly on the coast but possessed an ancient port which was called Ashdod Yam ("Ashdod-on-the-Sea"). With the decline of Assyrian power, the Egyptian pharaoh Psammetichus I conquered the city after a siege of 29 years (according to Herodotus, 2:157). Ashdod was the Philistine capital in the post-Exilic period, so that in the days of Nehemiah, an "Ashdodite" was synonymous with a "Philistine" (Neh. 4:1; 13:24). Nehemiah fought against Ashdod's influence which extended as far as Jerusalem.

The town continued to be a district capital in the

Philistine figurine of female deity, found at Ashdod. The lower part of the figure merges with the throne. Early 12th century B.C.E. 33

Hellenistic period when it was known as Azotus and it served as a Greek stronghold down to the days of the Hasmoneans (I Macc. 5:68). Its suburbs were burnt by Jonathan[7] (I Macc. 10:84; 11:4) and the city was captured by John Hyrcanus[8] (c. 165 B.C.E.; Jos., Ant. 13:324). Ashdod then remained in Hasmonean hands until its conquest by Pompey[9] (63 B.C.E.). It was rebuilt by Gabinius (55 B.C.E.) and later changed hands several times, eventually becoming the property of Herod, who gave it to his sister Salome; she bequeathed it to Livia, the wife of Augustus Caesar, from whom it was inherited by the emperor Tiberius (ibid., 14:75, 88; 17:189; 18:31). From the time of the Hasmoneans until the second century C.E., Ashdod appears to have been a Jewish town. It declined after Vespasian's conquest. In the Byzantine period, the Madaba Map distinguished between inland "Ashdod of the Horsemen" and the bigger coastal town "Ashdod-on-the-Sea." The discovery of a chancel screen of a synagogue at Ashdod-on-the-Sea (Mīnat al-Qal'a) with a Greco-Jewish inscription gives evidence of a Jewish community there in the sixth century C.E. Part of the Muslim-Arab townlet of Isdūd, which was in existence until the end of the Mandate period, was built on a tell called al-Ra's on the site of the ancient city. Excavations conducted by the Israel Department of Antiquities near the new Ashdod port at Tell Mor (Tell Murra) uncovered remains of Canaanite and Israelite fortifications and a Hellenistic plant for extracting purple dye from murex. A joint Israel-American expedition (directed by Moshe Dothan and for the first two seasons also with David Noel Freedman) started excavating the mound in 1962. This is situated in the arable coastal plain of Philistia, and lies about 2.8 mi. (4.5 kms.) from the sea and about 9.4 mi. (15 kms.) northeast of Ashkelon. Stratigraphical evidence (twenty-two strata were uncovered) shows nearly continuous occupation from the seven-

[7] Head of Jewish state (160–143 B.C.E.)
[8] Ruler of Judea and high priest (135–104 B.C.E.)
[9] Roman general (106–48 B.C.E.)

Part of the Madaba mosaic map (c. 500 C.E.), showing the original
Ashdod (as indicated by *) lying inland from the sea.

teenth century B.C.E. till the end of Byzantine times. The city was fortified from the end of the Middle Bronze II period onward until the Late Bronze Age (strata XXII-XIV). The Late Bronze Age city (mentioned frequently in Ugaritic texts) was destroyed by the Philistines and Ashdod became one of the cities of the Philistine Pentapolis. At least three Philistine strata have been uncovered (strata XIII-XI) revealing a rich material culture including seals inscribed in an unknown script. Cult objects, including a musician's stand and many *kernoi* and offering tables, which attest to the local religious practices of the Iron Age II period, were probably manufactured in the potters' quarter of the lower city. The excavation verified the biblical tradition of destructions by Uzziah and by Sargon II of Assyria. After its complete destruction the city reached a new peak in Hellenistic times, afterward gradually declining to a small, unimportant village.

iii AVEDAT.

Avedat—or Ovdat—was a former city in the central Negev, probably named after a Nabatean king. It is referred to in ancient sources as Oboda (*tabula Peutingeriana*) Eboda (Ptolemaeus 5: 16,4), and Oboda (Stephanus Byzantinus s.v.)

The ancient site was discovered and mapped in 1870 by E. H. Palmer, while a more detailed survey was made by A. Musil in 1902. Survey expeditions conducted more detailed investigations in 1904, 1912, and 1916. Large-scale excavations were undertaken from 1958–60 directed by Michael Avi-Yonah (1958) and Avraham Negev (1959–60). Avedat is situated near the point where the two main routes from Petra and Elath converge to form one road leading north to Haluzah and the Mediterranean coast. Here, in the third century B.C.E., the Nabateans established a road station for the supply of their caravans with water and food, as is shown by the pottery and coins dating back to that period. The diverse nature of the archaeological finds indicates that Avedat occupied a position of great importance in Indo-Arabian commerce. Little more is known of the first few centuries of the city's existence, but it is clear that the site was abandoned at the beginning of the first century B.C.E., perhaps as a result of Alexander Yannai's[10] conquests in the central Negev. The Nabatean settlement reached its zenith during the reign of Aretas IV (9 B.C.E.–40 C.E.), when the city's acropolis was fortified and a large temple built within it. From this period excavations have also uncovered two gate towers and massive retaining walls which encircled the high abutment upon which the acropolis stood. Very little of the temple has been preserved. The Nabatean city extended over the northern part of the mountain ridge at the edge of which the acropolis was situated. An army camp, north of the city, was apparently also built at that time. In the days of Aretas IV, Avedat was the site of a flourishing ceramic industry. A potter's workshop for the manufacture of the thin, delicate Nabatean ware was excavated in the eastern part of the city; the pottery has been dated also to the years 1–50 C.E. (the dating was made with the aid of imported ware also found there).

By the mid-first century C.E. the Nabatean trade diminished and Avedat began to decline. It was then that the inhabitants built a system of dams to exploit the meager rainfall for farming. Many Nabatean inscriptions engraved on large stone libation altars dating from 89–99 C.E. which were found in and around the city refer to these constructions. The Roman conquest in 106 C.E. and the city's annexation to the Roman Empire produced little change. Thamudic and Safa'itic tribes intruded into the area at the beginning of the second century C.E. and scores of inscriptions in their dialects have been found at Avedat. They indicate that these tribes were responsible for the city's destruction sometime after 126 C.E. In about the mid-third century the Romans incorporated southern Erez

[10] Hasmonean king of Judea and high priest (c. 126–76 B.C.E.)

Israel and Transjordan into their chain of defenses to protect the Empire's southern frontier. Avedat, situated on this line, became a settlement for discharged soldiers who received land grants and other benefits in return for guaranteed military service in times of emergency. The new settlement was erected on the southern end of the mountain ridge. It was not fortified, but consisted of a number of well-built houses along two short roads. A temple dedicated to Zeus-Obodas and to Aphrodite was built, or rebuilt, on the acropolis. The burial cave on the southwestern slope also dates to this period. The Roman settlement was short-lived and the latest Roman epigraphic remains are from the end of the third century.

Avedat was resettled in the Byzantine period (in the early sixth century). On the acropolis a large citadel, two churches, and a monastery were built. The settlement itself moved down to the western slopes of the mountain ridge. The Byzantine dwellings consisted of houses erected over rock-hewn caves. These caves served for storing and processing agricultural produce. A small bath-house which drew its water from a nearby well was built in the valley west of the city. Extensive remains of dams, irrigation canals, and the many other water-storage installations, as well as winepresses and fruit-drying apparatus, all demonstrate that in the Byzantine period Avedat's economy was based mainly on agriculture and wine production.

The citadel and two churches were razed and the city itself suffered partial destruction in the Persian invasion in 614. Twenty years later, the Arab invaders found there hardly more than a village. While there is evidence of partial rebuilding and repair, the total absence of early Arabic pottery indicates that after the middle of the seventh century the city was completely deserted. The ancient city of Avedat has been reconstructed by the Israel Department for Landscaping and Preservation of Historic Sites.

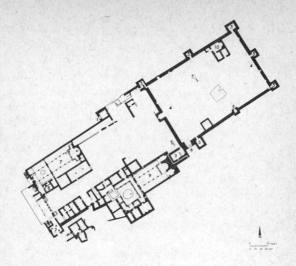

1. Nabatean Gate (9 B.C.E.—40 C.E.)
2. Nabatean entrance with portico
3. Late Roman tower (3rd century C.E.)
4. Byzantine citadel (middle of 6th century to 620/619 C.E.)
5. Towers around Citadel
6. Main gate of Citadel
7. Byzantine North Church and Atrium (Beginning of 6th century to 620/619 C.E.)
8. Baptismal font of North Church
9. Southern Church ("St. Theodorus Martirium") (middle 6th century to 620/619 C.E.)
10. Late Byzantine Chapel (620 C.E. to end of 6th century)

Plan of the reconstructed city of Avedat.

iv BEERSHEBA.

Beersheba is an important biblical city in the Negev on the southern border of Judah; its name has been preserved in the Arabic form Bir (Be'r) al-Sab'. The city was first settled in the Chalcolithic period. Excavations conducted at Tell Abu Matar by J. Perrot uncovered remains of cave dwellings dug in the earth from this age. The inhabitants of the caves engaged in raising cattle and the manufacture of metal tools. Their pottery and stone vessels and figurines carved out of ivory and bone display a highly developed craftsmanship. Evidence of the beginnings of a religious cult was also found.

According to the Bible, Abraham and Isaac dug wells at Beersheba and also formed alliances there with Abimelech "king of the Philistines." The allies bound themselves under oath to observe the treaties, and in one source Abraham set aside seven ewes as a sign of the oath, which the Pentateuch explains was the origin of the name of the city (Be'er, "well"; Sheva, "oath" or "seven"; see Gen. 21:31; 26:33). The sanctuary of "the Lord, the Everlasting God," which was apparently located there in very early times, was invested with great importance in the patriarchal period (Gen. 21:33; 26:23–24, 32–33; 46:1). After the Israelite conquest, Beersheba became a city of the tribe of Simeon and was later incorporated into the tribe of Judah (Josh. 19:2; 15:28). It appears to have been a center of the Israelite settlement in the Negev in the time of Samuel since his sons were sent there as judges (I Sam. 8:1–2). The sanctuary at Beersheba was regarded as the extreme southern point of the country in contradistinction to the sanctuary at Dan which was held to be the northern point (Amos 5:5; 8:14). Thus the phrase "from Dan to Beer-Sheba" (Judg. 20:1, etc.) was the customary designation, at least until the days of David and Solomon, for the entire area of the country. After the division of the

Bone carving of a human head from the Chalcolithic settlement at Tell Abu Maṭar near Beersheba (c. 4000 B.C.E.).

41

monarchy, Beersheba continued to be the southern frontier of the kingdom of Judah; the expression "from Dan to Beersheba" was then replaced by "from Beer-Sheba to the hill-country of Ephraim" (II Chron. 19:4) or "from Geba to Beersheba" (II Kings 23:8). Zibiah, the mother of Jehoash, king of Judah, originated from Beersheba (II Kings 12:2). Elijah set out on his journey to Horeb from Beersheba, the gateway to the desert (I Kings 19:3, 8). The city was settled by Jews after the return from Babylon (Neh. 11:27, 30). The biblical town of Beersheba is to be sought at Tell al-Sabʻ (Tell Beersheba), $2\frac{1}{2}$ mi. (4 km.) northeast of the new town, where remains of a fortress and potsherds from the Iron Age to the Roman period were found in excavations begun in 1969 by Y. Aharoni. According to Aharoni, Beersheba was established in the 12th–11th centuries B.C.E. The excavations at Beersheba yielded further information on the city plan, the walls, and the gate. Of special interest was the discovery of a main city drain leading toward the gate. Several rooms of the Persian and Hellenistic period were also excavated. Ten Aramaic ostraca from the fourth century B.C.E. were found, which deal with the distribution of wheat and barley. The names include typical Edomite names with the theophoric component qws.

After 70 C.E. Beersheba was included in the Roman frontier-line defenses against the Nabateans and continued to be a Roman garrison town after the Roman annexation of the Nabatean kingdom. A large village existed then at its present site, where many remains have been found including mosaic pavements and Greek inscriptions (including a sixth-century C.E. ordinance regarding tax payments, which was issued to the south of the country, and a synagogue inscription). In the fourth and fifth centuries C.E., Beersheba first belonged to the district of Gerar and was later annexed to "Palaestina Tertia." The town was abandoned in the Arab period.

v BET ALFA. Bet Alfa is a place situated in the eastern Jezreel Valley at the foot of Mount Gilboa. The name is historical and has been preserved in the Arab designation of the site Beit Ilfa which may have some connection with the proper name Ilfa or Hilfa which occurs in the Talmud (Ta'an. 21a). The foundations of an ancient synagogue were discovered in 1929 near Bet Alfa by E. L. Sukenik and N. Avigad, who were conducting excavations on behalf of the Hebrew University. The synagogue covered an area of 46×92 ft. (14×28 m) and included a courtyard, narthex, basilical type hall with a nave and two side aisles, and, apparently, a women's gallery. The apse at the end of the hall was oriented south toward Jerusalem, and a small cavity in its floor probably served as a *genizah;* above it once stood an ark for Scrolls of the Law. The entire floor of the structure is paved with mosaics: the courtyard, narthex, and aisles in simple geometric designs, and the floor of the

The mosaic floor in the nave of the synagogue at Bet Alfa executed in the 6th cent. C.E. Courtesy Government Press Office, Tel Aviv. **43**

nave is decorated with mosaic panels surrounded by a broad ornamental border. Two inscriptions were found at the entrance to the hall: one (in Aramaic) states that the mosaic was made during the reign of Emperor Justin (undoubtedly Justin I, 518–27); the other (in Greek) gives the names of the mosaicists, Marianos and his son Hanina. Symbolic animals are depicted on either side of the inscriptions: a lion on the right and a bull on the left. The three mosaic panels in the center of the hall depict (from north to south): (1) *The Offering of Isaac,* which shows Abraham pointing a drawn knife at Isaac who is bound near an altar; behind Abraham a ram is tied to a tree, and alongside it appears the inscription "And behold a ram." The hand of God is seen between the sun's rays above; Abraham's two servants and donkey stand behind him; a band of palm trees separate this scene from the next one. (2) *The Signs of the Zodiac,* with the sun in the center in the form of a youth riding a chariot drawn by four horses; each sign has its Hebrew designation inscribed above it. In the corners appear the four seasons of the year (Tishri, Tevet, Nisan, Tammuz), each in the form of the bust of a winged woman adorned with jewels. (3) *The Ark of the Synagogue,* in which the ark has a gable roof with an "eternal light" suspended from its top and two birds perched at its corners; on either side is a lion with a seven-branched *menorah* ("candelabrum") and above it and between them are depicted *lulavim* ("palm branches"), *etrogim* ("citrons"), and censers. Two curtains adorn the scene on the left and right sides.

The simple but strong style of the mosaic pavement represents a folk art that appears to have developed among the Jewish villagers of Galilee. The figures are depicted frontally and the artist took great pains to make each scene expressive. The mosaics of Bet Alfa are striking in their coloring and stylization and are among the finest examples of Jewish art in the Byzantine period. In 1960 the synagogue structure was renovated and the pavement repaired by the

Israel Government.

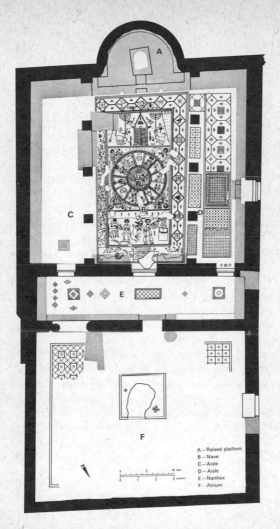

A — Raised platform
B — Nave
C — Aisle
D — Aisle
E — Narthex
F — Atrium

Plan of the Bet Alfa synagogue, showing the elaborate mosaic plan of the nave. After E. L. Sukenik, *The Ancient Synagogue of Beth Alpha.* Jerusalem, 1932.

vi BET(H)-EL. Beth-El is a Canaanite and Israelite town, 10½ mi. (17 km.) N. of Jerusalem, located at the intersection of the north–south mountain road along the watershed and the east–west road leading to the plains of Jericho and to the Coastal Plain (cf. Judg. 20:31). At present its site is occupied by the small Muslim village of Baytīn, 2,886 ft. (880 m.) above sea level. Excavations were conducted at Beth-El by W. F. Albright and J. L. Kelso in 1927 and 1934 and resumed by Kelso in 1954, 1957, and 1961.

Settlement at Beth-El apparently began at the turn of the third millennium B.C.E., when it inherited the position of neighboring Ai (et-Tell), which already lay in ruins. In the 16th century B.C.E. the settlement was enlarged and surrounded by an 11 ft. (3⅓ m.) thick stone wall. The biblical account of Abraham's building an altar to the Lord between Beth-El and Ai (Gen. 12:6–8) is usually assigned to this period. Beth-El's main importance, however, is derived from its traditional association with Jacob's dream. Fleeing from his brother Esau, Jacob spent the night there and dreamed he saw a ladder reaching to heaven with angels of God ascending and descending it. A voice then spoke to him and assured him of God's protection and confirmed the promise that the land on which he rested would be given to him and his descendants (**Gen.** 28:10–22). Arising the next morning, Jacob erected a *mazzevah* ("sacred pillar") over which he poured oil as a thanksgiving sacrifice. The name of the place, which was formerly Luz, was now called Beth-El (i.e., "home of God"; **Gen.** 5:19; 35:6, 15; 48:3; Josh. 18:13; according to Josh. 16:2, however, Beth-El was east of Luz).

Canaanite Beth-El continued to flourish in the Late Bronze Age (15th–14th centuries, B.C.E.), when it had commercial relations with Cyprus, indicated by the pottery finds. The remains of a house with rooms built around a

Ruins of ancient Beth-El, with the Arab village of Baytīn in the background. Photo Richard Cleave, Jerusalem.

large courtyard, plastered or stone floors, and masonry sewage channels belong to this period. A burnt layer indicates that the city was captured and burned down around the first half of the 13th century B.C.E. and resettled by an Israelite population (cf. Judg. 1:22ff.; Josh. 12:16). The city was on the southern border of Ephraim (Josh. 16:1-2; 18:13; I Chron. 7:28), but it is also listed as a Benjamite town (Josh. 18:22). There was a decline in the standard of living at Beth-El during the Israelite period, when the building became cruder, but a recovery is noticeable during the reigns of David and Solomon. The stormy epoch of the Judges is reflected in three building phases, while the relatively calm period of the United Monarchy is represented in a single building phase. The Tabernacle and the Ark were set there for a while, and in the conflict with Benjamin the Israelites prayed, fasted, and offered sacrifices there. They invoked the oracle of the Urim and the answer was provided by Phinehas (Judg. 20:18, 28). Deborah lived near the city (Judg. 4:5), and Samuel visited **47** it periodically to judge the people (I Sam. 7:16). During Saul's war with the Philistines, he concentrated his forces in the mount of Beth-El (I Sam. 13:2).

With the division of the Monarchy, Beth-El passed into the possession of Jeroboam I. In order to wean his people away from making pilgrimages to Jerusalem, he erected one of the two principal shrines of his kingdom there (the other one was at Dan), with its own priesthood. The golden calf he set there was apparently designed to serve as a substitute for the cherubim in the Temple of Jerusalem. In the same spirit he ordered the 15th day of the eighth month to be celebrated instead of the Feast of Ingathering (Sukkot), which was observed on the 15th of the seventh month in Jerusalem as the main pilgrim festival (I Kings 12:29–33). This schism aroused vehement opposition among the prophets (I Kings 13) and caused a rift between Jeroboam and Ahijah the Shilonite (I Kings 14:7ff.). The biblical story of Hiel the Bethelite, who ignored the curse of Joshua and rebuilt Jericho on its ruins (I Kings 16:34), and that of the children of Beth-El who mocked Elisha (II Kings 2:23) may serve as proof of the strained relations existing between the inhabitants of Beth-El and the prophetic circles. This antagonism assumed its most acute form in the days of Amos (3:14; 4:4; etc.) and Hosea (10:15), both of whom call Beth-El Beth-Aven ("The House of Iniquity"; Amos 5:5; Hos. 4:15; cf. Jer. 48:13).

Beth-El and its surroundings were conquered by Abijah, king of Judah, in his war against Jeroboam (II Chron. 13:19), but it was returned to Israel not later than the reign of Baasha and remained there until the fall of the kingdom. In the eighth century B.C.E., Beth-El was enclosed by a thick wall with towers that was repaired in the following century. Even after the destruction of Samaria (721 B.C.E.), priests still served at Beth-El (II Kings 17:28) until Josiah captured it, broke down its altar, destroyed its high place, and defiled the site (II Kings 23:15). Beth-El was destroyed during the Babylonian invasion (587 B.C.E.)

and remained in ruins until the Persian period. In the time

of Nehemiah, it was included in the territory of Judah (Ezra 2:28; Neh. 7:32). During the Hasmonean revolt, it was fortified by the Syrian general Bacchides (I Macc. 9:50). Beth-El is not mentioned again until its capture by Vespasian in 69 C.E. (Jos., Wars, 4:551). Coins found there date only from the period between 4 B.C.E. and its capture. In the Byzantine period, Beth-El was a village in the territory of "Aelia Capitolina" (Jerusalem), located 12 (Roman) miles from the capital "on the right, as one goes to Neapolis" (Eusebius, Onom. 192 etc.). The Christian traveler the Pilgrim of Bordeaux (333 C.E.) and the Christian writer Theodosius (c. 503 C.E.) also refer to it. According to Jerome (fifth century) a church was erected at Beth-El. On the Madaba Map "Luzah, which is also Beth-El" is also represented as a village north of Jerusalem. Very few remains of the Roman and Byzantine periods have been discovered at the site.

vii BET(H)-SHEAN. This historic city (also called Beisan) is in the fertile valley of Beth-Shean. The city Beth-Shean, situated at a main crossroads in a well-watered fertile region, is 390 ft. (120 m.) below sea level.

"Shean" or "Shan" (II Sam. 21:12) seems to be the name of an idol. Some scholars dispute the supposed mention of it in the Egyptian execration texts of the 20th–19th centuries B.C.E. It is mentioned in Egyptian sources from the time of Thutmose III (15th century B.C.E.) to that of Ramses III (12th century B.C.E.). The excavations of Tel Beth-Shean (Ar. *Tell al-Husn*) proved the importance of Beth-Shean as a station for caravans and as a center of Egyptian rule. An Egyptian basalt stele found dating from the reign of Pharaoh Seti I (late 14th century B.C.E.) mentions the Apiru, the Habiru (thought to be Hebrews) of the cuneiform writings, who disturb the peace and

This basalt relief from Beth-Shean, depicting a fight between a lion and a dog, is believed to be of Hittite workmanship, c. 1400 B.C.E.

undermine government authority in the region of Beth-Shean. Ramses II refortified the city of Beth-Shean and built a temple different from that of Seti I. His basalt stele mentions the suppression of the "Asians and the inhabitants of the sands": Ramses III also refortified the city and rebuilt its temples. Evidence of Aegean cultural influences, brought by Philistine laborers, was found in the vicinity of the cemetery beyond the tell. It was one of the strong Canaanite cities not captured at the beginning of the Israelite conquest of Erez Israel.

The valley of Beth-Shean was allotted to the tribe of Issachar, but the tribe of Manasseh extended its settlements to this territory (Josh. 17:11). During Saul's reign the city was in the hands of Philistines; they hanged Saul's body on the walls of Beth-Shean (I Sam. 31:10, 12). In the time of Solomon it was included in the district under the authority of Baana the son of Ahilud (I Kings, 4:12). The wall, the gate, and the style of stone cutting found in the hill belong to the Solomonic period. It is thought to have been destroyed by Sheshonk I (the biblical Shishak), king of Egypt.

Excavations conducted there by an American expedition between 1921 and 1933 uncovered 18 levels of occupation extending from the Chalcolithic (fourth millennium B.C.E.) to the early Arab period. The main discovery was a series of temples built by the Egyptians in honor of local deities. These apparently range in date from the el-Amarna period to the reign of Ramses III in the 12th century B.C.E. (strata IX–VI). Two later temples (stratum V) existed until c.1000 B.C.E.; one of them may be identical with the "house of Ashtaroth" in which the Philistines placed Saul's armor (I Sam. 31:10). Various Egyptian inscriptions were found including a stele dedicated to Mekal, the god of Beth-Shean; a lintel bearing the name of an Egyptian builder from the time of Ramses II; and three victory stelae, two from the reign of Seti I and the other from the reign of Ramses II.

A large number of burial caves from different periods were excavated on the slope opposite the tell. Some of these contained anthropomorphic sarcophagi that attest to the presence of the Philistines (or a related group of sea peoples). The blow struck at the Philistines before the war of Deborah (Judg. 3:31; 5:6) may have had the seizure of the Egyptian citadel at Beth-Shean and its mercenary troops as its objective. With the removal of the supreme Egyptian authority, the safety of the roads was disrupted and the

The tell of Beth-Shean. Photo Government Press Agency, Tel Aviv.

Aerial view of the tell of Beth-Shean. Photo Richard Cleave, Jerusalem.

Part of the lid of an anthropomorphic pottery sarcophagus from the Philistine necropolis at Beth-Shean, 12th century B.C.E. Jerusalem, Israel Museum. Photo Zev Radovan, Jerusalem

opportunity provided for the decisive battle between the Israelites and Canaanites in the north of the country.

During the rule of the Diadochi, the successors of Alexander the Great, Beth-Shean received the name of Scythopolis ("city of the Scythians"); this seems to refer to a colony of Scythian mercenaries, who were in the service of the Egyptian king Ptolemy II. It is first mentioned in the campaign of Antiochus Seleucus III, against Egypt in 218 B.C.E. Near the temple for the worship of Dionysus, a temple in honor of Zeus was built. The town accepted Seleucid rule and became a Greek city *(polis)* under Antiochus IV.

By the time of Judah Maccabee, many Jews lived in Beth-Shean. It was there that Jonathan, the brother of Judah, met Tryphon, the Syrian usurper. The city was conquered by the sons of John Hyrcanus I in 107 B.C.E. During the Hasmonean period Beth-Shean became an important administrative center, and Alexander Yannai built ramparts around the city. In 63 B.C.E. Pompey revived the Greek way of life, and Gabinius, proconsul in Syria from 57 to 54 B.C.E., improved the city and enlarged it. It became the capital of the federation of ten Greek cities known as the Decapolis alliance, the other nine centers of which were on the east bank of the Jordan. When the Jewish War broke out in 66 C.E., the Jews also attacked Beth-Shean. The Jewish and gentile inhabitants of the city alike resisted. However, the Gentiles deceived the Jews and massacred some 13,000 of them (Jos., Wars, 2:466–76).

During the mishnaic and talmudic periods (second and third centuries) Beth-Shean was inhabited by Jews (Av. Zar. 1:4; 4:12), whose principal occupations were the manufacture of thin linen garments, field-crops, and olive plantations (TJ, Pe'ah 7:4, 20a). They spoke in the Galilean dialect. At that time Beth-Shean was one of the world centers for the manufacture and export of textiles. Regular performances were held in the theater, amphitheater, and hippodrome. The theater, considerable remains of which are still visible, was built about 200 C.E. and had seating for 4,500–5,000 spectators.

A synagogue excavated north of the Byzantine wall of the city testifies to the presence of a Jewish population from the fourth century onward. The synagogue itself was in use about 200 years and there are signs of renovation. It is built in the form of a basilica and paved with a beautiful mosaic

Bronze handle in the shape of a *menorah*, believed to have been attached to the rim of an oil lamp, found in the synagogue at Beth-Shean. Jerusalem, Department of Antiquities and Museums.

of geometrical and plant patterns, and a beautiful Holy Ark with a candelabrum on each side, ritual horns *(shofarot)*, incense bowls, and three Greek inscriptions. In the adjoining rooms of the later Byzantine era a Samaritan inscription was also found. The synagogue seems to have burned down in 624.

At the beginning of the fifth century Beth-Shean became the capital of the province called Palestina Secunda and the seat of the commissioner and the tribunal. It was also the seat of the episcopate and had numerous churches. An interesting mosaic floor from one of these churches, found in the northern part of the city, is preserved in a new building. 55

The Roman theater at Beth-Shean, c. 200 C.E. Photo Richard Cleave. Jerusalem.

viii **BET SHE'ARIM.** This ancient city (also called Besara) on the southern slopes of Lower Galilee is located on the hill of al-Sheikh Burayk (near Kiryat Tivon on the Nazareth–Haifa road). Although settlement at Bet She'arim apparently started during the period of the divided monarchy, the first mention of the city occurs at the end of the Second Temple period, when it was a center of the estates of Berenice (the daughter of Agrippa I and sister of Agrippa II) in the Plain of Esdraelon. Josephus speaks of it as Besara (Life, 118–9). According to talmudic sources, important *tannaim* and *amoraim* lived there (Tosef., Ter. 7:14; Nid. 27a). Bet She'arim reached a position of great importance and prosperity in the late second century when Judah ha-Nasi[11]

---

[11] Patriarch of Judea and redactor of the Mishnah (later half of 2nd and beginning of 3rd cent. C.E.)

took up residence there and made it the seat of the Sanhedrin (RH 31a-b). From the beginning of the following century the necropolis of Bet She'arim became a central burial place for Jews of Palestine and the Diaspora (TJ, MK 3:5, 82c). The city was destroyed by Gallus[12] during the suppression of the Jewish revolt in 352 C.E. A small settlement nevertheless continued to exist there during the Byzantine and early Arab periods.

The hill of al-Sheikh Burayk has been partly excavated by B. Mazar (1935-40; 1960) and N. Avigad (1953-58) under the auspices of the Israel Exploration Society. An inscription found there contains the name Besara, confirming the identification of the site with Bet She'arim.

The city of Bet She'arim extended over the entire summit of the hill—an area of some 25 acres (100 dunams), 450 ft. (137 m.) above sea level. It was surrounded by a wall, two sections of which were exposed. Remains of various large buildings were uncovered on the northeastern part of the hill. The most important of these was a spacious basilical-type synagogue, 115×49 ft. (35×15 m.), built of ashlar blocks, of which only two courses have survived. The front of the synagogue was oriented toward Jerusalem and contained three entrances that led into the large columned hall; the bases of the columns have been preserved. The synagogue was decorated in the style characteristic of Galilean synagogues of the third century C.E., and many architectural fragments were found scattered among its ruins: column drums, capitals, jambs, lintels, and decorated friezes. The ruins of other buildings and courtyards were found in the vicinity of the synagogue, including a large two-story building with an outer wall 99 ft. (30 m.) long, built of fine ashlar blocks, as well as the remains of what was apparently a glassmaking workshop. Many small artifacts were found: metal, pottery, and glass vessels, inscribed marble slabs, and some 1,200 bronze coins, all of which were struck in the first half of the fourth century C.E.

[12] Co-emperor with Constantinus II, and commander of Roman army in Palestine (351-354 C.E.)

Entrance to the main catacomb of the Bet She'arim necropolis, second-fourth centuries C.E. It has been restored with stones found on the site. Photo Government Press Office, Tel Aviv.

These coins made it possible to determine the date of the destruction of all the buildings in the area. A gate and an oil press, used chiefly in the Byzantine period, were also found nearby.

The excavations, however, were concentrated mainly in the extensive ancient necropolis that stretched over the slope of the hill northeast, north, and west of the city and over the slopes of adjacent hills to the north and west. Rock-cut catacombs that were prepared to provide burial places to sell to people from outside Bet She'arim were found in all these areas. Some were family vaults, but the majority were for the general public. Each catacomb contained an open court and a number of tomb halls that were connected by a series of chambers to some of the branch burial compartments containing graves. The

The courtyard of catacomb no. 13. Its 12 doors leading to the burial chambers are constructed on three levels. All are made of solid blocks of stone moving on hinges. Photo Israel Department of Antiquities and Museums, Jerusalem.

Bas-relief of a *menorah* held by a man dressed in a Roman legionary's tunic. The seven-branched candelabrum is the decoration recurring most frequently among the many wall carvings in the Bet She'arim catacombs. Photo Government Press Office, Tel Aviv.

Man leading a horse. One of the many graffiti of the Bet She'arim necropolis.

openings between the chambers are arched. The usual form of a grave is the *arcosolium*—an arched niche cut into the wall with trough-like graves hewn at the bottom. *Kukhim* (*loculi*—"burial recesses") are also found frequently. Some of the catacombs lack all decoration, but many possess chambers that display a variegated ornamentation. The soft rock easily lent itself to carving and incision. The many reliefs, graffiti, and drawings adorning the walls are generally executed in the primitive style of the Jewish folk art popular in the Roman period. Jewish symbols and ritual objects are very common motifs, particularly the seven-branched candelabrum and the Ark of the Law, complete with columns and steps. The *shofar, lulav, etrog,* and incense shovel are also represented. But secular motifs also occur: human figures, animals, ships, geometric patterns, etc., as well as architectural ornaments that were carved in the rock (columns, capitals, arches, and niches). Ornamental stone doors were decorated to imitate wooden ones, complete with panels, nailheads, and knockers. These were locked by bolts, and lifted by keys. The doors still turn on their hinges. Some of the main entrances are adorned with built arches resting on pillars. The facades of two catacombs   61 (nos. 14 and 20) are built of smooth ashlar stones in the form of an arcade of three arches. Over these facades are structures of monumental steps with prayer niches. A mausoleum was built over catacomb no. 11 and contained rich architectural decorations and reliefs.

Of special importance are the epitaphs, of which some 250 have been discovered. The majority are in Greek and the others are written in Hebrew, Aramaic, and Palmyrean. They are incised in the soft rock of the chamber walls, on the sides of the tombs, on lintels, on stone or marble slabs, or are painted in red or black. Their contents are generally restricted to the name of the deceased and his patronymic (or other family descent), with the addition of a word of affection or praise. The rank or occupation of the deceased, and occasionally his place of origin, are sometimes mentioned. Among the callings and titles are teacher,

View of a series of burial chambers and sarcophagi. Photo Government Press Office, Tel Aviv.

Carving of a bearded face on the end of a sarcophagus, possibly representing the Greek god Zeus. Photo Government Press Office, Tel Aviv.

kohen, banker, goldsmith, government official, perfumer, chief warden of a community, chief of a synagogue, and rabbi (written *ribbi* and *bi-ribbi*). Typical examples of Hebrew inscriptions read: "Shalom to Judah," or "This tomb is (of) Rabbi Isaac bar Makim, shalom." An unusual Aramaic epitaph was found: "He who is buried here [is] Simeon, son of Johanan, and on oath, whoever shall open upon him shall die of an evil end." In catacomb no. 14 the following epitaphs were found: "Rabbi Simeon"; "This is the burial place of Rabbi Gamaliel"; and "Anina [Ḥanina] the Small." As it is known from the Talmud that before his death Judah ha-Nasi appointed his son Simeon *ḥakham*, Gamaliel (his second son) patriarch, and his most outstanding pupil, Hanina b. Hama, head of the academy (TB, Ket. 103b), one may assume that this catacomb was the burial place of the patriarch and his family. There are 218 Greek inscriptions and Greek was apparently the common language of the Jews at the time. Pure Greek names occur beside Hebrew ones in Greek transliteration. Some inscriptions express a belief in eternal life. The places of origin appearing in the epitaphs indicate that Bet She'arim was a central burial place for the Jews of Palestine—Ezion-Geber, the nearby Arabah and Baka, and of the Diaspora—Tadmor (Palmyra) in Syria, Antioch, Byblos, Tyre, Sidon, and Beirut, Melshan in northern Mesopotamia, and Himyar in southern Arabia. Two inscriptions found incised on marble slabs in the mausoleum over catacomb no. 11 and in catacomb no. 18 are arranged in the form of Greek epigrams in the Homeric style. The former reads:

Here lie I, son of Leontius, dead, son of Sappho-Justus,
And after I had plucked the fruit of all wisdom
I left the light, the miserable parents who mourn ceaselessly
And my brothers. Woe to me, in my Besara!
After descending to Hades, I, Justus, lie here
With many of my people, for so willed stern fate.
Be comforted, Justus, no man is immortal.

The mausoleum also contained a reused sarcophagus on which Greek mythological scenes were depicted.

The largest catacomb excavated (no. 20) was comprised of 24 burial chambers with over 200 coffins made of local limestone and many fragments of imported marble sarcophogi decorated with mythological figures. On the coffins birds and animals and even human beings were depicted. The inscriptions found in the catacomb (almost all in Hebrew) reveal that it was occupied by members of the patriarchal family, "holy" rabbis, and other sages.

Additional information on the industrial activities of Bet She'arim was supplied by the discovery of a huge glass slab (11×7 ft. (c. 3⅓×2 m.) and 18 in. (45 cm.) thick, weighing nine tons) in an underground cistern. It possibly served as raw material for village glassmakers in the region. The slab must have been heated for several days at about 1922°F (1050°C) in order to melt it.

ix BET(H)-SHEMESH. Beth-Shemesh was a city in the Shephelah on the northern border of the tribe of Judah, between Chesalon and Timnah (Josh. 15:10).

The name Beth-Shemesh, mentioned a number of times in the Bible, means "the house (temple) of (the sun-god) Shemesh." Beth-Shemesh appears on the list of cities of the tribe of Dan (Josh. 19:41, as Ir-Shemesh), but it was apparently never actually conquered by it (Judg. 1:35, if the identification of Harheres with Beth-Shemesh is correct). In the list of levitical cities, it is mentioned as belonging to the tribe of Judah (Josh. 21:16; I Chron. 6:44). Beth-Shemesh was located close to the border of Philistia, and the archaeological excavations there have shown that in the period of the Judges, the Philistines exerted a strong influence on the city. The Samson narratives all take place in the vicinity of Beth-Shemesh; his birthplace, Zorah, lay just to the south of it, and the Philistine city Timnah is to the west of it. It has even been suggested that the name Samson itself (Heb. *Shimshon*) indicates a connection with the city. When the Philistines returned the "Ark of God," which they had captured at the battle of Eben-Ezer, on an ox-driven cart, it was sent along the road that led straight from Ekron to Beth-Shemesh (I Sam. 6). In the period of the monarchy, the city was part of Solomon's second administrative district, which included the former cities of the territory of Dan (I Kings 4:9). The war between Amaziah and Jehoash, kings of Judah and Israel, in about 790 B.C.E. was fought near Beth-Shemesh, and Amaziah was taken prisoner there 65

(II Kings 14:11–13; II Chron. 25:21–23). The last reference to Beth-Shemesh in the Bible occurs during the reign of Ahaz, king of Judah, from whom it was captured by the Philistines in about 734 B.C.E. (II Chron. 28:18).

Beth-Shemesh is identified with Tell al-Rumayla, astride the Wadi al-Ṣarār (biblical Sorek Valley?) on one of the major highways connecting Jerusalem with the seacoast (the modern Jerusalem–Tel Aviv railroad follows this ancient route). The site was excavated by D. Mackenzie (1911–12) and E. Grant (1928–33); G. E. Wright assisted in analyzing the results. The excavations revealed that the first city (stratum VI) of Beth-Shemesh was established toward the close of the third millennium B.C.E. (end of the Early Bronze Age). The next city (stratum V), dating to the Hyksos period (c. 1750–1550 B.C.E.), is characterized by a high level of development. This Middle Bronze Age city was fortified by a massive wall with insets and offsets and towers. In the southern part of the wall, a strong gate was discovered with the entrance between two guardrooms, a style typical of the period. The city continued to flourish in the Late Bronze Age (stratum IV, c. 1550–1200 B.C.E.). In this stratum plastered water cisterns, installations for the manufacture of bronze, numerous imported vessels from the Aegean area and Egypt, an inscription in the Ugaritic cuneiform alphabet, and an ink-inscribed ostracon in early Canaanite-Phoenician script were found. The following stratum (III) dates to the period of the Judges (Early Iron Age). This city shows signs of a decline in the material culture as is also evident in other sites from this period. The decline, however, did not affect the metal industry, which continued to operate at its previous high level. The abundance of Philistine pottery found in this stratum is proof of the strong influence of the Philistines in the area during this period. The destruction of the city by fire in the second half of the 11th century B.C.E. was a result of the wars with the Philistines that preceded the establishment of the monarchy. The city was rebuilt (stratum IIa) sometime in the tenth century and was surrounded by a casemate

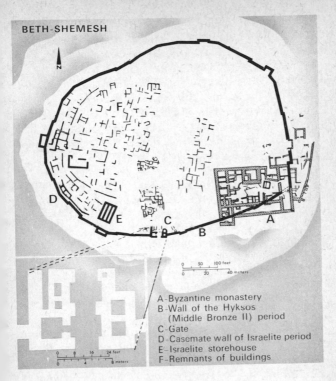

BETH-SHEMESH

A - Byzantine monastery
B - Wall of the Hyksos
     (Middle Bronze II) period
C - Gate
D - Casemate wall of Israelite period
E - Israelite storehouse
F - Remnants of buildings

Plan of the excavations at Beth-Shemesh.

wall—the typical fortification of Israelite cities in the period of the united monarchy. The large store house and granary erected in the city confirm the biblical description of the important administrative role held by Beth-Shemesh.

Settlement at Beth-Shemesh continued until the end of the First Temple period (strata IIb and IIc). The last city was unfortified. Between IIb and IIc there appears to have been some interruption in the occupation of the site, which may explain the absence of Beth-Shemesh from the detailed city list of Judah, where it would be expected to appear in the Zorah-Azekah district (Josh. 15:33–36). Scholars disagree as to whether the date of this gap in the history of Beth-Shemesh should be ascribed to Pharaoh Shishak's campaign in c. 924 B.C.E. or to the capture of the city by Jehoash, king of Judah, in the eighth century. In Roman times the settlement moved to nearby Ayn Shams, which preserves the ancient name. Talmudic sources describe Beth-Shemesh as a small village (Lam. R. 2:2; etc.) and Eusebius (Onom. 54:11-13) accurately locates it 10 miles from Eleutheropolis (Bet Govrin) on the road to Nicopolis (Emmaus).

x BET YERAḤ. This was a large Canaanite city on the shore of the Sea of Galilee extending over a tell of approximately 50 acres, from the site of the present-day moshavah Kinneret, to the outlet of the Jordan River from the lake near Deganyah. This location is based on the Jerusalem Talmud (Meg. 1:1, 70a) which speaks of two autonomous cities surrounded by walls, Bet-Yeraḥ and Ẓinabri (Sennabris), in the vicinity of the Sea of Galilee. An additional reference is found in *Bekhorot* 51a, which states that the Jordan River "began" at Bet Yeraḥ. Inasmuch as Sennabris is usually identified with Ḥaẓar Kinneret, it is probable that Bet Yeraḥ was situated on the site known to the Arabs as Khirbat al-Karak. Although not mentioned in the . Bible, the name points to an ancient Canaanite settlement whose deity was a moon god. Excavations were conducted there in 1944–46 by the Jewish Palestine Exploration Society and, from 1949, by the Department of Antiquities and the Oriental Institute, University of Chicago.

The earliest settlement at Bet Yeraḥ is dated at the end of the Chalcolithic and the beginning of the Early Bronze Age I (c. 3200 B.C.E.). The inhabitants lived in huts some of which were sunk into pits dug to a depth of about 11½ ft.

(3.5 m.). Traces of pavements and ovens were found in the pits. The erection of a brick wall, the first of Bet Yeraḥ's fortifications, was followed by the building of mud-brick houses and in the 29th century B.C.E. (Early Bronze Age II), stone houses made their appearance. A tomb from this period found at moshavah Kinneret contained gold ornaments in the style of Asia Minor. The settlement reached its zenith in the Early Bronze Age III (26th–24th centuries B.C.E.), when a large granary, 3,936 sq. ft. (1,200 sq. m.) in area, was constructed to the north of Bet Yeraḥ, indicating that at that time it was already the center of a large region of irrigated farmlands. The pottery of this epoch is light red or red-black burnished ware (a type common in Syria and Asia Minor) and its presence is apparently to be attributed to influences of northern peoples who penetrated through trade or invasion. In the Middle Bronze Age I the settlement was concentrated in the southern part of Bet Yeraḥ. No settlement existed there after that for about 1,500 years until the Persian period; to this period belong several graves found there. The city's location in ancient times east of the Jordan, on a narrow tongue between the river and the Sea of Galilee, necessitated building the main fortifications on the southern side. Here, where the Jordan now flows, the city lacked natural defenses in ancient times. The settlement at Bet Yeraḥ flourished again in the Hellenistic period. It has been identified with Philoteria, a Ptolemaic center, captured by Antiochus III in 198 B.C.E. and also mentioned among the cities conquered by Alexander Yannai (according to George Synkellus, 1:559). Remains uncovered from this period include a stone wall with vaulted openings and several houses, some with floors, plastered and painted walls, and windows overlooking the lake; numerous Rhodian stamped jar handles were also discovered.

In the early Roman period, a large Roman structure, covering an area of 105×59 ft. (32×18 m.), was erected on the ruins of the Hellenistic houses on the south. A large rectangular fort built of dressed masonry with towers at its

0 5 10 meters
0 33 feet

Above: Drawing of the base found at Bet Yeraḥ for a set of grain containers. Diam. 6 in. (15 cm.).

Opposite: Model of a similar set of containers from the tomb of Kamena at at-Kab, Upper Egypt, c. 2613–2494 B.C.E. Diam.11 in. (28 cm.), height 15¼ in. (39 cm.). Haifa, Dagon Museum.

corners was constructed on the northern part of the tell in the third century C.E. From this period there are several reports of a mixed Jewish-gentile population at Bet Yeraḥ (TJ, Meg. 1:1, 70a). After the Bar Kokhba war, priests of the Haaziah family settled there. The verse "Naphtali is a hind let loose" (Gen. 49:21) was interpreted by rabbis of the time as referring to Bet Yeraḥ, the territory of which was "entirely irrigated" (Gen. R. 98:22). The statement in the Jerusalem Talmud (loc. cit.) "The city was destroyed and became the possession of gentiles" also alludes to some event which occurred in the third century at Bet Yeraḥ or in its vicinity. In the fourth and fifth centuries, the fort seems to have been abandoned and its southern wall was used as the northern wall of a bathhouse. Excavations have shown that the bathhouse, the water for which was conducted through earthenware pipes from the aqueduct of Tiberias, had a central hall with a circular pool in the center and heated rooms. In the fifth century, a synagogue was

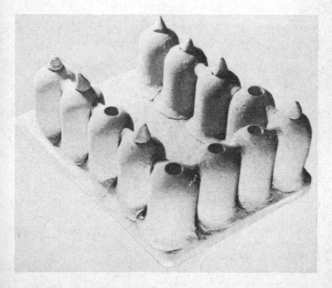

built within the fort. It was basilical, with an apse oriented to Jerusalem, and was one of the largest contemporary synagogues in the country, 121×72 ft. (37×22 m.). Its foundations have survived as well as part of its mosaic floor depicting a citron tree, a man and a horse (possibly a representation of the story of Mordecai and Haman), and also the base of a column incised with a seven-branched candelabrum.

North of the synagogue, a Christian church was built, basilical in form, with a central hall and two aisles; an atrium containing a well lay on its west side. The church had been enlarged to the north by a baptistery with a mosaic pavement dating from 529 C.E. Bet Yeraḥ was resettled in the seventh century after having been destroyed during the Persian or Arab invasion, but it was abandoned shortly afterward.

Pottery bowl of the Early Bronze Age III (26th-24th centuries B.C.E.) from Bet Yeraḥ, a typical specimen of the red and black burnished "Bet Yeraḥ ware." Jerusalem, Israel Department of Antiquities and Museums.

xi CAESAREA.

An ancient city on the coast midway between Tel Aviv and Haifa. Caesarea was originally called Straton's Tower after its founder Straton (Abd-Ashtart), who was probably a ruler of Sidon in the 4th century B.C.E. (Jos., Ant., 13:395). The city is first mentioned in 259 B.C.E. by Zeno, an official of Ptolemy II, as a harbor where he disembarked on his way to Jerusalem accompanying Apollonius on an economic mission to Erez Israel and Egypt. During the dissolution of the Seleucid kingdom it fell into the hands of a tyrant called Zoilus. In 104 B.C.E. Alexander Yannai captured the city and it remained part of the Hasmonean kingdom until its restoration as an autonomous city by Pompey; it was rebuilt by Gabinius[13] in 63 B.C.E. (Ant., 13:324ff., 395). For some time in the possession of Cleopatra,[14] it was returned by Augustus[15] to Herod[16] (Ant., 15:215ff.), who greatly enlarged the city and renamed it Caesarea in honor of the emperor. Herod surrounded it with a wall and built a deep sea harbor (called Sebastos, i.e., Augustus in Greek); the new city was officially inaugurated in about 13 B.C.E. The population of Caesarea was half gentile and half Jewish and the divergent claims of the two groups to citizenship and municipal rights led to frequent disputes (Ant., 20:173ff.; Wars, 2:266ff.; 284ff.). After Herod's death (4 B.C.E.) Caesarea fell to his son Archelaus, but after his banishment to Gaul in 6 C.E. it became the seat of the Roman procurators of Judea. Except for the brief reign of Agrippa I (41–44), who died in Caesarea (Acts 12:19–23), the city remained the capital of Roman and Byzantine Palestine. The clashes between Jewish and gentile communities finally sparked the Jewish war against Rome

[13] Roman general
[14] Egyptian queen
[15] First Roman emperor (63 B.C.E.–14 C.E.)
[16] King of Judea (?73–4 B.C.E.)

in 66 C.E. During the war Vespasian made Caesarea his headquarters and when he became emperor he raised it to the rank of a Roman colony—*Colonia Prima Flavia Caesarea.* The city prospered in the first and early second centuries but the harbor began to fill with sand in the late second century.

Caesarea was one of the first gentile cities visited by the apostles Peter and Paul (Acts 10:1, 24; 11:11; 21:8); Paul was imprisoned there before being sent to Rome (Acts 23: 23ff.). During the Bar Kokhba War (132–135) the city was the headquarters of the Roman commander Julius Severus and after the fall of Bethar several prominent Jewish leaders, including R. Akiva, were martyred there. In the third century Caesarea was a center of Christian learning; its celebrated scholars included Origen and later Eusebius, archbishop of Caesarea. Although it was the capital of Roman Palestine, Jewish life flourished there from the third century onward. The Talmud mentions judges or rabbis who lived in Caesarea, particularly R. Abba, R. Adda, R.

Aerial view of the theater at Caesarea, built by Herod between 22 and 10/9 B.C.E. It was in use until the 4th cent., when a Byzantine fortress was erected above it. Remains of the fortress can be seen in the foreground. Photo Government Press Office, Tel Aviv.

Ḥanina, R. Assi, R. Hosheya, R. Hezekiah, and R. Ahava b. Zeira (Er. 76b; TJ, Shab. passim). R. Abbahu, the most important local leader, represented the Jewish community before the Roman governor (Ket. 17a, et al.). The Talmud also refers to the synagogue of Caesarea (*Kenishta Maradta*—possibly the "Synagogue of the Revolt," TJ, Ber. 3:1, 6a, et al.); it was situated near the harbor and prayers were said there in Greek (*Alunistin*; "Hellenic": TJ, Sot. 7:1, 21b). Caesarea contained a large number of Samaritans who were recruited for the city guard (TJ, Av. Zar. 1:2, 39c). The city reached its greatest extent in Byzantine times when it was surrounded by a semicircular wall; it was then served by two aqueducts, one from Naḥal Tanninim and the other from the mountains near today's Zikhron Ya'akov. In the late Byzantine period Caesarea was the capital of the province of *Palaestina Prima*. It was the last Palestinian city to fall to the Muslims in 640. According to Arabic sources the Jewish inhabitants of Caesarea showed the conquerors a way into the fortress.

High-level aqueduct built by Herod to provide Caesarea with water from springs on Mount Carmel. It was restored by the Roman Second and Tenth Legions during Bar Kokhba's revolt (132–135). Photo Werner Braun, Jerusalem.

Statue of the fertility goddess, Artemis of Ephesus, found at Caesarea, third century C.E. Jerusalem, Israel Museum.

During the pillage that followed the capture of Caesarea in 1101 by Baldwin I, a leader of the First Crusade, Genoese soldiers discovered in a building some green glassware, among which was a bowl which the crusaders believed to be

Headless porphyry statue on a granite throne at Caesarea, Herodian period. Government Press Office, Tel Aviv.

the Holy Grail. Taken to Italy and still preserved in the Cathedral of San Lorenzo, Genoa, it became known as the *"Sacro Catino."* Utilizing the remains of Herod's large harbor at Caesarea the crusaders built a smaller harbor inside it and fortified the city, making it the seat of an archbishop, and building a cathedral there. The city was made a *signoria* of the larger feudal third, into which Palestine was divided. However, it was destroyed by Saladin in 1187 and again in 1191, but was restored by the Knights Hospitalers in 1218 when the city's citadel and southern breakwater were largely rebuilt. From 1251-52 it was splendidly reconstructed by Louis IX. This time the city too was strongly fortified, by a deep moat and high walls. The moat was transversed by two bridges. Most of the remains of the Crusader period now visible at Caesarea after recent excavations date to the time of Louis IX. Under Crusader rule the Jewish community dwindled until in 1170 only 20 Jews remained (according to Benjamin of Tudela).

In 1265 Caesarea fell to Baybars, and the Mamluks systematically destroyed the city, which remained in ruins—serving as a quarry for the pashas of Acre—until 1884, when it was resettled by Muslim refugees from Bosnia who lived there for a short time, and whose place was taken by Arabs. A few remains of Straton's Tower have been found north of the Crusader city. The Herodian city is represented by the remains of a harbor (moles and vaulted magazines), one vault possibly serving as foundation of the Temple of Augustus, and the remains of a wall with round towers. The Roman and Byzantine cities (although mostly still buried under 12 feet (4 m.) of sand) are also amply represented by a city wall, hippodrome, theater, and a paved square, with staircase and mosaics, where Roman statues were set up, in secondary use in Byzantine times. The foundations of a cathedral and of another church outside the wall, paved with fine mosaics depicting beasts and birds, as well as the remains of a synagogue, have been uncovered near the harbor at its northern end. From the Crusader period, the wall of Louis IX, with its sloping fosse, gateways, and towers, has been cleared and partly restored. Many remains of sculpture (including a very large porphyry statue) and hundreds of inscriptions (among them the first epigraphic mention of Pontius Pilate and of Nazareth) have been found in this site. Caesarea's exploration has been undertaken by the Israel Department of Antiquities, the Hebrew University, the Instituto Lombardo of Milan, the Link Underwater Expedition, and the Israel Department for the Preservation of Antiquities and Landscape. The full investigation of the huge site has, however, hardly begun.

xii CAPERNAUM. An ancient village on the N.W. shore of the Sea of Galilee, its name is derived from the Hebrew *Kefar* ("village of") *Nahum* (an unknown personage). It is first mentioned by Josephus as a village on his line of advance toward the issue of the Jordan into the Sea of Galilee and is described by him as "a highly fertile spring called by the inhabitants Capharnaum" (Wars, 3:519–20). In the New Testament it appears as the place of residence chosen by Jesus on the shore of the lake and it is sometimes even termed "his own city" (Matt. 4:13; 9:1), and it is also stated that he preached in the synagogue of Capernaum one Sabbath (Mark 1:21; John 6:59). It was the seat of a customs house (Matt. 9:9) and at least five of the apostles, including the very first ones, were fishermen from Capernaum. Although Jesus in the end reproved the people of Capernaum for their lack of belief (Matt. 11:23; Luke 10:15), a Judeo-Christian community continued there into talmudic times (Eccles. R. 1:8). Capernaum is identified

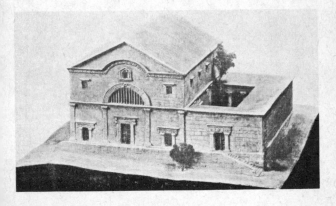

Facade of a reconstructed model of the synagogue. From H. Kohl-C. Watzinger, *Antike Synagogen in Galilea,* Leipzig, 1916.

Ruins of the synagogue at Capernaum, second–third century C.E. In the foreground are the steps leading from the eastern courtyard to the synagogue proper. Government Press Office, Tel Aviv.

The pentagram known as Solomon's Seal, from the gallery frieze of the synagogue. Government Press Office, Tel Aviv.

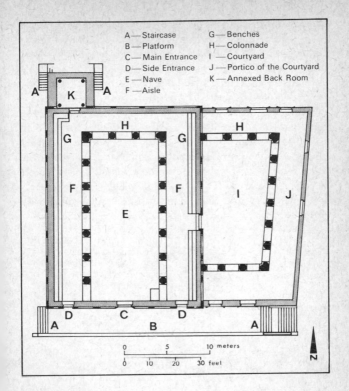

A — Staircase	G — Benches
B — Platform	H — Colonnade
C — Main Entrance	I — Courtyard
D — Side Entrance	J — Portico of the Courtyard
E — Nave	K — Annexed Back Room
F — Aisle	

0   5   10 meters
0 10 20 30 feet

N

Plan of the Capernaum synagogue, third century C.E. E. L. Sukenik, *Ancient Synagogues in Palestine and Greece,* London, 1934.

with a ruin called Tell Ḥūm in Arabic. Remains of a synagogue were excavated there by H. Kohl and C. Watzinger in 1905; it was entirely cleared and partly restored by the Franciscan fathers who own the site. Dating from the late second or early third century, it is one of the best preserved Galilean synagogues of the early type. The synagogue measures 360 sq. m. (c. 3,960 sq. ft.) and consists of a main basilica-shaped hall with one large and two small entrances in the facade which faces south toward Jerusalem.

The facade is ornately decorated: above the main entrance is a large semicircular window with a sculptured frieze running round it. The base of the triangular gable is arched in the "Syrian" style. The hall contains two parallel rows of columns along its length and one transverse row, and stone benches along the walls. The interior is undecorated and no evidence was found of a fixed Torah ark. Steps outside the building led to an upper gallery (probably for women worshipers). The wall of the gallery was adorned with an elaborate stone frieze depicting symbols of the plants of the Holy Land, Jewish religious symbols, including the Tabernacle, *menorah,* and Torah ark, and magic symbols such as the pentagram and hexagram. A colonnaded court with porches east of the hall probably served as a guest house.

Detail from the gallery frieze of the synagogue, showing what is believed to be the Ark of the Covenant on a wagon.

Government Press Office, Tel Aviv.

xiii EN-GEDI. En-Gedi is an oasis on the western shore of the Dead Sea and one of the most important archaeological sites in the Judean Desert. En-Gedi (En-Gaddi in Greek and Latin; 'Ayn Jiddī in Arabic) is actually the name of the perennial spring which flows from a height of 661 ft.(200 m.) above the Dead Sea. In the Bible, the wasteland near the spring where David sought refuge from Saul is called "the wilderness of En-Gedi" and the enclosed camps at the top of the mountains, the "strongholds of En-Gedi" (I Sam. 24:1–2). En-Gedi is also mentioned among the cities of the tribe of Judah in the Judean Desert (Josh. 15:62). A later biblical source (II Chron. 20:2) identifies En-Gedi with Hazazon-Tamar but this is rejected by most scholars. In the Song of Songs 1:14 the beloved is compared to "a cluster of henna in the vineyards of En-Gedi"; the "fishers" of En-Gedi are mentioned in Ezekiel 47:10.

In later literary sources, Josephus speaks of En-Gedi as the capital of a Judean toparchy and tells of its destruction during the Jewish War (Wars, 3:55; 4:402). From documents found in the Cave of the Letters[17] in Naḥal Hever, it appears that in the period before the Bar Kokhba War (132–135), the Jewish town of En-Gedi was imperial property and Roman garrison troops were stationed there. But in the time of Bar Kokhba, it was under his control, and was one of his military and administrative centers in the Judean Desert. In the Roman-Byzantine period, the settlement of En-Gedi is mentioned by the Church Fathers; Eusebius describes it as a very large Jewish village (Onom. 86:18). En-Gedi was then famous for its fine dates and rare spices.

After surveys of the area, five seasons of excavations were conducted at En-Gedi by B. Mazar, T. Dothan, and I.

---

[17] One of the Judean Desert Caves in which 15 letters from Bar Kokhba were found

Menorah discovered in the 1970 excavations at En-Gedi. Israel Department of Antiquities and Museums, Jerusalem.

Dunayevsky between the years 1961–62 and 1964–65. The settlement of En-Gedi was found to have been established only in the seventh century B.C.E. with no evidence of occupation in the time of David (tenth century B.C.E.). Excavations showed that Tell Goren (Tell el-Jurn), a small hill above the southwestern part of the plain near Naḥal Arugot, was one of the main centers in the oasis beginning with the Israelite and especially in the Iron II, Hellenistic, and Roman-Byzantine periods. Surveys of the area revealed that the inhabitants of En-Gedi had developed an efficient irrigation system and engaged in intensive agriculture. The combination of abundant water and warm climate made it possible for them to cultivate the rare spices for which En-Gedi was renowned. The settlement was apparently administered by a central authority which was responsible for building terraces, aqueducts, and reservoirs, as well as a network of strongholds and watchtowers.

Five periods of occupation were uncovered on Tell Goren. The earliest settlement, Stratum V, was a flourishing town which had spread down the slopes of the tell dating

The synagogue at En-Gedi. G.P.O., Tel Aviv

from the Judean kingdom (c. 630–582 B.C.E.). Various installations, especially a series of large clay "barrels" fixed in the ground, together with pottery, metal tools, and ovens indicated that workshops had been set up for some special industry. This discovery conforms with literary sources (Josephus and others) which mention En-Gedi as a center for the production of *opobalsamon* ("balsam"). It can thus be assumed that En-Gedi was a royal estate which ran this costly industry in the service of the king. This first settlement was apparently destroyed and burned by Nebuchadnezzar in 582/1 B.C.E.

The next town on the tell (Stratum IV) belongs to the Persian period (fifth fourth centuries B.C.E.). Its area was more extensive than the Israelite one and its buildings were larger and well-built. A very large house, part of it two-storied, which contained 23 rooms, was found on the northern slope of the tell. En-Gedi at this time was part of the province of Judah as attested by the many sherds inscribed "Yehud," the official name of the province.

Stratum III belongs to Hellenistic times. Its famous dates are mentioned in this era by Ben Sira[18] (Ecclus. 24:10).

---

[8] 2nd cent. B.C.E. Hebrew aphorist sage, and scribe, the author of the Wisdom of Ben Sira (Ecclesiasticus)

En-Gedi flourished in the Hasmonean period, especially in the time of Alexander Yannai and his successors (103–37 B.C.E.). A large fortress on the tell was probably destroyed in the period of the Parthian invasion and the last war of the Hasmoneans against Herod.

The next occupation (Stratum II) contains a strong fortress on the top of the tell surrounded by a thick stone wall with a rectangular tower. This settlement is attributed to the time of Herod's successors (4–68 C.E.); it was destroyed and burned apparently during the Jewish War in 68 C.E. Coins from the "Year Two" of the war were found in the area of the conflagration.

During the Roman-Byzantine period (Stratum I) the inhabitants of the tell lived in temporary structures and cultivated the slopes of the hill (third–fifth centuries C.E.). It appears that at least from the time of the Herodian period the main settlement at En-Gedi moved down to the plain, east and northeast of Tell Goren between Naḥal David and Naḥal Arugot. A Roman bath was found in the center of this plain about 660 ft. (200 m.) west of the shore of the Dead Sea. It is dated by finds, especially six bronze coins, to the period between the fall of the Second Temple and the Bar Kokhba War.

A sacred enclosure from the Chalcolithic period was found on a terrace above the spring. It consists of a group of stone structures of very high architectural standard. The main building was apparently a temple which served as the central sanctuary for the inhabitants of the region.

Recent excavations have brought to light the remains of a Jewish community in the Byzantine period. Their synagogue had a beautiful mosaic floor depicting peacocks eating grapes, and the words "Peace on Israel," as well as a unique inscription consisting of 18 lines which, inter alia, calls down a curse on "anyone causing a controversy between a man and his fellows or who (says) slanders his friends before the gentiles or steals the property of his friends, or anyone revealing the secret of the town to the gentiles..." (According to Lieberman, it was designed against those revealing the secrets of the balsam industry.) A seven branched menorah of bronze and more than 5,000 coins (found in the synagogue's cash box by the ark) were also uncovered.

Later, En Gedi was abandoned and remained in ruins.

xiv GEZER. Gezer was a major city in ancient times located in the northern Shephelah at Tell Jazar (also called Tell Abu-Shūsha). Gezer was first settled in the Chalcolithic period (fourth millennium B.C.E.). In the Early Bronze Age I it was occupied by a non-Semitic people who followed the custom of burning their dead. Semitic settlers established there in the Early Bronze Age II–IV (3rd millennium B.C.E.) enclosed the city with a wall. The Canaanite occupation reached its peak of prosperity in the Middle Bronze and Late Bronze I

1. Outer wall of the Late Bronze Age.
2. Inner wall of the Middle Bronze Age.
3. Part of the inner wall.
4. Gate of the inner wall, three entry way.
5. Part of the casemate wall.
6. Water tunnel of the Late Bronze Age.
7. Four entry way gate of the Solomonic period.
8. High place of the Middle Bronze Age.
9. Wêli (a hole to obtain water).
10. Part of the inner wall (excavation of 1934).

Plan of the Gezer excavations. Courtesy William G. Dever, Herew Union College, Biblical and Archaeological School, Jerusalem.

A "high place" at Gezer, with ten pillars and a stone basin or altar. Middle Bronze Age II, c. 1600 B.C.E. Courtesy William G. Dever, Hebrew Union College, Biblical and Archaeological School, Jerusalem.

Ages (20th–14th centuries B.C.E.), when a stone wall 10ft. (3 m.) wide with square towers was built around the city. This period at Gezer also yielded objects testifying to links with Egypt as well as a potsherd in ancient Canaanite script. The city is first mentioned in Egyptian documents in the list of cities captured by Thutmose III (c. 1469 B.C.E.). The importance of Gezer in the 14th century is evident from the Tell el-Amarna letters. Milkilu, king of Gezer, and his successor Yapahu controlled an extensive area which also included Aijalon and Zorah; their chief rival was the king of Jerusalem. The capture of Gezer is mentioned in the "Israel stele" of Pharaoh Merneptah (c. 1220 B.C.E.) together with Ashkelon and Yeno'am. During the Israelite conquest, Horam, king of Gezer, was defeated in battle by the Israelites (Josh. 10:33). His city was assigned to the Levites in Ephraim (Josh. 16:3, 21:21) but its population remained predominantly Canaanite (Josh. 16:10, Judg. 1:29)

Solomonic city gate at Gezer, with finely dressed ashlar masonry at the threshold. (1) On the sides of the street, divided by a large drain (2), are four sets of piers guarding the entry. Courtesy William G. Dever, Hebrew Union College, Biblical and Archaeological School, Jerusalem.

Pharaoh Siamun (?) conquered Gezer and ceded it to Israel "for a portion unto his daughter, Solomon's wife," Commanding the approaches to Jerusalem, the city became one of the major strongholds of Solomon who built a gate there identical in plan with gates he erected at Hazor and Megiddo (I Kings 9:15–17). Part of the Solomonic city gate, built of dressed stones, and an adjacent casemate wall have been discovered there. A stepped tunnel 216 ft. (66 m.) long cut to provide access to the water table may date to this period. The Gezer Calander, a Hebrew inscription of seven lines, dated to the tenth century B.C.E., and citing an annual cycle of agricultural activities was found there. Gezer was conquered by Shishak according to that Pharaoh's inscriptions (c. 924 B.C.E.) and archaeological finds indicate that the city declined at that time. Tiglath-Pileser III's cap-

The "Gezer Calendar," an ancient Hebrew record of the annual cycle of agricultural occupations, late tenth century B.C.E. Replica in the Israel Museum, Jerusalem.

ture of the city (probably in 74 B.C.E.) is depicted on a relief found at Calah. In the Assyrian period Gezer's population was augmented by foreign settlers; contracts of two of these, written in cuneiform from the years 651 and 649 B.C.E., have survived. The city recovered in the Persian period and under the Hellenistic kings it again became an important royal fortress. During the Hasmonean wars Gezer was a major Greek base and remained in Greek hands until its capture in 142 B.C.E. by Simeon who expelled the aliens. He refortified the city and made it the military center of his state, under the command of his son John Hyrcanus, second only to Jerusalem (I Macc. 4:15; 9:52: 13:43; 16:19). A Hasmonean palace discovered there was apparently built by Greek prisoners of war; a curse was found scratched on one of its stones: "May fire descend from heaven and devour the house of Simeon." Gezer's importance declined after the Hasmonean period and the center of the district was transferred to Emmaus. Eusebius mentions it as a village four miles north (this should read "south") of Emmaus (Onom. 66:19ff.). It does not appear in other ancient sources but a Roman bathhouse and several Christian lamps found there testify to its continued occupation. On the Madaba Map, the legend "Gedor also Gidirtha" apparently refers to Gezer. It was known as Montgisart in the crusader period; there King Baldwin II defeated the forces of Saladin[19] in 1177, by 1191 it was in the hands of the Muslims and served as their headquarters in the war against Richard the Lionhearted.

After crusader times the site was completely forgotten. It was reidentified by C. Clermont-Ganneau in 1873 and investigated in excavations conducted at Tell Jazar by R.A.S. Macalister from 1902 to 1912, A. Rowe in 1934–35, and from 1964, by the Hebrew Union College under G. E. Wright, William G. Dever, and others.

[19] Sultan of Egypt and Syria (1138–1193)

xv HAZOR. Hazor is a large Canaanite and Israelite city in Upper Galilee. It is identified with Tell al-Qidāḥ (also called Tell Waqqāṣ), 8¾ mi. (14 km.) north of the Sea of Galilee and 5 mi. (8 km.) southwest of Lake Ḥuleh. The city was strategically located in ancient times and dominates the main branches of the Via Maris ("Way of the Sea") leading from Egypt to Mesopotamia, Syria, and Anatolia.

Canaanite Hazor is mentioned in the Egyptian Execration Texts [20] (19th, 18th century B.C.E.) and is the only Palestinian town mentioned (together with Laish) in the Mari documents (18th century B.C.E.) where it appears as a major commercial center of the Fertile Crescent with caravans traveling between it and Babylon. It is also frequently mentioned in Egyptian documents of the New Kingdom: in the city lists of Thutmoses III (where it appears together with Laish (Dan), Pella, and Kinnereth), and of Amenhotep II and Seti I. In the Tell el-Amarna letters the kings of Ashtaroth and Tyre accuse Abdi-Tirshi, king of Hazor, of taking several of their cities. The king of Tyre furthermore states that the king of Hazor left his city to join the Habiru. In other letters, however, Abdi-Tirshi—one of the few Canaanite rulers to call himself king—proclaims his loyalty to Egypt. Hazor is also referred to in the Papyrus Anastasi I (probably from the time of Ramses II).

The Bible contains a direct reference to the role of Hazor at the time of Joshua's conquests. Jabin, king of Hazor, headed a league of several Canaanite cities against Joshua in the battle at the waters of Merom: "And Joshua turned back at that time, and took Hazor, and smote the king thereof with the sword: for Hazor beforetime was the head of all those kingdoms . . . and he burnt Hazor with fire . . . But as for the cities that stood on their mounds,

[20] Curses which were inscribed on pottery bowls or crude human figurines in clay

Israel burned none of them, save Hazor only—that did Joshua burn" (Josh. 11:10-13). Hazor is also indirectly mentioned in the prose account of Deborah's wars (Judg. 4) in contrast to the "Song of Deborah" (Judg. 5) which deals with a battle in the Jezreel Valley and does not mention Hazor. According to I Kings 9:15, the city was rebuilt by Solomon together with Megiddo and Gezer. The last biblical reference to Hazor records its conquest, with other Galilean cities, by Tiglath-Pileser III in 732 B.C.E. (II Kings 15:29). In Hasmonean times, Jonathan and his army, marching northward from the Ginnosar (Gennesar) Valley during his wars against Demetrius, camped on the plain of Hazor near Kedesh (I Macc. 11:67). Josephus locates the city above Lake Semachonitis (Ant. 5:199).

Hazor was first identified with Tell al-Qidāḥ by J. L. Porter in 1875 and again by J. Garstang in 1926. The latter conducted soundings at the site in 1928. Four large campaigns of excavations—the James A. de Rothschild Expedition—took place between 1955 and 1958, under the direction of Y. Yadin on behalf of the Hebrew University, with the aid of P.I.C.A., the Anglo-Israel Exploration Society, and the Israel government. A fifth campaign took place in 1968.

The site of Hazor is composed of two separate areas—the tell proper covering some 30 acres (120 dunams) and rising some 130 ft. (40 m.) above the surrounding plain, and a large rectangular plateau, about 175 acres (700 dunams) in area, north of the tell. The latter is protected on its western side by a huge rampart of beaten earth and a deep fosse, on the north by a rampart and on the other sides by its natural steep slopes reinforced by glacis and walls.

Lower City. Garstang had concluded from his soundings that the large plateau (enclosure) was a camp site for infantry and chariots and since he found no Mycenean pottery (which first appears in the area after 1400 B.C.E.), he dated Hazor's final destruction to about 1400, the date he ascribed to Joshua's conquest. The excavations, however, revealed that the enclosure was not a camp site but that the

Aerial photograph of Hazor showing the tell proper (1), the plateau north of the tell (2), and the rampart of beaten earth west of the plateau (3). Courtesy Yigael Yadin, Jerusalem.

entire area was occupied by a city with five levels of occupation. It was first settled in the mid-18th century B.C.E. (Middle Bronze Age II), to which the fortifications date, and was finally destroyed sometime before the end of the 13th century B.C.E. The discovery of Mycenean and local ware from the 13th century helped to disprove Garstang's date of its fall. Seven areas in different parts of the lower city were excavated and the same chronology was found in all. The first city (stratum 4) was followed by a settlement (stratum 3) from the end of the Middle Bronze Age II (17th–16th centuries) which was razed by fire. The city was rebuilt in the Late Bronze Age I (stratum 2, 15th century). This stratum represents the peak of Hazor's prosperity together with the 14th-century city (stratum Ib) in which times Hazor was the largest city in the area in the land of Canaan; City Ib suffered destruction in undetermined circumstances. The last settlement in the lower city (stratum Ia) was a reconstruction of the previous one and with its fall, before the end of the 13th century, occupation ceased in the lower city. Its destruction, both here and in the contemporary city on the tell, is to be ascribed to the conquering Israelite tribes, as is related in detail in the Book of Joshua.

In the southwestern corner of the lower city (area C) a small sanctuary was found on the foot of the inner slope of the rampart. It dates from stratum Ib and was rebuilt in Ia. A number of basalt steles and statuettes were found in a niche in one of the walls, one with two hands raised toward a divine lunar symbol—a crescent and a circle, and a statuette of a seated male figure with its head intentionally broken off. Benches for offerings line the walls of the temple. A pottery cult mask was found in a potter's workshop nearby as well as a bronze standard plated with silver and bearing a relief of a snake goddess.

Reconstruction of a sanctuary found in the lower city of Hazor, 14th–13th century B.C.E. Jerusalem, Israel Museum. Courtesy Yigael Yadin, Jerusalem.

95

Rock-cut tombs with an elaborate network of tunnels connecting them were found in the eastern sector of the lower city (area F), dating from the earliest stratum. A large building (probably a temple) with thick walls was constructed there in the next city which used the older tunnels for a drainage system. In the next stratum (stratum II) a temple was built. In stratum Ib the area assumed a definite cultic character and a large monolithic altar with depressions for draining the sacrificial blood stood there.

In several areas, a large number of infant burials in jars were found beneath the floors of houses from stratum III.

Four superimposed temples were found in area H, at the northern edge of the lower city. The earliest (stratum III) consisted of a broad hall with a small niche—a sort of holy of holies. South of the hall was a raised platform reached by several finely dressed basalt steps. The next temple was substantially the same in plan but a closed court was added and an open courtyard south of it. The court was entered through a broad propyleum. The courtyard contained a large rectangular *bamah* ("high place") and several altars. A clay model of a liver, inscribed in Akkadian, found in a pile of debris nearby, was intended for use by the priest-diviners and mentioned various evil omens. A bronze plaque of a Canaanite dignitary wrapped in a long robe was also found. In stratum Ib, the temple was composed of three chambers built on a single axis from south to north: a porch, a main hall, and a broad holy of holies with a rectangular niche in its northern wall. In its general plan it resembles several temples found at Alalakh in northern Syria as well as the temple of Solomon. A row of basalt orthostats (which may have belonged originally to the previous temple) forming a dado around the interior of the porch and the holy of holies which is very similar to some found at Alalakh and other sites, shows distinct evidence of northern influence. On either side of the entrance to the porch stood a basalt orthostat with a lion in relief (only one was found, buried in a pit). The following temple (stratum Ia) shows only minor alterations. Two round bases found in front of the entrance to the hall are apparently similar to the Jachin and Boaz of Solomon's temple. The many ritual vessels (probably reused from the previous temple) include a basalt incense altar, with the emblem of the storm god in relief—a circle with a cross in the center, ritual tables and bowls, a statuette of a seated figure, cylinder seals and a scarab bearing the name of Amenhotep III. Outside the sanctuary were found fragments of a statue of a deity with the symbol of the storm god on its chest. The god had stood on a bull-shaped base.

A succession of city gates and walls ranging in date from the founding of the city to its final end was found in area K on the northeastern edge of the lower city. The gate from stratum III was strongly fortified, with towers on either side and three pairs of pilasters in the passage. A casemate wall adjoining it is the earliest example of this type found thus far in Erez Israel. A similar series of gates was found in the 1968 season on the eastern edge of the lower city.

Upper City. Five areas were excavated on the tell proper where 21 levels (with additional sub-phases) of occupation were uncovered. Settlement began here in the 27th century B.C.E. (end of the Early Bronze Age II), and, after a gap between the 24th and 22nd centuries, it was resettled in the Middle Bronze Age I (stratum XVIII). From the period of Hazor's zenith (15th century) parts of a large palace (the residence of the king?) and temple were uncovered which contained part of an orthostat with a lioness in relief similar to the lion orthostat from the contemporary temple in the lower city. Stratum XIII, the last Late Bronze Age city on the tell, shows the same signs of destruction in the 13th century as were found in the lower city. The upper city, however, in contrast, was resettled after a short interruption, but not in the form of a true city. Most of its constructions are still of a seminomadic character—silos, hearths, and foundations for tents and huts. These remains are essentially identical with those of the Israelite settlements in Galilee in the 12th century and indicate that the majority of this settlement occurred only after the fall of the cities and provinces of Canaan.

A part of the upper city of Hazor, showing Solomon's gate (1), a casemate wall of the tenth century B.C.E. (2), and a large storehouse, thought to have been built in the ninth century B.C.E. by the House of Omri (3). Courtesy Yigael Yadin, Jerusalem.

Stratum XI is an 11th-century, unfortified Israelite settlement, with a small high place. Only from the time of Solomon onward did Hazor return to its former splendor, though on a smaller scale than in Canaanite times. Solomon rebuilt and fortified the upper city (stratum X) with a casemate wall and a large gate with three chambers on either side and two towers flanking the passage. These are identical with the fortifications he constructed at Gezer and Megiddo (cf. I Kings 9:15). The following city was destroyed by fire and rebuilt by the House of Omri in the ninth century (stratum VIII) which erected a strong citadel covering most of the western part of the tell (area B). The citadel is symmetrical in plan with two long halls running from east to west and surrounded on three sides by chambers. The entrance was ornamented with proto-Aeolic capitals and a monolithic lintel. Near the citadel were a number of public buildings. The citadel was strengthened in the eighth century and continued in use until Hazor's conquest by Tiglath-Pileser III in 732 B.C.E.

A large storehouse with two rows of pillars in the center (mistakenly interpreted as Solomon's stables by Garstang) also dates to stratum VIII (House of Omri). Stratum VI (eighth century) was destroyed by an earthquake, possibly the one which occurred in the days of Jeroboam II, mentioned in the Book of Amos. The last fortified city at Hazor is represented by stratum V, and after its destruction by the Assyrians the city remained uninhabited except for a temporary unfortified settlement (stratum IV). A large citadel in stratum III was evidently constructed by the Assyrians and continued in use in the Persian period. Another citadel, from stratum I, is attributed to the second century, i.e., the Hellenistic period.

In the 1968 season a large underground water system was discovered at the center of the southern edge of the mound facing the natural spring below. It has the same plan (although on a much larger scale) as the famous one at Megiddo, and was hewn out of the rock at the same period, i.e., the ninth century B.C.E. (Hazor stratum VIII).

xvi HEBRON. Hebron is a biblical city in Ereẓ Israel, 19 mi. (32 km.) S. of Jerusalem in the Judean Hills, 3,050 ft. (930 m.) above sea level. The name Hebron is explained as deriving from the root ḥbr (friend), the name *Habiru*, or the Arabic word *ḥaber* ("granary"). In the Bible, Hebron is also referred to as Kiriath-Arba: "Now the name of Hebron formerly was Kiriath-Arba; this Arba was the greatest among the Anakim . . ." (Josh. 14:15) and "was the father of Anak" (Josh. 15:13). B. Mazar maintains that the name Kiriath-Arba implies that the city was a member of four *(arba)* neighboring confederated settlements in which the families of Aner, Eshkol, and Mamre resided around the citadel of Hebron.

In the Canaanite period Hebron was located to the south of modern Hebron, on the strategic hill known as Jebel al-Rumayda, which was also the site of the later Israelite city. Numbers 13:22 states that Hebron was founded seven years before Zoan, the capital of the Hyksos which was founded in about 1720 B.C.E. (cf. Jos., Wars, 4:530). Artifacts from this period—the middle Bronze Age—were found in a tomb in Wādī al-Tutāḥ; these included pottery, alabaster objects, and personal articles. At this time the name Hebron is connected with the Patriarchs, especially the purchase of the Cave of Machpelah (see below) by Abraham from Ephron the Hittite. Hebron, however, remained a Canaanite city: it was one of the important localities visited by the 12 spies (Num. 13:22). Hoham, the king of Hebron (Josh. 10:3), participated in the Battle of Aijalon against Joshua and was defeated there together with the other kings of Canaan. His city was conquered by Caleb son of Jephunneh (Josh. 15:13; Judg. 1:20).

After the death of Saul, David chose Hebron as his royal city and was anointed there as king over Judah (II Sam. 2:1–4). In addition, Abner was buried there (3:32)—his traditional tomb is still standing. The assassins of Ish-Bosheth, the son of Saul, brought Ish-Bosheth's head to David in Hebron, and he ordered that they be hanged next to the pool in the town (4:12). Eventually David was anointed king over all Israel in Hebron (5:1-3). The city was also one of the levitical cities and a city of refuge

Jar handle from the time of King Hezekiah, eighth century B.C.E., bearing a royal stamp consisting of a four-winged beetle with the words "to the king" above and "Hebron" below.

Courtesy Israel Department of Antiquities, Jerusalem.

(Josh. 21:13; I Chron. 6:42); it was an important administrative center and this was the reason why Rehoboam fortified it (II Chron. 11:10). In the division of Judah into districts during the Monarchy (cf. Josh. 15:54) Hebron was a city of the mountain district.

With the Babylonian conquest and destruction of the First Temple the Jewish inhabitants of Hebron were exiled and their place was taken by Edomites, whose border extended to Beth-Zur. According to Nehemiah 11:25, however, there were still some Jewish families living in the town; nevertheless, the Jews of Hebron did not participate in the construction of the walls of Jerusalem.

In I Maccabees 5:65 it is stated that Edomite Hebron was attacked by Judah Maccabee and its towers set on fire; the incorporation of the town into Judah, however, only took place after the conquest of Idumea by John Hyrcanus at the end of the second century B.C.E. With the conversion of the Idumeans, Hebron again became a Jewish city. King Herod built the wall which still surrounds the Cave of Machpelah. During the first war against the Romans, Hebron was conquered by Simeon Bar Giora, the leader of the Zealots (Jos., Wars, 4:529), and the city was plundered; it was later burned down by the Roman commander Cerealius (Jos., Wars, 4:554), but the Jews continued to live there. It appears that the population did not suffer during the Bar Kokhba revolt. There are remains in the city of a synagogue from the Byzantine period. It was during this period that a church was erected over the Cave of Machpelah: the "very large village" of Hebron then formed part (together with the Botna fortress to the north) of the fortified southern border of the country.

The Cave of Machpelah site is identified with Kharam el-Khalīl in modern Hebron. Surrounding the area, to a height of 39 ft. (12 m.), is a magnificent wall, distinguished by its hewn stones which are up to 23 ft. (7.5 m.) in length. Because of their style they have been attributed to Herod even though this style of stonecutting existed previously. Josephus, who describes the tombs of the patriarchs as "of

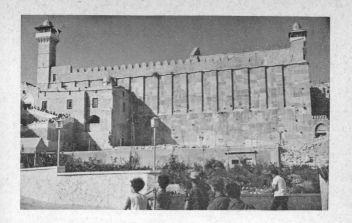

Site of the cave of Machpelah at Hebron, sacred to Jews and
Moslems as the burial place of the patriarchs. The wall, of
Herodian and Mamluk construction, surrounds a mosque built
over the cave itself. Courtesy Ministry of Tourism, Tel Aviv.
Photo David Harris, Jerusalem.

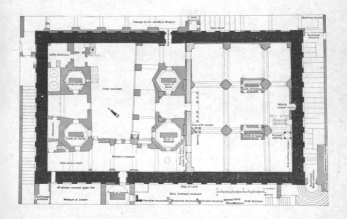

Plan of the mosque above the Cave of Machpelah, drawn by E.
J. H. Mackay and L. H. Vincent, 1932. From *Sefer Ḥevron*.

really fine marble and exquisite workmanship" (Jos., Wars
4:532), does not, however, mention the surrounding wall.
The earliest source on the arrangement of the graves is in
the Book of Jubilees (36:21) which states that "Leah is
buried to the left of Sarah." According to the Jerusalem
Talmud, the graves of the patriarchs are situated in the form
used for the partaking of a meal; the most prominent
reclining at the head, on the middle couch, the second
above him and the third below him (TJ, Ta'an. 4:2). The
two structures, which today mark the tombs of Abraham
and Sarah, are indeed in the center of the compound area.
The tombs of Jacob and Leah are at the northwestern end
so that when facing the tombs from the southwest—the
probable original entrance—the tomb of Leah is in fact to
the left of Sarah's. The area inside the compound was

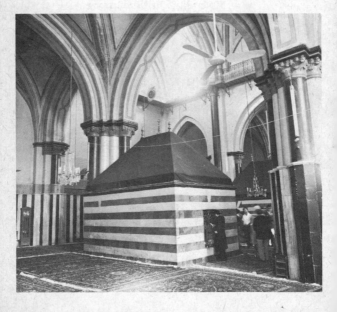

Traditional tomb of Rebekah in the cave of Machpelah at Hebron.
Photo Werner Braun, Jerusalem.

evidently originally left roofless. The Byzantines built a church, later converted by the Muslims into a mosque, at the southeastern extremity, which left the two constructions marking Isaac and Rebekah's tombs inside, while those for Abraham and Sarah were outside, at the entrance. In the floor, inside the mosque, are two openings leading to the cave underneath. One of these, at the southeast wall, is covered by stone slabs fixed with iron hooks. The other, at the opposite wall, is open, as a Muslim custom requires the lowering of an oil lamp which is continually lit. The actual form of the cavern is uncertain but from the accounts of travelers it seems safe to conclude that there are at least two caves joined by a passage and possibly a third inner chamber. The entrance to the caves (apart from the two openings) is not known today. Rabbinic sources mention the burial of Adam and Eve in the Machpelah and the alternative biblical name for Hebron, Kiriath-Arba ("the town of the four"), is explained to refer to the four couples buried there. According to Josephus and apocryphal sources, the sons of Jacob were also buried in the Machpelah. A Muslim tradition maintains that Joseph was buried here, his tomb and the Mosque of Joseph being just outside the southwest exit of the compound. This tradition is probably due to a corruption of the Arabic name for Esau, whose head, according to aggadic sources, fell within the cave after he had been killed in a battle for the right of burial in the Machpelah (Sot. 13a; PdRE 39).

During the Byzantine period, the Jews were authorized to pray within the area. The Christians entered through one gate and the Jews through another, offering incense while doing so; when the Arabs conquered the country they handed over the supervision of the cave of Machpelah to the Jews, in recognition of their assistance. During the late 11th century, the official responsible for the area bore the title of "The Servant to the Fathers of the World." The Jews of Hebron were accustomed to pray daily in the cave of Machpelah for the welfare of the head of the Palestinian aonate. Many Jews sought to be buried in the vicinity of

105

the cave of Machpelah. It was then written of them that "their resting-place was with that of the Fathers of the World." Benjamin of Tudela, the 12th-century traveler, relates that "many barrels, full of the remains of Jews, were brought there and they are still laid to rest there to this day." The Mamluk sultan Baybars prohibited the Jews and Christians from praying within the area (1267). Jews, however, were permitted to ascend five, later seven, steps on the side of the eastern wall and to insert petitions into a hole opposite the fourth step. This hole pierces the entire thickness of the wall, to a depth of 6 ft. 6 in. (2.25 m.). It is first mentioned in 1521, and it can almost certainly be assumed to have been made at the request of the Jews of Hebron, possibly on payment of a large sum, so that their supplications would fall into the cave situated under the floor of the area. The extremity of the hole is below the blocked opening in the mosque floor and leads to the cave.

In the hills of Hebron there are sites of archaeological interest. One such place is Eshtemoa. The site is occupied by the Arab village of al-Samū' 9 mi. (14 km.) S.S.W. of Hebron where many fragments of synagogue ornamentation, such as reliefs of candelabra, have been found. Remains of an ancient synagogue were uncovered by excavations conducted by L.A. Mayer and A. Reifenberg in 1935–36.

Excavations which were conducted by S. Yeivin in 1969 led to the discovery of a mosaic pavement with an Aramaic inscription. The synagogue differs in plan and details from the type common in Galilee in the third and fourth centuries C.E.

North of Hebron stand the remains of Beth-Zur. Remains of the Maccabean fortress, containing large rock-hewn cisterns, were uncovered in excavations conducted in 193 and resumed in 1957. The city was destroyed and abandoned, apparently during Vespasian's campaigns, but as shown by the Madaba Map, it was reestablished in th

Byzantine period, probably on the opposite hill, Khirbat Burj al-Ṣūr, whose ruins date from Crusader times.

At Khirbat Susiyyah, 2 mi. (3 km.) north-east of Eshtemoa, a synagogue, identical with the one in Eshtemoa, with numerous inscriptions and mosaics, was excavated. It was in use as late as the 9th cent. C.E.

The remains of the main entrance to the synagogue at Eshtemoa, fourth century C.E. The decorated lintel above the door is probably not the original. Israel Department of Antiquities and Museums, Jerusalem. Photo Emka, Jerusalem.

Excavations at Ramat al-Khalil, 1¼ mi. (2 km.) north of Hebron in 1926–28 revealed remains of a Herodian enclosure surrounded by a strong wall, as well as a Constantinian church, an altar, and a sacred well filled with the offerings (money, figurines, etc.) of worshipers. Its identification is uncertain.

xvii JAFFA. Jaffa is an ancient port city in the central sector of the Erez Israel coast. The meaning of the name Jaffa (Yaffo) is "lovely" or "pretty." The ancient city was built on a hill jutting out slightly from the coastline on the west and overlooking the open sea. At the foot of the rise on the western side extends the port, which was protected by a chain of rocks jutting out above the water; on the northern side there is a small bay that is protected from the southwest winds but open to the stormy winds from the north. Storms were probably overcome by using the mouth of the Yarkon River ("Me-Jarkon," Josh. 19: 46) at a distance of 3.7 mi. (6 km.) from the northern corner, where boats took shelter in the winter.

Jonah the prophet, unwilling to fulfill his mission to Nineveh, boarded a ship at Jaffa bound for Tarshish (Jonah 1:3). Some scholars assume that the expression "the Jaffa sea," mentioned in the Bible in connection with the transport of the cedars of Lebanon to the Temple (II Chron. 2:15; Ezra 3:7) and in Josephus in connection with the defense line built by Alexander Yannai "from the mountainside above Antipatris to the coast at Jaffa sea" (Wars 1:99), is a reference to the jetties of the Yarkon at Tell Kadadi and Tel Qasīla. Archaeological excavations were conducted at the Jaffa tell from 1955 by Y. Kaplan on behalf of the Tel Aviv-Jaffa Antiquities Museum.

One of the oldest remains found at Jaffa are pieces of wall of sun-dried clay bricks in the eastern part of the ancient Jaffa fortress and dated from the 16th century B.C.E. Remains were also found from the 15th to the 13th centuries B.C.E., which was the period of Egyptian rule in Jaffa. The name Jaffa is mentioned among the Canaanite cities that were conquered by Thutmose III in 1469 B.C.E. A folktale that came into being about 200 years afterward describes the conquest of Jaffa by Thutmose's military chief by cunning, rather than by war, through introducing soldiers into the fort in baskets. In the Tell el-Amarna letters, Jaffa is mentioned as an Egyptian district in which the king's stores were located. In the Anastasi Papyrus I, from the time of Ramses II (13th century B.C.E.), the Egyptian fort is described as being located on the side of the Canaanite city and containing workshops and arms stores. Excavations uncovered three stones of the fortress gate from the 13th century with inscriptions of the five titles of Ramses II.

The remains of the fortress gate (fourth level in the excavations) belong to the period of Israelite settlement, in the second half of the 13th century, and near the threshold a bronze bar that supported the corner of the left gate was uncovered. There are no written documents from this period; the description of the border of the tribe of Dan, which ran "over against Jaffa" (Josh. 19:46) is now dated by most scholars to the Davidic period. The appearance of the Sea Peoples at the beginning of the 12th century B.C.E. left its mark in the signs of destruction at the fourth level of settlement and in the few Philistine remains. However, there is basis for the supposition that the connection between the Greek legend of Perseus and Andromeda and the rocks off Jaffa is rooted in this period. It appears that Jaffa remained outside the boundary of Israelite settlement. Excavations have uncovered a part of the fortifications from the ninth century comprising a glacis covered with slabs of stone, beneath which were alternate strata of pressed earth and sun-dried clay bricks whose general width in some place reached four to five meters.

In the last third of the eighth century B.C.E., the period of 109 the Assyrian invasions of Erez Israel, Jaffa became, from what can be seen, part of the "province of Ashdod." At the end of the eighth century it was under the protection of Ashkelon, according to Sennacherib, king of Assyria, who conquered it together with Bene-Berak and Bet Dagon on his way to fight Hezekiah, king of Judah, and his Egyptian allies. In the fifth century B.C.E. the coastal cities were held by Tyre and Sidon with the support of the Persian rulers. Jaffa was under the control of Sidon according to the description of the coastal cities of Syria and Erez Israel of Pseudo-Scylax (fourth century B.C.E.) and the inscription of Eshmunezer, king of Sidon, which relates that the "lord of kings" (the king of Persia) gave Sidon two cities on the Erez Israel coast—Jaffa and Dor—as a sign of his gratitude. A Sidonian stone dedicatory inscription was discovered in 1892 in Jaffa and mentions the establishment of a Sidonian temple in the city. To these should be added the discovery of a part of the wall of the Sidonian fortress uncovered in excavations in Jaffa in 1955.

During the Greek period, after the Macedonian conquest and the death of Alexander the Great, Jaffa passed from one military commander to another until finally, in about 301 B.C.E., it fell, together with the rest of the country, to the Ptolemaic governors of Egypt. Jaffa quickly became a Greek city and its name changed to Ioppe ('Ιόππη), which is a Greek-sounding name. From the period of the Ptolemaic dynasty, which lasted a few hundred years, it is known that coins were minted in Jaffa during the reign of Ptolemy II and III bearing the name Ioppe. Another source of information on Jaffa in this period is the Zeno Papyri (mid-third century B.C.E.). In the excavations of Jaffa in 1961, a cave of tombs built of hewn-out stones and part of a dedicatory inscription in Greek that mentions the name of Ptolemy Philopater (the IV), from the end of the third century B.C.E., were found. At the beginning of the second century B.C.E. Erez Israel, and Jaffa together with it, was conquered by Antiochus III of the Seleucid dynasty.

In the time of the Hasmoneans, the leader of the revolt,

Judah Maccabee attacked the city and burned the harbor in retaliation against its foreign inhabitants for drowning about 200 Jaffa Jews (II Macc. 12:3-7). Afterward, his brother Jonathan conquered the city, and following his death, Simon finally annexed it to the Jewish state, after its military governor, Jonathan b. Absalom, drove the foreigners out of the city: "And he turned aside to Joppa, and took possession of it for he had heard that they were minded to deliver the stronghold unto the men of Demetrius; and he placed a garrison there to keep it" (I Macc. 12:34). During the 31 year reign of John Hyrcanus, the Syrians made repeated attempts to regain the income from Jaffa, but with the aid and political support of the Roman senate the city remained in Jewish hands (Jos., Ant. 13:261). Excavations have uncovered a portion of the fortress wall from the Hasmonean period that was built on the remains of an older fortress, which belongs to the end of the third century, or the beginning of the second century.

With Pompey's conquest of Erez Israel (66 B.C.E.), Jaffa was separated from the Jewish state and became, as did the other coastal cities, a free city in the district given over to the authority of the Syrian commissioner. Only in 47 did Julius Caesar return the city to Judea (Jos., Ant., 14:202, 205). In 38 Herod captured Jaffa on his way to Jerusalem to establish his reign there. Afterward he built the harbor of Caesarea, which was a strong competitor to Jaffa. During the reign of Antony in the east, Jaffa, together with the other coastal cities, was given to Cleopatra, the queen of Egypt; only in the year 30 was it returned to Herod by Augustus Caesar. A part of a house that was uncovered in the excavations belongs to the Augustan period. The structure included an entrance yard, a water hole, and a wall that was part of a room with an entrance. Jaffa is mentioned in the Christian chronicles in the context of the stories of Tabitha (Dorcas) and Simon the tanner. The New Testament contains the story of the miracle of Tabitha, who was resurrected by Peter (Acts 9:36-42). While in Jaffa, Peter stayed in the house of Simon the tanner and on his roof dreamed the dream that has been interpreted to allow Christians to eat the flesh of unclean animals. It was also there that he heard the voice calling him to convert pagans, as well as Jews, to Christianity (Acts 10:9ff.). With the outbreak of war with the Romans, Cestius Gallus destroyed Jaffa, but the city was quickly rebuilt by the Jews. They stationed a fleet of ships in the sea that attacked the ships passing on the maritime route from Egypt to Syria. Prior to his arrival in Jerusalem, Vespasian sent foot soldiers and cavalry to Jaffa, under cover of darkness, and they surprised the defenders of the city. The startled inhabitants quickly fled the city to take shelter in the boats, but, to add to the tragedy, a stormy wind broke early in the morning and dashed the boats and those in them against the rocks of the shore. The survivors were massacred by the Romans, who were waiting on the shore (Jos., Wars, 3:414–431). Vespasian then destroyed the city and built a fort on its ruins that contained a guard from the Tenth Legion. In the excavations, a piece of a tile was discovered with the seal of the Tenth Roman Legion on it.

Jaffa was rebuilt, it appears, still during the reign of Vespasian, who turned it into an autonomous city by the name of Flavia Ioppe. This is known from the coins that were minted during the reign of Heliogabalus (218–222), on which this name is mentioned. Three identical inscriptions engraved on a stone uncovered during the excavations tell of the Jewish community in Jaffa during the period between the destruction of the Second Temple and the Bar Kokhba revolt. The inscriptions contain the name "Yehudah," who was the inspector of weights and measures in the Jaffa market during the reign of Trajan. Another discovery is the floor of a cellar that belongs to the period of Trajan; above it were found many clay jars and bronze and silver coins. The Mishnah and Talmud, as well as tombstones discovered in the cemetery of Jaffa Jews in Abu-Kabir, are sources of information on Jewish Jaffa during the second to fourth centuries C.E. Among the scholars of Jaffa mentioned in the Talmud are R. Ada

(Meg. 16b; Ta'an. 16b), R. Naḥman (Lev. R. 6:5), R. Yudan (Lev. R. 20:10), and others. From the tombstones it is possible to learn of the occupations and origins of the dead. It becomes clear that the Jews of Jaffa during this period lived in neighborhoods according to their country of origin. Jews from Alexandria, Cyrenaica, Cappadocia, and other places are mentioned on the stones. Among the professions were trade in cloth, perfumes, rags, fishing, etc. Jerome, who visited Jaffa in 382, expressed his surprise at the sight of "the harbor of fleeing Jonah"; he also tells that he saw the rock on which Andromeda was bound.

From this period until the Arab conquest (636 C.E.), the information about Jaffa becomes more scarce. Cyril the Holy, from Alexandria, who wrote during the first half of the fifth century, described Jaffa as an important commercial center and a port of exit for all travelers from Judea to the countries of the Mediterranean. During this period, it seems that after its Christian population grew, Jaffa became the seat of the episcopate, and thus the name of the bishop of Jaffa, Phidus, is mentioned in the list of the church council that was convened in 431 in Ephesus. The name of another bishop, Elias, who participated in the council that convened in Jerusalem in 536, is also mentioned.

xviii JERICHO. Jericho is the oldest town known in Erez Israel. It is identified with Tell al-Sulṭān, near the 'Ayn al-Sulṭān spring (Spring of Elisha), about 1 mi. (1½ km.) N.W. of modern Jericho (Ar. al-Rīḥā) and 4½ mi. (7 km.) W. of the Jordan on the road leading to Jerusalem. The tell, covering an area of about 8½ acres (34 dunams) is 65 ft. (20 m.) high and 820 ft. (250 m.) below sea level. Its warm climate and abundant waters made Jericho an oasis attracting settlers from earliest times and it is a major site of the beginnings of civilization. The first systematic examination of Jericho was 113

Tell al-Sulṭān, the site of ancient Jericho, showing trenches cut
during successive archaeological excavations by K. Kenyon.
Photo Richard Cleave, Jerusalem.

conducted by E. Sellin and C. Watzinger in 1901–09.
Extensive excavations were carried out by J. Garstang in
1930–36 and K. Kenyon in 1952–61. Jericho was first settled
at the dawn of civilization, sometime during the eighth
millennium B.C.E. (Mesolithic period). From this period,
when the settlers lived as hunters and food-gatherers, flint
tools have been found and also the ruins of a building which
apparently served some cultic purpose. Two Neolithic
sub-periods are distinguished at Jericho; their main
difference is the absence of pottery in the first and its
appearance in the second. The pre-pottery Neolithic period
(seventh millennium) is characterized by irrigation farming
and the development of an urban culture represented by the
building of defensive walls—the earliest discovered so far in
the history of man. These undertakings are clear evidence of
the existence of a developed social organization. Two stages
in Jericho's development can be distinguished along with the
transition of man as a nomadic hunter to a sedentary
member of an organized community. In the first pre-pottery

Neolithic phase, after the settlers had apparently lived in huts, they constructed the first permanent houses discovered in Ereẓ Israel. These were round in shape and built of plano-convex bricks (flat with curved tops). The town was surrounded by a stone wall, 6½ ft. (2 m.) thick, to which a stone tower was attached, 30 ft. (9 m.) high and 28 ft. (8½ m.) in diameter with an inner staircase leading to the top of

Circular tower from the Neolithic Period (8000–7000 B.C.E.), of the Jericho city wall. Diam. 30 ft. (9 m.). From J. B. Pritchard, *Ancient Near Eastern Pictures*, Princeton, 1950.

the wall. For this phase radioactive carbon-14 tests of organic material establish a date of 6850±210 B.C.E., i.e., between 7060 and 6640 B.C.E. Following the destruction of this town, a new one was built on its ruins and also enclosed by a stone wall erected on new foundations. Rectangular-shaped houses, of elongated mud-bricks, contained plastered floors colored red or yellow and burnished to a high polish. On several were found impressions of rush mats once spread on them. Several structures from this level may have served as public buildings or perhaps temples. Eleven building phases and 22 superimposed plastered floors were distinguished in this city. Throughout its long history, the settlers had no knowledge of the art of manufacturing pottery but they possessed a highly developed standard of sculpture. An outstanding example of their artistic skill is a flat head modeled from clay with shells inset for eyes in a unique style. Beneath the floor of one of the houses were discovered human skulls coated with a limey clay with features molded into realistic human portraits. These skulls were probably connected with some cultic practice. Finds such as flint sickle blades, querns, mortars and pestles, and various types of grain indicate that the occupants of this city were agriculturists. Carbon-14 tests from various levels gave dates of 6520±200 (6720–6320) and 5820±160 (5980–5660 B.C.E.). In the fifth millennium, newcomers seem to have arrived at Jericho. No building remains date to this time but they brought with them a new culture—the art of manufacturing pottery. Their products are the earliest known pottery in Erez Israel. The vessels of this Neolithic period pottery are handmade, coarse and primitive, but some are finer and decorated with a red, well-burnished zigzag design. The latest pottery from this period, decorated with incised herringbone patterns, parallels the Yarmukian culture of northern Erez Israel. In the Chalcolithic period (fourth millennium), Jericho was uninhabited but remains were found at nearby Tulūl Abu al-ʿAlāyiq. Judging from the many changes in the fortifications and the appearance of the remains, the Early Bronze Age (third millennium) was one of great upheaval for Jericho and it was the scene of frequent wars and earthquakes. The walls were destroyed, repaired and rebuilt 17 times during this time. The thick walls, of unbaked bricks, built almost exactly over the Neolithic ones, had a semicircular tower—one of the rare examples of a tower known from this period in Erez Israel. Round structures, whose purpose is unknown, were found as well as a large rectangular tower, rectangular-shaped houses and tombs. Jericho flourished in this period and was destroyed by nomadic tribes which penetrated into Canaan in the Middle Bronze Age I (2100–1900 B.C.E.). The city was not rebuilt and the remains from this time are mainly a great number of tombs with weapons and pottery. In the Middle Bronze Age II (19th–17th centuries B.C.E.) the city again became prosperous and it was defended by an imposing system of fortifications consisting of a huge glacis of beaten earth on the slopes of the tell and supported at its foot by a massive stone retaining wall 20 ft. (6 m.) high. The fortifications are typical of the Hyksos period. Many tombs were found outside the city with rich offerings in alabaster and bronze, scarabs and jewelry as well as wooden objects and reed mats and baskets which are rarely preserved in Israel. The city was probably destroyed at the time of the expulsion of the Hyksos by the Egyptians; from the period of the latter's rule of Canaan (15th–13th centuries) little remained at Jericho but it is clear that the city was inhabited in the 13th century. This was the city encountered by the Israelites when they entered the Promised Land and whose conquest was essential for their advance into the interior of the country. Joshua sent two spies to investigate the city which the Bible describes as walled (Josh. 2:1). It was not captured in battle but by divine command: the Israelites were to encircle the city once a day for six days and seven times on the seventh day and then to the blare of trumpets and the sound of a great shout the wall of the city fell and it was burnt. The city and all that was in it was consecrated to the Lord and only Rahab, the harlot, who had hidden the messengers, and her household were saved (Josh. 6). In excavations at Jericho, no wall was found which could be attributed to the Canaanite city captured by Joshua. To resolve this discrepancy, some scholars suggest that the mud-brick wall was washed away by rain and erosion during the long period that it stood in ruins. Others maintain that the Canaanite city did not possess its own wall but reused the wall of the earlier city and still others consider the biblical tradition to be an etiological story invented to explain the destruction of the earlier city. At all events, the archaeological evidence does not help establish an exact date for the Israelite conquest of Jericho. The Bible contains many references to Jericho in the Israelite period (12th–6th centuries). The city was included in the territory of Benjamin (Josh. 18:21) and after Joshua's conquest of the city and his curse against anyone rebuilding it (Josh. 6:26), it apparently remained uninhabited as no remains from the 12th century were found. The Bible records the capture of "the city of palm-trees" by Eglon, king of Moab (Judg. 3:13). Evidence was found of a small settlement dating to the end of the period of the Judges and the beginning of the monarchy. A large public building of four rooms which was probably a royal storehouse is attributed to the tenth century B.C.E., i.e., the time of David. On their return from the Ammonite king, David's messengers remained at Jericho until their beards grew again (II Sam. 10:5). The city was rebuilt by Hiel, the Bethelite, in the days of Ahab, and for this act he was revenged by the fulfillment of Joshua's curse (I Kings 16:34). Some building remains from this time were found. The prophets Elijah and Elisha lived there (II Kings 2:4, 18–22) and the Judahite prisoners captured by the Israelites in the time of Pekah were returned to the "city of palm-trees" (II Chron. 28:15). The city expanded considerably at the end of the Israelite period (seventh, sixth centuries) but it remained unfortified and unimportant up to its destruction by the Babylonians in 587 B.C.E. The city was resettled by 345 Babylonian exiles (Neh. 7:36) and they participated in rebuilding the wall of Jerusalem (3:2). A small settlement lived there in the post-Exilic period. Jar handles inscribed "Yehud," the Aramaic name of the province of Judea under Persian rule, indicate that Jericho was included in the Judean state. On one handle, after the name "Yehud" appears "Urio"; he was apparently the official in charge of the fiscal affairs of the state. Jericho was abandoned in the Hellenistic period and became a cemetery; some buildings and burials were found from the Byzantine and early Arab periods. Hellenistic and Roman Jericho moved farther west to Tulūl Abu al-'Alāyiq where Wadi al-Qilt enters the Jordan Valley. Remains of a Hellenistic fortress are identified with the fortifications erected by Bacchides during his war with the Hasmoneans. Gabinius made it the seat of one of his councils (synhedria) when he reorganized Judea into five districts. Remains of imposing structures constructed by Herod were also found. Because of its vast groves of dates and persimmons, it was a state possession. The city was destroyed during the Jewish War (66–70) and military installations were again built there in the time of Hadrian. In the time of the Bordeaux pilgrim[21] (333), it was still occupied. In the Byzantine period Jericho moved about 1 m. (1½ km.) east to its present location. Near the city were remains of a seventh-century basilical-shaped synagogue. It was oriented toward Jerusalem and had a mosaic pavement decorated with a *menorah*, the inscription "peace on Israel," and a memorial inscription in Aramaic.

Jericho is mentioned in the *Onomasticon* of Eusebius (fourth century) and was depicted as a flourishing city on the Madaba Map (sixth century) where the well, which supplied the ancient city with water, is shown as a church and called the "Spring of Elisha" ($\tau\grave{o}$ $\tau[o\tilde{v}]$ $\dot{\alpha}\gamma\iota[o\tilde{v}]$ $\text{'}E\lambda\iota\sigma\alpha\acute{\iota}ov$). This according to tradition was the site of the story of Elisha in the Bible (II Kings 2:18–22). It seems that by the seventh century Jericho was again in ruins but Jewish refugees from the tribe of Banu Nadir fled there from before Muhammad. A new synagogue arose on the site of

[21] Anonymous author, the writer of an itinerary in which he describes his journey to Ereẓ Israel

Mosaic floor from a seventh-century synagogue in Jericho.
Seen in the disc at the bottom are a *menorah, lulav,* and *etrog,*
and the words "peace unto Israel." Courtesy Israel Department of
Antiquities, Jerusalem.

the Byzantine one and the Masoretes mention a "Jericho Codex" existing there. With the Arab conquest the Omayyad Khalif, Hisham, built a winter palace in 724 at Khirbat Mafjar nearby. Excavations in 1935 brought to light beautiful mosaics and engravings there. By 891 Jericho was the district capital of the Ghauer (cleft of the lower Jordan; Ya'kūbī, 113) and by the early Middle Ages was important for the production of indigo and sugarcane (Yākūt, 3:823, 913). It was captured by the Crusaders in 1099 and used by Raymond IV, count of Toulouse, as an encampment when his rival Godfrey de Bouillon gained Jerusalem. Queen Melisande endowed the whole of Jericho and its surrounding lands to her newly established convent of St. Lazarus (at Bethany) in 1147 and fortified Jericho with a tower. It was recaptured by Saladin without a struggle in 1187. The present Jericho is on the site of the Crusader town. Close by is the site of ancient Dok on the summit of which is the Byzantine Monastery of the Temptation (Qarantal) where Jesus was said to have fasted for forty days and nights (cf. Matt. 4:1-5; hence its medieval name, Mons Quarantana). The Knights Templar built a fortress on the summit, called Castellum Dok and the monastery was granted the tithes of Jericho city and the rights of the sugar mills in 1136. At the foot of the hill are the remains of three Crusader sugar mills (one nearly intact) which were referred to as early as 1116. They were driven by water systems originally built by Herod and repaired by the Crusaders. Nearby a Crusader building for boiling the sugar is in a good state of preservation. The town itself was practically uninhabited from then until the 19th century.

xix JERUSALEM. Since the mid-19th c. when the earliest research started in Erez Israel, Jerusalem has been the main attraction for archaeologists because of its historical and religious significance. The fact that Jerusalem was populated by layer upon layer of ancient civilizations and included many sites sacred to the various religions made methodical archaeological research a difficult and challenging task.

Investigation of the ancient remains on the surface began at the beginning of the 19th century. An appreciable part of the scientific surveys by E. Robinson (1824, 1852), T. Tobler (1845), C. J. M. de-Vogüé (1853, 1861) are devoted to ancient Jerusalem and contain descriptions and sketches of some of the remnants found on the surface. These works are particularly important because subsequent building activities in the city covered a good part of the remains. Charles Wilson (1864–66) conducted the first detailed survey and published an exact map of the city.

BIBLICAL PERIOD. *The City and Its Fortifications.* Charles Warren (1867–70) was the first to try to follow the line of the ancient wall by excavations, pits, and tunnels. In the S.E. corner of the Temple Mount he discovered what he identified as the wall of the Ophel, which continues for 750 ft. (230 m.) to the south on the top of the eastern slope of the two hills on which ancient Jerusalem was built. Although Warren perceived correctly that this wall was of later date than the First Temple, those who followed him assumed that at least the lower part of the wall belonged to the Jebusite city and to the City of David. Warren's work turned the attention of archaeologists to the eastern hill south of Jerusalem, whose form was like an elongated triangle based on the Temple Mount—the eastern side being the Kidron Valley, and the western side the Tyropoeon Valley, which divides the eastern from the western hill. This area, with the exception of the Temple Mount, is called the City of David in archaeological terminology.

Clermont-Ganneau and H. Guthe (1881) found additional sectors that extended the line of the "Jebusite wall" along the eastern slope of the City of David. In the southern end of the City of David, at the opening of the Tyropoeon Valley near the Siloam Pool, F. J. Bliss and A. C. Dickie (1894–97) discovered massive sectors of walls that served to dam the opening of the Tyropoeon Valley and fortify this weak point, which was the lowest in the whole city. They

Warren's dig at the southeastern corner of the Temple Mount, showing Herodian layers of the wall of the Mount (1) and adjoining it (2) what Warren identified as the wall of the Ophel. This was subsequently proved to be of a much later period, probably Hasmonean. In the background are the Mt. of Olives (3) and the Kidron Valley (4). Photo David Eisenberg, Jerusalem.

also discovered the continuation of the wall on the slopes of the western hill above the Ben Hinnom Valley. The lower of the wall's two levels was mistakenly attributed by them to the period of the First Temple. (This opinion served as the basis for including the western, as well as the eastern, hill in the Jerusalem of the early monarchy.) M. Parker's expedition (1909–11) dug in the area of the Gihon Spring and the slope above it, where an additional sector of the wall was discovered (the results of Parker's expedition were published by L. H. Vincent). The southern end of the City of David was investigated by the Weill expedition (1913–14, 1923–24), which revealed additional built-up sectors of the line of fortifications.

R.A.S. Macalister and J. G. Duncan (1923–25) excavated a considerable area in the north of the City of David over the Gihon Spring. They discovered sectors of the wall, towers, and revetment whose early use they attributed to the Jebusite city and subsequent use to Jerusalem during the period of David and Solomon. Inside the line of fortifications they uncovered a number of population strata, the lowest of which they attributed to the Canaanite and the Israelite cities. The J. W. Crowfoot and G.M. Fitzgerald expedition (1927–28) dug close to the area mentioned above. The results of the systematic excavation show that most of the remnants discovered there cannot be dated earlier than the Roman and Byzantine periods. They were additions to the system of fortifications then accepted as belonging to the Jebusite city—the splendid gate (the "Gate of the Valley"), which is above the Tyropoeon Valley in the west of the city (the width of the wall in the area of the gate is approximately 28 ft. (8.5 m.)). K. Galling, G. Dalman, J. Simons, L.H. Vincent, M. Avi-Yonah, N. Avigad, B. Mazar, and other scholars published theoretical studies based on these findings, while the efforts of archaeologists were directed to other areas of ancient Jerusalem.

There is a difference of opinion concerning the basic problem of the topography of ancient Jerusalem: the area of the city in the biblical period, particularly from the time of David and Solomon. Those who accepted the narrow concept (Galling, A. Alt, Mazar, and Avi-Yonah) claimed that the area of Jerusalem in that period spread over the

extension of the City of David—the eastern hill between the

Kathleen Kenyon's excavations in the eastern hill, south of the Temple Mount. Photo Werner Braun, Jerusalem.

Kidron Valley and the Tyropoeon Valley—at the top of which stood the Temple and the king's palaces within the boundaries of the Temple Mount and its vicinity, as they are today. The exponents of the wider concept (Vincent, Simons, Dalman and others) claim that the western hill, Mount Zion, and the Armenian and Jewish quarters of the present day should be added to this area. For their conclusions in this matter, the scholars employed the descriptions in the Bible far more than they used the archaeological findings then available.

The excavations of Kathleen Kenyon (1961–67) opened a new period in the history of archaeological research of the city. She dug in many places, although in limited areas, in the eastern and western hills and a few inside the Old City. The fact that the areas of excavations were so limited was detrimental to the important conclusions she published. On the other hand, in the great cut A, which was carried out between the Gihon Spring and the sectors of the upper wall discovered by Macalister and Duncan in 1925, the key to understanding the topography and the boundaries of the city in biblical times was made clear. The system of fortifications discovered by Macalister and Duncan was found to have been built on the remnants of the biblical city, which were demolished with the destruction of Jerusalem at the end of the First Temple period. It thus becomes clear that the line of fortifications discovered by Macalister and Duncan did not precede the Return to Zion or the Hasmonean period. This conclusion also holds for the rest of the remnants of fortifications discovered on the top of the eastern slope described above.

A series of soundings on the eastern slope of the western hill confirmed the opinion that there was no continuation of Israelite population west of the Tyropoeon Valley. Kenyon's cut A was deepened in some places to the rock, where ceramics were found from the Early Bronze Age and the Middle Bronze Age. The most ancient architectural

structure was a thick wall built from hunks of rock in the

Middle Bronze Age, discovered at the bottom of the slope, some 82 ft. (25 m.) above the Gihon Spring. This was the wall of Jerusalem until the eighth century B.C.E. During the reign of Hezekiah a new wall, whose width was approximately 18 ft. (5.5 m.), was built in the same place.

The discovery of the site of the city walls in the biblical period solved another difficult problem, i.e., the relation between the entrance to Warren's shaft (which was 43 ft. high) and the line of the upper wall, which in the past had been attributed to the period of the Jebusite city and the City of David, placing the upper entrance to the ancient waterworks outside of the fortified area. Such an arrangement would have differed completely from those in every other ancient city and negated the very purpose for which the waterworks were constructed, i.e., to ensure a regular supply of water in the event of a siege. The inclusion of this water system within the limits of the fortified city, as a result of the discovery of the new range of walls, solved this problem.

Organizing the city's area was a problem because of the narrowness of its circumference, due to the steepness of its eastern slope. This problem was overcome by a series of graduated terraces filled in with stones and supported by stone walls that rose from the base of the city—the eastern wall—upward. According to Kenyon, this system was used in Jerusalem from the 14th century B.C.E. and throughout the Israelite period. It should be identified with the "Millo," mentioned in I Kings 9:15. Today it is clear that the Canaanite city extended only on the eastern hill, and its area was approximately 15 acres (60 dunams). There is ceramic evidence from the tenth century B.C.E. of the extension of the population northward to the Temple Mount, which had been built by Solomon as the upper city (the administrative and religious center). Its total area was then approximately 120 dunams. Remnants of buildings of hewn stone and proto-Aeolian capitals, found by Kenyon, hint at the splendid buildings of Jerusalem in the period of the kings (similar to those in Samaria and Megiddo). While

Kenyon produced archaeological evidence of the development of the ancient city on the entire eastern hill and Temple Mount, excavations carried out after the Six-Day War (1967) produced new evidence about the history of the western hill and the area today known as the Old City. In his excavations at the Citadel, Johns (1934–40) found ceramics from the late Israelite period not prior to the seventh century B.C.E. This fact was proved in the excavations of R. Amiran and A. Eitan (1968–69), in which floors of dwellings from that period were discerned. Similar ceramics were discovered close to the rock by Tushingham, working with Kenyon, in the soundings made in the Armenian Quarter and the Muristan Bazaar.

In N. Avigad's excavations (1969ff.) in the center of the Jewish Quarter, parts of buildings dated to the end of the Israelite period were discovered for the first time, in addition to late Israelite ceramics. His main find (1970) was a segment of the city wall, some 130 ft. long by 25 ft. broad (40 m. by 8 m.), running in a northeast–southwest direction across the western hill. B. Mazar's excavations (from 1968 onward) south of the Temple Mount uncovered a whole series of tombs hewn in the rock whose style suggests Phoenician influence and which he dated to the ninth-eighth century B.C.E. Their site is beyond the Tyropoeon Valley on the beginning of the rocky slope of the western hill. It is clear that this sector had not been included in the limits of the city in the period when it evidently served as a cemetery for the aristocracy. It is therefore now possible to conjecture cautiously that in the late eighth century B.C.E. an Israelite settlement was initiated on the western hill. The buildings which were dug out in the 1960s by Kenyon provide clear signs of the Babylonian conquest of the year 586 B.C.E. and serve as physical evidence of the destruction of Jerusalem at the end of the First Temple period.

Necropolises. The graves discovered by Parker (1909–11) on the slope above the Gihon are the most ancient finds in Jerusalem. They were dated to the beginning of the Early Bronze Age. Kenyon discovered a series of graves from the Middle Bronze Age on the Mount of Olives. Graves rich in remnants from the Middle Bronze and Late Bronze Ages were found near the Dominus Flevit Church and were excavated by S. Saller (1954). Graves with many important implements of the Late Bronze Age were also found in Naḥalat Aḥim (Amiran, 1961) and in the area of the UN headquarters. A series of graves of the First Temple period cut into rock were found east and west of the City of David. In some of them, the influence of the

The "Daughter of Pharaoh Tomb" of the First Temple period hewn out of the rock in Siloam village. Above the entrance to the square structure are the remnants of an inscription in ancient Hebrew characters. Photo David Eisenberg, Jerusalem.

Phoenician style is noticeable in the planning of the hewn graves, as well as in the cemetery area. As early as 1865 F. de Saulcy investigated the monolithic "Tomb of the Daughter of Pharaoh." Clermont-Ganneau examined a series of graves hewn in the rock of the Siloam village (among them was the grave with the inscription "[ ]yahu who is over the house"). In the southern end of the City of David, Weill (1913–14) found monumental tombs that he identified as the graves of the House of David, but it seems that this identification requires further proof. A summary study of the graves and accompanying inscriptions in the Kidron Valley and village of Siloam was made by Avigad (1945–47). A new survey of all the graves hewn in rock in Siloam was made by D. Ussishkin (1968). (For tombs discovered by Mazar south of the Temple Mount, see above.)

SECOND TEMPLE PERIOD. *The City and Its Fortifications.* Remains from the period of the Second Temple, and particularly from the time of King Herod (37–4 B.C.E.) served as a starting point for archaeological research. Terms and names connected with the period are mainly obtained from the descriptions of the city by Josephus. In 1867–70, Wilson and Warren were engaged in an investigation of the Herodian walls of the Temple Mount. Warren's description and precise sketches of the topography of Jerusalem, particularly of the structure of the Herodian walls, are still in use. "Robinson's Arch" and "Wilson's Arch" were studied in detail and the nature of their original function was examined. Warren uncovered a part of the foundation of the first arch of "Robinson's Arch" (revealed in its entirety by Mazar from 1969 and the concept of its having served as the base of an extensive bridge was abandoned). He investigated the Herodian subterranean structure in the south of the Temple Mount, which is called "Solomon's Stables." He also correctly identified the site of the Antonia fortress, adjoining the northwest corner of the Temple Mount, which was investigated by Clermont-Ganneau (1871) and Vincent and Marie-Aline de Sion (1955): (the foundation and stone floor of the fortress can be seen today in the cellars of the monasteries at the start of Via Dolorosa, for example in the convent of the Soeurs de Sion). C. N. Johns (1934–40) revealed three fortification systems in the court of the Citadel near Jaffa Gate. The two earlier systems belonged to the Hasmonean period and the third to the period of Herod. The most impressive remnant is Phasael's Tower, commonly called David's Tower (its original remnants are preserved to a height of 66 ft. (20 m.). It became clear that on the eastern side the city's fortification system rested on the walls of the Temple Mount and on the western side on the Citadel.

The remnants of the First Wall were uncovered south of the Citadel around Mt. Zion, along the Valley of Hinnom to the Kidron Valley. Schick and H. Maudsley (1871–75) located remnants of half a house in the rock that served as a base for the wall and its towers in the western sector between the Citadel and Mt. Zion. In the section between Mt. Zion and the Kidron Valley, Bliss and Dickie uncovered two fortification systems; the earlier was mistakenly ascribed to the period of the First Temple, but later comparisons with the findings of Johns' excavation in the Citadel show that it belonged to the Hasmonean period. The remnants of the walls found at the top of the eastern hill, which had been attributed to the First Temple period, were shown by Kenyon's excavations to belong to the continuation of the First Wall, which extended to the southeastern corner of the Temple Mount. Sections of the line of the First Wall, which descend eastward from Phasael's Tower directly to Wilson's Arch on the Temple Mount, were revealed by Warren in the area of the markets of the Old City.

The line of the Second Wall was reconstructed on the basis of the sources, rather than on archaeological findings (the scientific contentions of a number of scholars about this wall are influenced by the location of the Church of the Holy Sepulcher in this area). Fixing of the course of the Second Wall north or south of this church determines the

Dedicatory stone from a first-century C.E. synagogue in Ophel (City of David), Jerusalem. The inscription reads: Theodotus son of Vettenus who was priest and/Archisynagogos, son of Archisynagol/gos, and grandson of Archisynagogos, built/this synagogue for reading/the law and teaching the commandments also/the hospice, chambers, and water installa-/tions for the service of visiting guests/from abroad. This synagogue was/founded by his ancestors and the/elders and Simonides.

Photograph taken during C. N. Johns' excavations at the Jaffa Gate Citadel, showing two Hasmonean fortification systems (1 and 2) and the remnants of Herod's Phasael Tower (3). Courtesy Israel Department of Antiquities, Jerusalem.

"Robinson's Arch." Photo David Eisenberg, Jerusalem.

degree of scientific authenticity in the identification of this building, which, according to Christian tradition, is outside the course of the Second Wall. Established facts, however, are few. The line of the wall began at the First Wall near the Citadel, passing the area of the Church of the Holy Sepulcher, and reaching the Damascus Gate. Below this gate R. W. Hamilton (1931–37; 1938) and J. B. Hennessy (1964–66) uncovered a gate from the late Roman period, and under its foundations was found an Herodian construction, thought by Hamilton and Avi-Yonah to be the original gate of the Second Wall. Hennessy's attribution of the remains below the Damascus Gate to the time of Agrippa I, regarding them as part of the Third Wall, is based on insufficient evidence. From there the wall turned to the southeast toward Antonia. Kenyon dug near the Muristan Bazaar in the Old City and reported locating the fosse that is cut in the rock of the Second Wall, thus placing the area of the Church of the Holy Sepulcher outside of the market quarter fortified by this wall. Most scholars date the building of the Second Wall to the Hasmonean period.

The course of the Third Wall, the construction of which was begun at the time of Agrippa I (37 C.E.) is in dispute. Vincent, Simons, Kenyon, and Henessy fix the course parallel to the line of the Turkish Wall in the northern part of the Old City of today. The opinion of E. L. Sukenik and Mayer (1925–27), however, seems better founded. They identify the Third Wall with the line of the wall they uncovered along a distance of approximately 1,600 ft. (500 m.) from the Italian Hospital to the W.F. Albright Institute of Archaeological Research. (Sectors of wall, towers, and gate were revealed parallel to the line of the northern wall of the Old City, approximately 1,600 ft. (500 m.) to the north.) Sections of this wall had been examined by Robinson (1838), V. Schultze (1845), and C. Schick (1878).

Additional portions of the wall are still being disclosed today in digs along its course, which begins at the Citadel, continues northward to the Russian Compound, turns 134 northeast to the northern Kidron Valley, and there turns southward to the northeastern corner of the Temple Mount. The wall is built carelessly and is far simpler than the Herodian walls. This description is in keeping with the historical conditions at the time of its construction; it was begun in the day of Agrippa I and completed hastily before the outbreak of the revolt in 66 C.E. in order to protect the "New City."

The excavations of Macalister and J. G. Duncan, J. W. Crowfoot and G. M. Fitzgerald, and Kenyon on the eastern hill revealed the usual remnants of domiciles from the period of the Second Temple. Kenyon produced conclusive archaeological evidence as to the date of the destruction of those buildings, which coincides with the destruction of Jerusalem in 70 C.E. (Her other conclusion, that settlement on the eastern slope of the western hill did not begin before the time of Agrippa I, does not accord with the findings of other archaeologists.)

Remnants of the buildings of the Upper City were first revealed in the excavations of the Citadel. Amiran and Eitan (1968–69) revealed two levels of building; the earlier belongs to the Hasmonean city, while the latter is from Herodian times and was demolished with the destruction of Jerusalem. Avigad's excavations (1969ff.) in the Jewish Quarter disclosed remnants from the Hasmonean and Herodian periods. Beautiful architectural details and large quantities of plaster fragments, painted with a variety of geometric designs and plants, suggest the existence of a splendid building from the Herodian period. A seven-branched *menorah*—one of the most ancient known examples—engraved with great precision was found on one of the plaster fragments. Also uncovered was the large dwelling of the Bar Kathros family, rich in findings, which was completely covered with an accumulation of ash from the fire that razed it at the time of the destruction of the Upper City in 70 C.E.

The layout of the area around the southwestern corner of Temple Mount is becoming progressively clearer due to Mazar's excavations (beginning 1968). Alongside the 135 southern wall of the Temple Mount a wide street, paved with stone slabs, leading to Hulda's Gates, was discovered. It was supported by a high wall on its southern side, which separated it from the continuation of the slope of the eastern hill. The extent of the remains of "Robinson's Arch" was revealed. A monumental stairway was uncovered leading from the plaza in front of the Temple up to the street in front of one Huldah Gate (the "Double Gate"). Remains of a parallel stairway led up to the other Huldah Gate (the "Triple Gate"). The details of the southern and western walls of the Temple Mount serve as an example of the Herodian building system. The extent of the work and the expanse of the area involved resulted in the discovery of thousands of small items (pottery, coins, etc.).

A summary of archaeological research today shows that the Second Temple city grew from the ancient kernel of the City of David and part of the western hill, in which the

B. Mazar's excavations along the west wall of the Temple Mount showing "Robinson's Arch" (1), and the base of a pillar (2). Herodian stones (3) were reused by the Umayyads.

Photo David Eisenberg, Jerusalem.

returnees to Zion settled. Dynamic expansion began when Jerusalem became the capital of the Hasmonean kingdom in the second century B.C.E. and the capital of the Herodian kingdom in the first century B.C.E. and this expansion reached the Armenian Quarter of today. By then most of the area of the western hill was built up, and the population began to spread to the northern areas of the city—the "New City"—which reached its peak on the eve of the revolt in 66 C.E., when the area of the fortified city extended over 1,800 dunams (450 acres).

Necropolises. The burial areas of Jerusalem form a belt surrounding the city from Sanhedriyyah in the northwest, through Givat ha-Mivtar, Mt. Scopus, the Mt. of Olives, and the hill of the UN headquarters, to Talpiyyot and Ramat Rahel in the south. A few graves were also found west of the city. Hundreds of rock-hewn tombs—some simple and some very elaborate—were uncovered. The inside plan of the tombs is simple, as was the custom then. On the sides of central rooms are burial rooms that contain separate sepulchral chambers. The bones of the poor were gathered in limestone ossuaries. Some of the larger tombs have decorated fronts influenced by the architectural style of the West and by the east Hellenistic style; the combination created a hybrid style, which may be defined as Jewish art of the Second Temple period. As early as 1863 de Saulcy cleaned out the tombs of the kings and discovered there the decorated sarcophagi that probably belonged to the family of Queen Helena of Adiabene. Clermont-Ganneau completed the excavation of those tombs in 1867. He also partially cleaned the tomb known as Absalom's Tomb (1891). In 1891 Schick published the discovery of the tomb of the House of Herod, found near the site on which the King David Hotel was built later. In 1924 N. Slouschz cleared Absalom's Tomb. From 1926 to 1940 E. L. Sukenik studied approximately 40 Jewish funerary complexes in the city (such as the tomb of the Nicanor family discovered on Mt. Scopus). Avigad investigated the various burial sites of Jerusalem, especially in the Kidron Valley (1945–47).

Jason's Tomb from the Hasmonean period was excavated in Reḥavyah by L. Raḥmani (1954), who also investigated the burial sites of Sanhedriyyah (1961). In 1968 V. Tsaferis excavated several tombs at Givat ha-Mivtar, northeast of the city. One of them contained 35 burials, including one of a young man called Yoḥanan, who had died by crucifixion. Hundreds of limestone ossuaries and simple graves were disclosed on the western slope of the Mt. of Olives, near the Church of Dominus Flevit by P. B. Bagatti and J. T. Milik (1953–55). The major findings in this cemetery are from the Herodian period; however, it was used from the Hasmonean period to the Byzantine period.

THE LATE ROMAN PERIOD. After the destruction of the Second Temple and the suppression of the Bar Kokhba revolt (135 C.E.), the boundaries of the city became narrower. Remnants of the late Roman city, whose name was changed to Aelia Capitolina in the second century C.E., were uncovered in a number of places in the Old City. In the buildings of the Tenth Roman Legion, stationed at the time in Jerusalem, were found marks of its seal (LXF) on white tiles and clay pipes. In the excavations in the Citadel by Johns (1934–40) and Amiran and Eitan (1968–69), many remnants were revealed of the permanent camp of the Tenth Legion. Similar remnants were found in the excavations of Avi-Yonah on Givat Ram (1963, 1969). The new line of fortifications was uncovered extending from the area of the Citadel and continuing under the line of the Turkish Wall of the Old City. Hamilton (1937–38) and Hennessy (1964–66) revealed sectors of this wall and its towers on both sides of the Damascus Gate. The gate of Aelia Capitolina was found under the Damascus Gate, and an inscription mentioning the Roman name of the city was found fixed upon the gate. At the beginning of the Via Dolorosa, above the remnants of Antonia, a Roman triumphal arch, now called Ecce Homo, was discovered. Clermont-Ganneau investigated it in 1873–74. Kenyon (1961–67) found that the Muristan Area in the Old
City, which in her opinion had not been included within the

boundaries of the Second Temple city, had been filled in and leveled at that time for settlement purposes. The soundings of J. Pinkerfeld (1949) in the foundations of "David's Tomb" on Mt. Zion disclosed a previous level built from stone. In his opinion it probably contains remnants of a fourth-century synagogue. In Mazar's excavations (beginning 1968) dwellings from this same period were found. An inscription engraved on a stone tablet dates to the days of Septimius Severus (beginning of the third century C.E.) and is dedicated to the emperor and his family. The southern aqueduct was duplicated in Roman times by a high-level line from Ein Etam.

THE BYZANTINE PERIOD. During this period Jerusalem flourished anew. The city became the focal point for Christian pilgrimages. The main changes concentrated around sites associated with Christian tradition. Near these sites, churches, monasteries, and hospices were built. The city again spread out over the eastern and western hills to the south of the Temple Mount. The excavations of Macalister and Duncan, Crowfoot and Fitzgerald, Weill, Hamilton, Kenyon, and Mazar reveal remnants of streets, dwellings, and public buildings covering the south of the city, which was once again encircled by a wall. Remnants of that wall had been discovered by Warren near the Ophel, and long sectors were uncovered above the Valley of Hinnom by Bliss and Dickie. The construction of this wall is dated to the middle of the fifth century C.E. and is connected with the building activities of Empress Eudocia in Jerusalem. Mazar concludes from his findings that the Byzantine buildings near the Western Wall were destroyed by the Jews in preparation for the rebuilding of the Temple in the time of Julian (362–63).

Avigad's excavations carried out in the Jewish Quarter (1970) revealed a bathhouse whose accessories were well preserved and a part of the Nea Church, built by Justinian in the sixth century C.E. Some of these have been incorporated into newer buildings. The Church of the Holy Sepulcher was examined in part by Wilson (1863), M. Harvey (1933–34), and 139

V. Corbo (1961–63). The original church was founded in the fourth century C.E. The entrance, contrary to the accepted form, is in the east. This change resulted from the architectural incorporation into the church of the site of the Holy Sepulcher, which was surrounded by a special round structure; the "Rock of Golgotha" was included as well. The order of the White Fathers and Ch. Mauss (1863–1900) excavated the remnants of the church built above the Pool of Bethesda. Nearby they found remnants of a second Byzantine church that had been incorporated into the crusader Church of St. Anne. Bliss and Dickie (1894–97) dug above the Siloam Pool and uncovered the remains of the Church of Eudocia. J. Germer-Durand, who dug in the eastern slope of Mt. Zion at the end of the 19th century, revealed dwellings and a church. P. G. Orfali (1909, 1919–20) excavated the remains of the Gethsemane Church in the Kidron Valley. Vincent (1959) and Corbo (1959) discovered the remains of the Church of the Ascension on the top of the Mt. of Olives. Avi-Yonah (1949) discovered remains of a church and a monastery in the area of Givat Ram. Bagatti and Milik (1953–55) uncovered a cemetery of the Byzantine period in Dominus Flevit on the Mt. of Olives.

The Byzantine city was destroyed with the Persian conquest in 614 and the Muslim conquest in 638. Parts of numerous Byzantine structures served as building material for the Muslim structures that were constructed in the city by the end of the seventh century and in the eighth century. Much evidence of that was found in the excavations of Mazar (beginning 1968). It became clear that a large structure was built close to the southern wall of the Temple Mount in the period of the Umayyads at the beginning of the eighth century. On one of the stones in the Herodian Wall of the Temple Mount, Mazar discovered an inscription that he believes was engraved by a Jewish pilgrim in the fourth century C.E. The text of the inscription was taken from Isaiah 66:14; "And when you see this your heart shall rejoice and your bones shall flourish like young grass." This

B. Mazar's excavations near the south wall of the Temple Mount, revealing remains of the Umayyad period (eighth century C.E.). Below the street skirting the wall on the left was discovered a Herodian pavement leading to Huldah's Gates. In the background is the dome of the al-Aqṣā Mosque. Photo David Eisenberg, Jerusalem.

141

inscription undoubtedly indicates that among the masses of Christian pilgrims who arrived in Jerusalem during the Byzantine period, there were Jewish pilgrims visiting the ruins of the Temple Mount.

The excavations carried out in Jerusalem since early 1968 have shed new light on the topography of ancient Jerusalem and indicate that those who accepted the narrow concept (see 124) were mistaken. The city spread to the western hill in the First Temple period and the "second quarter" (Zeph. 1:10) existed. The city wall found in the Jewish Quarter (see 128) (it may be the "broad wall" of Neh. 3:8) seems to have run south, turned to the east, and joined with the wall of the City of David, and thus the Siloam Pool was included within the walls. It was also revealed that there was only one bridge, the one passing on "Wilson Arch," that connected the Temple Mount with the Upper City, and that the "Robinson Arch" was only a passage to a post of a monumental stairway. It was also suggested that the stone floor in the convent of the Soeurs de Sion (see 131) is not of the Antonia fortress, that there is no archaeological basis to the common restoration of this fortress, and that the Antonia was probably standing in the narrow area between the Temple Mount and Via Dolorosa.

xx JUDEAN DESERT CAVES. Following the discovery of the Dead Sea Scrolls in the Qumran caves, frantic searches for additional documents were carried out by Bedouin in all the cavities of the valleys adjoining the Dead Sea. As a result of evidence of such activities by Arab infiltrators from Jordanian territory into the territory of Israel, an expedition directed by Y. Aharoni set out to survey the area (November-December 1953). This was followed by a full-scale expedition, divided into four groups, which was undertaken jointly by the Hebrew University, the Israel Department of Antiquities, and the Israel Exploration Society, assisted by the Israel Defense Forces. In two campaigns (March 24–April 5,1960; March 15–27, 1961) caves were explored in the valleys between

Archaeologists in one of the Judean Desert caves. Courtesy
Ministry for Foreign Affairs, Jerusalem.

Masada and En-Gedi as far as the Jordanian border. The
investigations revealed two major periods of occupation in
the Judean Desert Caves during the Chalcolithic period
and as shelters at the time of the Bar Kokhba War
(132–135); some had also been inhabited during the First
Jewish War (66–70/73). Expedition A, directed by N. Avigad, explored the vicinity of En-Gedi, clearing burial caves
from the Second Temple period (including one which
contained a wooden sarcophagus inlaid with bone ornaments) and the "Cave of the Pool," which had been
inhabited by refugees who had constructed a reservoir to
ensure a sufficient water supply; they apparently survived
and left the cave when the danger had passed. Expedition B,
directed by Y. Aharoni, investigated the caves of Naḥal
Ẓe'elim where they discovered several biblical texts and
Greek papyri containing lists of names. They also explored
the "Cave of Horror" on the southern bank of Naḥal
Ḥever where some 40 fugitives took refuge at the end of the

Bar Kokhba War. A Roman camp was perched above them on the cliff. In the end the besieged succumbed from lack of water; they buried their dead and made a bonfire of their possessions, apparently choosing to die rather than surrender. Expedition C, led by P. Bar-Adon, explored the "Cave of the Treasure" in the Mishmar Valley. The main finds dated to the Chalcolithic period and consisted of a cache of 429 objects, 416 of copper, six of hematite, six of ivory, and one of stone. These included 240 mace heads of metal, six of hematite, one of stone, about 20 metal chisels and axes, 80 metal wands, ten metal "crowns" ornamented with birds and gate-like structures, five sickle-shaped objects made from hippopotamus teeth, and a box of elephant tusks. These were apparently ritual articles and may represent the treasures of a temple which were hidden from or by robbers. Other finds in this cave include plant remains, among them grains of emmer, which is the "missing link" between wild emmer and durum wheat. Expedition D, under Y. Yadin, worked in the "Cave of the Letters" on the northern bank of Nahal Hever. In this cave, also guarded from above by a Roman camp, Jonathan b. Bayan, one of Bar Kokhba's commanders at En-Gedi, took refuge together with his family which included a woman named Babatha. Objects found here included 19 metal vessels (a patera, jugs, and incense shovels), apparently booty from the Romans; several glass plates, a great number of keys, clothing, sandals, etc., as well as palm mats, a hunting net, and wool for working. Together with these articles were hidden 15 letters from Bar Kokhba to the commanders of En-Gedi, and an archive of 35 documents (17 in Greek; 6 in Nabatean; 3 in Aramaic; and 9 in Greek with Nabatean or Aramaic subscriptions). They are dated to 93/4–132 and represent the family and property archives of Babatha who was related by marriage to the Jonathan mentioned above. The absence of jewelry or coins in the cave together with the meticulous care with which the objects were cached suggests that the inhabitants of the cave survived and left it in the end.

Along with the finds at the Murabba'at caves these discoveries have revolutionized the conception of the Bar Kokhba War and have opened new vistas on the material and religious culture of the Chalcolithic period. By providing precisely dated material they are of great significance for the archaeology of the Roman and talmudic periods.

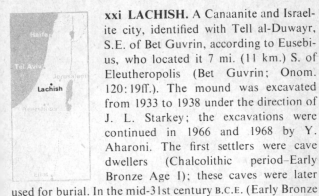

xxi LACHISH. A Canaanite and Israelite city, identified with Tell al-Duwayr, S.E. of Bet Guvrin, according to Eusebius, who located it 7 mi. (11 km.) S. of Eleutheropolis (Bet Guvrin; Onom. 120:19ff.). The mound was excavated from 1933 to 1938 under the direction of J. L. Starkey; the excavations were continued in 1966 and 1968 by Y. Aharoni. The first settlers were cave dwellers (Chalcolithic period–Early Bronze Age I); these caves were later used for burial. In the mid-31st century B.C.E. (Early Bronze Age II), settlement moved to the present mound. The city was fortified in the Middle Bronze Age. In the Late Bronze Age, it came under Egyptian sovereignty. At this time, a temple was constructed in the fosse, which had previously been part of the Middle Bronze Age II fortifications. The temple yielded a rich collection of gold and ivory ritual objects, including an ewer inscribed in Proto-Canaanite script. To this period belong two Tell el-Amarna letters written by two rulers of Lachish, Yabniilu and Zimreda (nos. 328, 329). Zimreda was accused of conspiring with the Habiru against the pharaoh (EA, no. 333). Japhia, king of Lachish, joined the Amorite coalition against Joshua (Josh. 10:3, 5); he was defeated at Aijalon and killed at Makkedah, the city falling to the Israelites (Josh. 10:32). Evidence of this destruction was found in the fosse temple and on the tell. A broken Egyptian inscription dated to the fourth year of an unknown pharaoh, who is either 145

Merneptah or Ramses III, was found in the debris and helps to date the fall of the city to 1220 B.C.E. or slightly later.

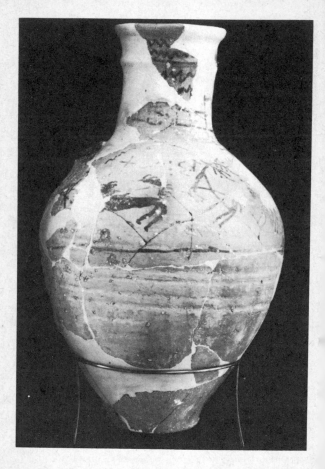

Ewer from the temple of Lachish, 13th century B.C.E., with an inscription in proto-Canaanite script dedicating it to the chief goddess. Jerusalem, Israel Department of Antiquities.

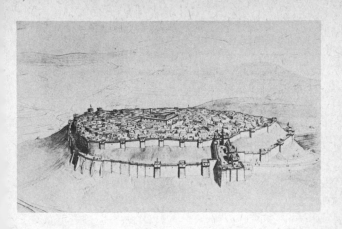

Conceptual sketch of Lachish by H. H. McWilliams, showing the double-wall fortifications built by Rehoboam and the palace-fort in the center. From N. H. Torcyzner, *Lachish*, Oxford, 1938.

Lachish remained partially in ruins until c. 1000 B.C.E., when the foundations of the first fortified palace were laid by either David or Solomon. Rehoboam included the city in his fortifications (II Chron. 11:9). It was expanded under Asa and Jehoshaphat, the citadel enlarged and the city walls rebuilt. Amaziah was killed there by conspirators (II Kings 14:19). Hezekiah strengthened the city's defenses and apparently tried to dig a large water shaft, a project which was abandoned. Under Hezekiah, the city was besieged and captured by Sennacherib. This event was recorded on a relief from Nineveh; the city's defenses represented there are identical to those uncovered in the excavation. From Lachish, Sennacherib sent messengers to Jerusalem (II Chron. 32:9; Isa. 36:2; cf. 37:8). The city was rebuilt in the seventh century. The guardhouse in the gate of this period contained 21 ostraca (the Lachish ostraca). Eighteen were discovered in 1935 in a room adjacent to the city gate, among the ruins of stratum II, which was destroyed by

Nebuchadnezzar of Babylonia, and in 1938, three more sherds were found. With the exception of two lists of names (nos. 1 and 19) and a docket (no. 20), the sherds are letters which were sent to Ya'ush, an army commander stationed at Lachish and responsible for the southwestern Shephelah. His correspondent was Hoshaiah, apparently an officer under Ya'ush in command of a garrison stationed in one of the towns between Lachish and Jerusalem. Ya'ush had accused Hoshaiah of reading secret documents sent from Jerusalem to the commander at Lachish and of revealing their contents to others. Hoshaiah denies the charge, humbly appealing to his superior. The usual opening salutation ("May the Lord cause my lord to hear tidings of peace!"; no. 2) is sometimes followed by the self-demeaning question "Who is your servant, a dog that . . . ?" (nos. 2, 5, and 6; cf. II Sam. 9:8; II Kings 8:13).

Another recurrent theme concerns the activities of a certain prophet, which were detrimental to the soldiers. Letter No. 3 appears to deal with this prophet: "The army commander, Coniah the son of Elnathan, has gone down to Egypt . . ." This incident strongly resembles the incident of the king Jehoiakim and the prophet Uriah from Kiriath-Jearim (Jer. 26); according to H. Torczyner (Tur-Sinai), the same event was recorded in both the ostracon and the Bible. In No. 4, Hoshaiah informs Ya'ush that he has carried out his orders, reporting what was done at his command and ending "We are watching for the fire signals of Lachish, according to all the signs my lord gave, because we do not see Azekah" (Tel Zakariyyeh (Tel 'Azeqah), at the entrance to the Elah Valley, north of Lachish). Hoshaiah's message that he does not see Azekah (or reading אות for את, the signal of Azekah has not been approved) because it has possibly already fallen, was sent probably after the situation described in Jeremiah 34:7: ". . . When the king of Babylon's army fought against Jerusalem, and against all the cities of Judah that were left, against Lachish and against Azekah; for these alone remained of the cities of Judah as fortified cities."

These ostraca constitute the latest corpus of Hebrew documents from the time of the First Temple. They are of great importance for linguistic and orthographic research and for the study of ancient Hebrew script. The various

One of the Lachish ostraca. Jerusalem, Israel Department of Antiquities.

Lachish Letters are written in a cursive script, the most developed form of the Paleo-Hebraic (ancient Hebrew) script, whose use was very much restricted after the destruction of the First Temple.

To this period belong many *la-melekh* seals, the impression of a seal of Gedaliah, the son of Ahikam, and Hebrew-inscribed weights, and a collection of impressions on clay bullae. Nebuchadnezzar destroyed Lachish in 588 B.C.E. A splendid palace built on the spot of the earlier Israelite citadels, perhaps by the Assyrian governor after Sennacherib's conquest, was repaired in 450 B.C.E. for use as a Persian residence. A temple rebuilt in c. 200 B.C.E. is the latest structure uncovered on the mound. The site was finally abandoned in 150 B.C.E.

xxii MASADA. Masada is the famous royal citadel of Herod and the last outpost of the Zealots during the Jewish War against Rome (66–70/73). Masada is situated on the top of an isolated rock on the edge of the Judean Desert and the Dead Sea Valley, approximately 15½ mi. (25 km.) south of En-Gedi. On the east the rock drops sharply approximately 1,300 ft. (400 m.) to the shore of the Dead Sea; its western side is approximately 330 ft. (100 m.) high above sea level. The rock is rhomboid shaped, very narrow in the north and broad in the center and measures approximately 1,950 ft. (600 m.) from north to south and approximately 1,000 ft. (300 m.) from east to west in the center. Its natural approaches are steep and arduous and include the "snake path" mentioned by Josephus on the east; the "white rock" (the Leuce of Josephus) on the west; and approaches on the cliff's northern and southern sides. The name Masada appears only in Greek transcription; it may be an Aramaic form meaning the *meẓad* ("stronghold").

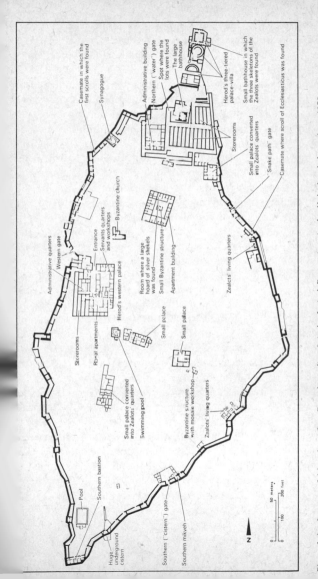

Plan of the fortress of Masada. After *Encyclopaedia of Archeological Excavations in the Holy Land.* Jerusalem, 1970.

Labels on the plan:

- Casemate in which the first scrolls were found
- Synagogue
- Administrative building
- Northern ("water") gate
- Spot where the lots were found
- The large bathhouse
- Herod's three-tiered palace-villa
- Small bathhouse in which the the three skeletons of the Zealots were found
- Storerooms
- Small palace converted into Zealots' quarters
- Snake path' gate
- Casemate where scroll of Ecclesiasticus was found
- Zealots' living quarters
- Byzantine church
- Room where a large hoard of silver shekels was found
- Small Byzantine structure
- Apartment building
- Small palace
- Small palace
- Byzantine structure with mosaic workshop
- Zealots' living quarters
- Administrative quarters
- Western gate
- Entrance
- Servants' quarters and workshops
- Herod's western palace
- Storerooms
- Royal apartments
- Small palace converted into Zealots' quarters
- Swimming pool
- Southern bastion
- Pool
- Southern ('cistern') gate
- Southern mikveh
- Huge underground cistern

50 meters
100
200 feet
0
0

N

History. The only significant source of information about Masada are the writings of Josephus (Ant., 14, 15; Wars, 1, 2, 4, 7) who relates that it was first fortified by the high priest Jonathan and named Masada by him (Wars, 7:285). Scholars disagree as to the identity of this Jonathan — whether he was referring to the brother of Judah Maccabee (mid-second century B.C.E.) or Alexander Yannai (103–76 B.C.E.) who was also called Jonathan. In another passage Josephus attributes Masada's construction to "ancient kings" (Wars, 4:399). In 40 B.C.E. Herod fled from Jerusalem to Masada with his family to escape from Mattathias Antigonus, who had been made king by the Parthians. He left his family, his brother Joseph and 800 men there to defend it against a siege by Antigonus (Ant., 14:361–2; Wars, 1:264, 267). According to Josephus the defenders almost died of thirst during the siege but were saved when a sudden rainstorm filled the creeks and pits on the summit of the rock. Herod, returning from a trip to Rome, raised the siege and carried his family off to safety (Ant., 14:390–1; 396, 400; Wars, 1:286–7, 292–4). Subsequently "Herod furnished this fortress as a refuge for himself, suspecting a twofold danger: peril on the one hand from the Jewish people, lest they should depose him and restore their former dynasty to power; the greater and more serious from Cleopatra, queen of Egypt" (Wars, 7:300). Herod's transformation of the rock of Masada into a mighty fort apparently took place between 37 and 31 B.C.E. when most of its buildings and fortifications were erected. Although there is no information on Masada immediately after Herod's death, it can be assumed that a Roman garrison was probably stationed there from 6 to 66 C.E. when, at the outbreak of the Jewish War Menahem, son of Judah the Galilean, attacked Masada at the head of a band of Zealots and captured it "by stratagem" (Wars, 2:408, 433). After Menahem was murdered in Jerusalem by Jewish rivals, Eleazar, son of Jair, son of Judah (i.e., Menahem' nephew) escaped to Masada where he became its "tyrant" until its fall in 73 C.E. During this period Masada served a a place of refuge for all who were in danger of capture; Simeon bar Giora also stayed there for a time. In 72 C.E. the Roman governor Flavius Silva marched against Masada the last remaining Zealot stronghold — at the head of the Tenth Legion, its auxiliary troops, and thousands of Jewish prisoners of war. After a prolonged siege a breach was made in the wall of Masada, whereupon Eleazar persuaded his followers to kill themselves rather than fall into the hands of the Romans. Josephus describes the dramatic last hours of Masada, Eleazar's speech to the Jewish defenders, the mass suicide of 960 men, women, and children and the burning of the buildings and stores of food. He quotes the story told by two women who together with five children survived by hiding in a cave. After Masada's conquest, Silva left a garrison there. Masada is also briefly mentioned by Pliny (*Natural History* 5: 17, 73).

History of Exploration. Masada was correctly identified for the first time in 1838 by the Americans E. Robinson and E. Smith who viewed the rock which the Arabs called al-Sabba through a telescope from En-Gedi. The site was first visited in 1842 by the American missionary S. W. Wolcott and the English painter Tipping and next by members of an American naval expedition in 1848. Ten years later, F. de Saulcy drew the first plan of Masada. C. Warren in 1867 heading the "Survey of Western Palestine" climbed Masada from the east along the "snake path" and in 1875, C. R. Conder, on behalf of the survey, drew plans which were the most accurate up to that time. The first detailed study of the Roman camps was made by A. V. Domaszewski and R. E. Bruennow in 1909. Others followed in the beginning of the 20th century, foremost among them, the German A. Schulten, who surveyed Masada for a month in 1932. The major impetus for the extensive excavations of the site was provided by enthusiastic Israel scholars and amateurs, especially S. Guttman who correctly traced the serpentine twistings of the "snake path" and, with A. Alon studied Herod's water system (1953). He also excavated and restored one of the Roman camps. 153

Large-scale Israel surveys were conducted for ten days in 1955 (headed by M. Avi-Yonah, N. Avigad et al.) and again in 1956 (headed by Y. Aharoni and S. Guttman) which established the general outline of the buildings and prepared new plans of the rock. Masada was mainly excavated in two seasons of 11 months (1963–65) by Y. Yadin, a large staff of archaeologists, and thousands of volunteers from all parts of the world. Almost the entire built-up area of the rock was uncovered as well as one of the Roman camps, and restoration of the buildings was carried out at the site simultaneously.

Early Settlements. Remains of a Chalcolithic settlement (4th millenium B.C.E.) including plants, cloth, mats, and potsherds were found in a small cave on the lower part of the southern cliff. Some sherds, but no evidence of building, were found on the summit from the Iron Age II (tenth–seventh centuries B.C.E.). As to the buildings attributed by Josephus to "Jonathan the high priest," only a few of the cisterns may possibly be pre-Herodian, but the discovery of tens of coins from the reign of Alexander Yannai indicates that Josephus' reference was most likely to Yannai and not to Jonathan the Hasmonean.

Herodian Period. One of Herod's first undertakings at Masada was undoubtedly the water system he constructed to ensure an adequate supply of water. It consisted of a drainage system to carry rainwater from the two wadis west of Masada to a group of cisterns in the northwestern slope of the rock. The water was deflected by dams and flowed along open plastered channels to 12 cisterns which were cut in two parallel rows. Each cistern had a capacity of up to 140,000 cu. ft. (4,000 cu. m.) and together could hold about 1,400,000 cu. ft. (40,000 cu. m.) The cisterns are mostly square in shape and have two openings, one leading from the aqueduct, and a second higher one, connected with an inner staircase for drawing out water. Other cisterns dug into the summit of Masada were filled with water brought by hand from the cisterns on the slope. Herod enclosed the entire summit of Masada, except for the northern tip, with a casemate wall (a double wall with the inner space divided into rooms). Its circumference measures about 1,400 m. (1,530 yd.) which corresponds exactly with the 7 *stadia* of Josephus' description. About 70 rooms, 30 towers, and four gates were found in the wall. The gates were elaborately built and consisted of a square room with two entrances, benches along the walls, stone slab pavements, and frescoes. They include the "snake path" gate in the northeast; the western gate in the middle of the western wall; the southern ("cistern") gate which led to a group of cisterns; and the northern ("water") gate near the bathhouse which served mainly for bringing water from the upper row of cisterns and was probably also the gate for the northern part of Masada.

NORTHERN PALACE. Herod constructed the most important buildings in the northern part of Masada—the highest point of the rock. Josephus gives a detailed account of a royal palace situated beneath the walls of the fortress on the western side facing north. Up to the 1950s this was believed to be a large building on the western side of the site but Israel explorers, including members of youth movements, discovered that the palace described was actually located on the north where it was daringly constructed on the very edge of the precipice. This palace, or more correctly, royal villa commanded a magnificent view of the surroundings as far as En Gedi, and was built in three tiers, the upper containing the living quarters whereas the lower ones were designed for pleasure. The upper terrace is an extension of the narrow tip of the summit and contains a large semicircular balcony bounded by a double wall. A four-room building south of it with two rooms on each side of a court was apparently Herod's private abode. Its black and white mosaic floor in geometric designs is one of the earliest mosaics found in Israel. The walls and ceilings were decorated with frescoes. To the south a great white plastered wall separated the palace from the rest of Masada and left only a narrow passageway at its eastern end for a staircase. Columns had probably stood on the facade of the 155 building and round the semicircular balcony. The middle terrace, approximately 65 ft. (20 m.) beneath the upper one, contained two concentric circular walls which served as a platform for a columned building. A staircase on the west led to the upper level and on the east stood a large room with traces of frescoes; between them was a roofed colonnade. This terrace was apparently designed for relaxation and a leisurely enjoyment of the view. The bottom terrace, approximately 50 ft. (15 m.) below the middle one, tapers to a narrow point; great supporting walls were built to form a raised square platform which was surrounded by low walls forming porticoes. Both the inner and exterior walls contained columns composed of sandstone drums plastered and fluted to resemble large monolithic columns. Frescoes on the lower part of the walls were painted to imitate stone and marble paneling. In the eastern corner of the terrace was a small bathhouse built in Roman style.

WESTERN PALACE. In addition to the palace-villa, Herod constructed a main official palace on the western side of Masada in the largest building found on the site, covering an area of nearly 43,000 sq. ft. (4,000 sq. m.). Containing scores of rooms and installations this palace was a self-sufficient unit and consisted of four wings: (1) Royal apartments in the southeast built around a large central court with a large reception hall leading into the throne room. In the hall was a magnificent richly colored mosaic pavement with circles and border ornaments of plant and geometric designs. This wing also contained service rooms as well as bathrooms with tubs, a cold water pool, and other installations, all paved with mosaics. (2) Servants' quarters and workshops in the northeast around a central court and including a potter's workshop. (3) Storerooms in the southwest. (4) Administrative quarters in the northwest. Three small richly decorated palaces nearby probably housed members of Herod's family. Near one of them was a large swimming pool with broad plastered steps leading to the water. Two large rectangular buildings, apparently an

Volunteer cleaning a floor mosaic in the Western Palace. Courtesy National Parks Authority, Tel Aviv.

administrative center and residence of high officials, were found in the north. A circular building with some 80 small niches set in rows in the inner walls on the southern part of the summit may have served as a columbarium for the gentile garrison troops.

BATHHOUSE. South of the Northern Palace was a large bathhouse with four rooms and a court built in traditional Roman style. The largest room, the *caldarium* (hot room), 157 had a *hypocaust* (heating room) beneath it and its floor stood on about 200 tiny columns, mostly made of brick. The walls of the rooms were faced with perforated clay pipes through which an adjacent furnace drove hot air into the room. Its general plan resembles Roman bathhouses at Pompei and Herculaneum and especially in Herodian palaces at Jericho, Herodium, etc. The other rooms, the *frigidarium* (cold room), *tepidarium* (tepid room), and *apodyterium* (entrance room) were lavishly decorated with frescoes and mosaic floors which were later replaced by triangular tiles.

STOREHOUSES. The public storerooms, situated east and south of the bathhouse, consisted of long narrow rooms built of large stone slabs in two main blocks: a small one containing four rooms in the north and a larger one in the south with 11 rooms. Oil, wine, flour, etc. were each kept in a separate room in special storage jars. Food, weapons, and other costly goods were also stored in small storerooms attached to public buildings. During the Herodian period at Masada, the buildings were constructed in two main phases over a long period of time. Many amphoras for holding wine were dated (the year of the consul C. Sentius Saturninus, i.e., 19 B.C.E.), and inscribed that they had been sent to Herod, king of Judea. From the period of the Roman garrison stationed at Masada between the time of Herod and the Jewish War hundreds of coins were found from the reigns of Archelaus, Agrippa, and the procurators.

Period of the Zealots (66–73). The many finds from this brief seven-year period throw much light on the character of the Zealots, their way of life at Masada, and the end of the Jewish War. The sumptuous palaces and small number of dwelling rooms in the Herodian buildings could not be easily adapted for dwellings for the Zealots and were therefore used as command posts, public buildings, etc. Their decorative architectural parts were dismantled for building materials and furniture: floors, roofs, columns, tables, etc. The Northern Palace, which was covered with a thick layer of ashes, apparently served as an administrative center and defense post. On the bottom level near the bathhouse were parts of skeletons of a man, woman, and child. The woman's scalp and braids and leather sandals were preserved intact and nearby were hundreds of silverplated armor scales, arrows, and fragments of a *tallit*. The skeletons undoubtedly represent the remains of an important commander of Masada and his family. The Western Palace was also found covered with a thick conflagration layer. The rooms and courts of the small

Plaits and sandals of a young woman *in situ*. Courtesy Y. Yadin, Jerusalem.

palaces were partitioned to serve as dwellings for large numbers of Zealot families. Alabaster and gold vessels and two hoards of shekels found under floors indicate that important leaders were housed in them. Some of the storerooms were found completely destroyed by fire while others had been left intact, apparently, as stated by Josephus, to prove to the Romans that they had not been driven to death by hunger. Most of the Zealots were housed in the casemate wall and in shacks of mud and small stones adjoining the wall and other buildings. Cooking stoves and niches for the cupboards were built into the wall. In rooms which had not been burnt remains of their daily life were strewn on the floors: clothing, leather, baskets, glass, stone and bronze objects, etc. Piles of charcoal with remnants of personal belongings indicate that they had collected all their possessions at the end and had set fire to them. Hundreds of coins and several scroll fragments were found in the rooms. The towers served mainly as public rooms or workshops, such as bakeries or tanneries.

MIKVA'OT (ritual baths). Two *mikva'ot* were found, one at the north and the other at the south, built exactly according to halakhic law which prescribed that part of the water of a *mikveh* must be supplied by rainwater flowing directly into it. The southern *mikveh* was built in a casemate and consists of three plastered pools. The largest one was for storing rainwater collected from the roof through a conduit and was connected by a narrow hole with a smaller pool (for immersion). Through the hole some of the rainwater could be mixed with other water brought by hand. A third small pool served for actual washing. An entrance hall and dressing room were added outside the wall. An elongated hall with a bench extending along three sides of the wall in one of the small palaces may have been a *bet midrash*.

SYNAGOGUE. A rectangular building from the time of the Zealots was found in the wall. Oriented toward Jerusalem, it contained four tiers of plastered benches along the walls and two rows of columns in the center. Lamps and an

160

Mikveh built by the Zealots in the southern casemate wall, c. 66-73 C.E. 1. water conduit; 2, 3, 4. pools; 5. opening in the inner wall leading to the *mikveh*. At right, 6, 7, 8. three of the camps built by the Romans at the foot of the mountain, 73 C.E. Courtesy Y. Yadin.

Stone vessels found in Zealot dwelling chamber within the casemate wall. Courtesy Y. Yadin, Jerusalem.

161

ostracon inscribed *ma'aser kohen* ("priest's tithe") were found here as well as parts of two biblical scrolls, Ezekiel and Deuteronomy, hidden in pits dug into the floor. In a corner was a room for ritual objects. This building, which was undoubtedly a synagogue, is the earliest known and the only one preserved from the time of the Second Temple (a similar synagogue was found later—in Herodium). It had originally been built by Herod on a different plan and may also have served as a synagogue in his time.

ZEALOT REMAINS. Twenty-five skeletons of men, women, and children were found thrown in a heap in a small cave on the southern cliff. Most of the skulls were of the type found in the Bar Kokhba caves in Naḥal Ḥever and it can be assumed that they are remains of Zealots. They were buried at Masada with full military honors in 1969.

COINS. Numerous coins struck during the Jewish War (66–70) were found both in large hoards (of 350, 200, and 100 coins) and in small numbers. Mostly ordinary bronze coins, they also include 37 silver shekels and 35 half-shekels representing all the years of the war and including the rare Year Five. This was the first discovery of shekels in a dated archaeological stratum.

OSTRACA. More than 700 ostraca were found mostly written in Hebrew or Aramaic. Since they can be dated exactly between 66 and 73 C.E. they are of great paleographic value and they also shed much light on the organization of life at Masada and the national and religious character of the defenders who scrupulously observed the ritual laws. About half of them were found near the storerooms. These bore single or several letters in Hebrew and may have been connected with the Zealot's rationing system during the siege. Others indicate tithes and names on others may be those of priests or levites. Eleven small ostraca each inscribed with a single name and all written by the same person may be the lots described by Josephus which the last ten survivors at Masada drew to choose who would kill the other nine and then himself. The names appear to be nicknames; one inscribed "ben Jair" may stand for Eleazar son of Jair, the commander of the Zealots.

SCROLLS. Parts of 14 biblical, apocryphal, and sectarian scrolls found at Masada are the first scrolls discovered outside of caves in a dated archaeological stratum. The biblical scrolls are mostly identical with the Masoretic Text but some show slight variations. These include parts of the books of Psalms, Genesis, Leviticus, Deuteronomy, and Ezekiel. Apocryphal scrolls include part of the original Hebrew text of the Wisdom of Ben Sira 39–44, dated to the first century B.C.E. and several lines of the Book of Jubilees. A fragment of a sectarian scroll of the Songs of Sabbath Service is identical with a scroll found at Qumran. It is important for dating the Dead Sea Scrolls and because it indicates that members of the Dead Sea Sect (apparently Essenes) took part in the Jewish War.

Roman Siege. Flavius Silva's effort to conquer Masada is still clearly visible. He surrounded the fortress with a siege wall (circumvallation) fortified by towers to prevent the 960 defenders from escaping. Round the base of Masada he set up eight camps including a large one in the east (Camp B) and in the northwest (Γ). The latter served as his headquarters and near it on the western slope he built an assault ramp of beaten earth and large stones on which was erected a siege tower from which the wall was attacked with a battering ram, catapults, and flaming torchs. After the fall of Masada a Roman garrison was stationed there for at least 40 years, from 73 to 111, to which the latest coin find dates. Remains of the garrison troops were found in Camp F and also on Masada itself.

Byzantine Period. A group of monks settled at Masada in the fifth and sixth centuries, after a series of earthquakes had caused considerable damage to many of the buildings. They erected a small church with mosaic pavements of which little remains aside from a beautiful colored floor in a side room with 16 round medallions containing representations of fruits, flowers, plants, etc. West of the church was a refectory and kitchen. These last occupants of Masada dwelt in small stone cells scattered over the summit and in caves.

Since the completion of Masada's reconstruction, it has become one of Israel's major tourist sites. In 1971 a cable car was inaugurated on the eastern (Dead Sea) side.

xxiii MEGIDDO. This ancient Canaanite and Israelite city is identified with Tell al-Mutasallim on the southern side of the Jezreel Valley, approximately 22 mi. (35 km.) S.E. of Haifa. The site was excavated in 1903–05 by G. Schumacher and in 1925–39 by the Oriental Institute in Chicago, under the direction of C.S. Fisher, P.L.O. Guy, and G. Loud. Small additional soundings were made by Y. Yadin in 1960 and later years. The excavations revealed the existence of over 20 levels, beginning with the Chalcolithic period in the fourth millennium (Stratum XX). In the Early Bronze Age (Canaanite period), represented in Strata XIX–XVI, the first temples were built, as well as a round high-place and a wall, 26 ft. (8 m.) thick. Three temples of the megaron type, consisting of a porch with two columns, a hall with a roof supported by two columns and an altar near the southern wall, may also have been built in the Early Bronze Age, although originally attributed to Stratum XV. The Middle Bronze Age city is represented by Strata XV–X, with Strata XIV–XIII corresponding in time to the 12th dynasty of Egypt. The statue of an Egyptian official called Thuthotep, which was found in the excavations, indicates that an Egyptian governor probably resided there at that time. Like all the Canaanite cities, Megiddo fell to the Hyksos (Strata XII–X: 18th–16th centuries B.C.E.). The conquerors strengthened the wall and built a glacis and a gate with the entrance between two guardrooms in the style typical of the period. In a large palace near the gate were found jewels and ivories, which attest to the prosperity of the city at that time. In approximately 1469 B.C.E. (Stratum IX), Thutmose III suddenly appeared before the walls of Megiddo, after passing through the Aruna Valley giving the city access to the coast. He overcame a coalition of Canaanites and Hittites and captured the city after a siege of seven months; the rich plunder he seized indicates the wealth of Megiddo. From then until Stratum VII the city remained under Egyptian sovereignty, with the presence of both a local king and an Egyptian commander and garrison. In the el-Amarna period, the king of Megiddo, Biridya (an Indo-Iranian name), was hard pressed by the Habiru and Labaya of Shechem (EA, 242-5). This Late Bronze Age city, dating to the period of Egyptian rule, witnessed the erection of a fortified temple, similar to that discovered at Shechem; according to the latest researches, such temples originate in the last phase of the Middle Bronze Age. Under one of the rooms of the Stratum VII palace (el-Amarna period) was

Tell Megiddo from the north, with the Jezreel Valley in the background. The major visible structures are: 1. gate area; 2. water installation pit; 3. south stables complex; 4. silo; 5. Schumacher's shaft; 6. round high place; 7. three temples of the megaron type; 8. north stables complex; 9. Israelite fortifications. Photo Werner Braun, Jerusalem.

found a rich treasure of gold, ivory, and lapis lazuli. A cuneiform tablet dating to this level contains a fragment of the Gilgamesh epic. The palace was rebuilt in Stratum VIIA and in it were discovered inscriptions of Ramses III and

The gate area on the north side of the tell, showing buildings of various periods: 1. earliest gate, with part of its break wall, 19th century B.C.E.; 2.gate from Late Bronze period (16th–15th century B.C.E.); 3. street and basalt steps leading from Late Bronze gate; 4. eastern section of Solomonic gateway (tenth century B.C.E.); 5. part of Ahab's gate (9th century B.C.E.). Photo Richard Cleave, Jerusalem.

Ramses VI and a hoard of 200 ivory tablets. This stratum marks the last wealthy and fortified Canaanite city, which was destroyed in the second half of the 12th century B.C.E. The next city, Stratum VI (late 12th–11th centuries B.C.E.),

Tablets from the ivory hoard found in the palace of stratum VIIa (1350–1150 B.C.E.). Jerusalem, Rockefeller Museum, Israel Department of Antiquities.

was unfortified and of an unclear ethnic composition.

According to biblical tradition, Megiddo did not fall to Joshua, although its king was defeated (Josh. 12:21; cf. Josh. 17:11–13; Judg. 1:27–28). Most scholars date its capture only to the time of David. Solomon fortified the city (I Kings 9:15) and included it in his fifth district (I Kings 4:12). The Solomonic gate with three guardrooms is identical in plan with the gates at Hazor and Gezer (cf. I Kings 9:15). A large palace built of well-hewn ashlar masonry and adorned with proto-Aeolic capitals was probably the residency of Solomon's governor, Baana, son of Ahilud. The city was largely occupied by three units of five rectangular stables and one unit of two stables, with feeding troughs between pillars and a capacity of 492 horses. Yadin, however, attributes these stables only to the time of Ahab, who rallied 2,000 chariots against Shalmaneser III at the Battle of Karkar. A water installation, built sometime in the Israelite period consists of a pit 81 ft. (25 m.) deep, with stairs leading to a horizontal tunnel 224 ft. (70 m.) long and to a spring in the slope of the hill, which was thus connected with the city inside the walls. The Israelite city (Stratum IV) perished in 733/2 B.C.E. with the conquest of Tiglath-Pileser III. The Assyrian king made Megiddo the capital of a province, which included Galilee and the Jezreel Valley. The Stratum III city was rebuilt on a uniform plan, with two large public buildings in the Assyrian style. Within the city was a silo, 23 ft. (7 m.) deep, with stairs curving around the inside and leading to the bottom. Stratum II (630–609 B.C.E.) probably dates to the time of Josiah of Judah, who fell in the battle against Pharaoh Necoh near Megiddo. To this event can be attributed the association of war with the Megiddo Valley in Zechariah 12:11 and with Armageddon in Revelation 16:16. The last settlement at Megiddo was a small city of the Persian period. Both Napoleon (in 1799) and Allenby[22] (1918) defeated the Turks at Megiddo. The tell has been developed for visitors with a small

[22] British commander in Egypt and Palestine (1861–1936)

museum demonstrating the history of Megiddo. On his visit to Israel in 1964 Pope Paul VI was received by President Shazar at Tell Megiddo.

xxiv QUMRAN. This region on the north-west shore of the Dead Sea has become famous since 1947 as the site of the discovery of the Dead Sea Scrolls. The name belongs more particularly to Wadi Qumran, a precipitous watercourse which runs down to the sea from the west, and to Khirbet Qumran, a ruin standing less than a mile west of the sea on the marl terrace north of the wadi. Visitors to the region in earlier days, impressed by the fortuitous similarity of names, thought that Khirbet Qumran might be all that was left of Gomorrah. In 1873 C.S. Clermont-Ganneau inspected the ruin, but was more interested in a cemetery lying between it and the sea. He came to no positive conclusions as a result of his inspection.

Occupation of Khirbet Qumran. In 1949, the possibility was raised of a connection between the discoveries in the first scroll cave and Khirbet Qumran. A trial excavation was made on the site, but nothing was found which suggested any connection. In November and December 1951, three rooms were excavated. In the floor of one of them was found a jar of the same type as those in which the scrolls in Cave 1 had been placed, and along with it was a coin bearing a date equivalent to 10 C.E. Systematic campaigns of exploration were mounted in 1953, 1954, 1955, and 1956, in which the Jordan Department of Antiquities, the Palestine Archaeological Museum, and the French Dominican Ecole Biblique collaborated.

It soon became evident that the building complex had formed the headquarters of a fairly large and well-organized community. R. de Vaux, soon after the excavations began, expressed the belief that these were the headquarters of the Essenes referred to by Pliny the Elder in his *Natural History* (5:73), partly on the ground that nothing else in that region could correspond to Pliny's description. Pliny says that "below" the Essene headquarters lies En-Gedi; since he is describing the Jordan Valley and Dead Sea region from north to south he may mean that En-Gedi lies south of the Essene headquarters; En-Gedi in fact lies some 22 miles (34 km.) south of Khirbet Qumran. But the identification of the community of Yaḥad that occupied Khirbet Qumran cannot be determined on archaeological grounds alone.

The cemetery to the east of Khirbet Qumran proved to contain about 1,200 graves, laid out in parallel rows lying north and south, with the head to the south. The burials were as simple as possible; the bodies were neither placed in coffins nor accompanied by funeral offerings. In an eastern extension of the cemetery, skeletons of four women and one child were found. Skeletons of women and children were also identified in two subsidiary cemeteries lying north and south respectively of Wadi Qumran. Pottery in the earth-filling of the graves indicated that the burials belonged to the same general period as the community occupation of Khirbet Qumran.

The site of Khirbet Qumran had been occupied at various times in antiquity. At a low level were found the remains of walls and pottery of Iron Age II (8th–7th centuries B.C.E.). A potsherd inscribed with Phoenician characters and a royal seal stamped on a jar handle belonged to this period, as did also a deep circular cistern which, centuries later, was incorporated in an elaborate system of aqueducts and reservoirs. This phase of occupation may be correlated with the statement that Uzziah king of Judah (c. 790–740 B.C.E.) "built towers in the wilderness and hewed out many cisterns" (II Chron. 26:10). M. Noth has suggested that at this period the site was known as Ir ha-Melaḥ ("city of salt," Josh. 15:61). At the nearer end of the record there is evidence of brief and sporadic occupation during the Arab period.

170 Chief interest attaches to the abundant evidence for the

occupation of the site in the Greco-Roman period. In this period archaeologists have distinguished the following phases of occupation: Ia. Occupation (c. 130 B.C.E.) by people who cleared the circular cistern, built two rectangular cisterns beside it, constructed a few rooms around these, and installed two pottery kilns in the Iron Age enclosure. Ib. Occupation of a much enlarged area, with two- and three-storey buildings, and an elaborate system of cisterns (incorporating the earlier ones) connected by channels and supplied by an aqueduct from a dam built to store the water which runs down Wadi Qumran in the rainy season. This phase began shortly before 100 B.C.E.; its termination is marked by an extensive fire followed by a severe earthquake (probably that otherwise attested for 31 B.C.E.) II. Occupation of a restored building complex, which in general followed the lines of phases Ib but was reinforced at various points against earthquake damage. This phase came to an end during the war of 66–73 C.E. III. Occupation by a Roman garrison for some 20 years until c. 90 C.E. IV. Occupation by Jewish freedom fighters in the second war against Rome, 132–135 C.E.

Description of Khirbet Qumran. The main building of the complex in phases Ib and II was roughly 37 meters square, of large undressed stones, with a strong tower at the northwest corner. There were several large rooms suitable for assembly rooms or refectories. Adjoining the largest of these rooms (on the south side of the building) was a smaller room containing over 1,000 earthenware vessels—all the varieties necessary for kitchen and refectory use. They may have been manufactured on the spot, since the excavations brought to light the best preserved pottery factory thus far found in ancient Palestine, complete with kilns and levigating pit. A first-story room in the southwest part of the building was evidently furnished as a writing-room (*scriptorium*). Flour mills, storage bins, ovens, a laundry, a stable, smelting furnaces, and workshops with metal implements were also uncovered. The occupants apparently aimed at being as self-sufficient as possible. The building complex does not seem to have included sleeping quarters; tents or the neighboring caves may have served the occupants for rest and shelter.

The elaborate series of cisterns, designed to ensure a plentiful water supply, has excited special interest; there has been a tendency to relate these to the prescriptions regarding cleansing in water laid down in the Manual of Discipline[23] found in the Qumran caves. It is not certain that the water supply was used for ceremonial purposes; these might have been served more acceptably by the running water of the Jordan or the spring-water of Ein Feshkha. Water reservoirs like those of Khirbet Qumran, with steps leading down into them, are known from other Palestinian sites. It is especially in some of these cisterns that the damage from the earthquake is still most clearly visible. The 14 stone steps of the largest cistern, to the east of the site, show a central crack running down from top to bottom, so that their eastern half has sunk nearly half a foot below the level of the western half. When the site was reoccupied some 30 years after the earthquake, this cistern could not be used as it no longer held water; a new one was excavated southeast of the building. Other major repairs were effected at the same time: the walls were strengthened and the northwestern tower reinforced.

Chronology of Khirbet Qumran. The record of the phases of the occupation of Khirbet Qumran is indicated most clearly by the coins found in the course of excavations on the site. About 650 coins of the Greco-Roman period have come to light. The coin record starts with Antiochus VII of the Seleucid dynasty (139–129 B.C.E.) and his contemporary John Hyrcanus (135–104 B.C.E.) and goes on without a break to Antigonus, the last Hasmonean king (40–37 B.C.E.). Coins of Alexander Yannai (103–76 B.C.E.) are especially frequent. Only five coins from Herod's reign (37–4 B.C.E.) have come to light. The record is resumed with

---

[23] One of the Dead Sea Scrolls, a religious document focused on various

aspects of life within the community

coins of Archelaus (4 B.C.E.–6 C.E.) and continues with those of the procurators and a particularly large number of Herod Agrippa's coins (37–44 C.E.). There are 73 coins from the second year of the war against Rome (67–68 C.E.) and several from the following year, contemporary with these are coins minted in the coastal cities of Caesarea, Dor, and Ashkelon; later are a coin of Agrippa II (86 C.E.), one of Vespasian (69–79 C.E.), three of Trajan (98–117 C.E.), one of the type struck by the liberation leaders during the second revolt. It is doubtful whether a hoard of 563 silver coins hidden in three pots in a floor to the west of the building can be related to the occupation of Khirbet Qumran. The hoard was comprised of coins of Antiochus VII and tetradrachms of Tyre, the latest of which was dated 9 B.C.E. These coins may have been hidden there toward the end of the period when the building was unoccupied between Phases Ib and II.

A sample of charcoal from the room where the large number of earthenware vessels was found was subjected to the radiocarbon test, which yielded a date of 16 C.E. (with a margin or deviation of 80 years either way) for the age of the wood, and a date of 66 C.E. (with a similar margin of deviation) for the burning. Phase II of the occupation of Khirbet Qumran was brought to an end not by earthquake but by fire and sword. The destruction was much more thorough than that caused by the earthquake 100 years earlier. The walls were demolished, a layer of black ash covered the site, and a quantity of arrowheads added their silent testimony to the picture. It can hardly be doubted that the building was attacked and stormed by the Romans in the course of the war of 66–73.

A few rooms were built over the ruins and occupied by a Roman garrison which appears to have been stationed there for some 20 years. The brief occupation of the site by an insurgent garrison during the second revolt was followed by the complete destruction of its surviving fortifications.

The chronology of the occupation of Khirbet Qumran, archaeologically established, agrees remarkably well with that of the nearby manuscript caves and their contents,   173

Tefillin found at Qumran thought to be from the first half of the first century C.E.:   (a) interior of container with four separate compartments, each containing a folded parchment, (approx. ¾ in. × 1 in. (2 × 2.8 cm.); (b) Parchment number two, after opening, the text, written with black ink, is Deut. 5: 22–33 and 6:1 9 (approx. 1 × 1½ in.; 2.7 × 4.3 cm.). Courtesy Y. Yadin, Jerusalem.

b

paleographically established. (The paleographical evidence is supplemented by the application of pottery dating to the jars in which the manuscripts of Cave 1 were placed and by the application of the radiocarbon test to some of the linen in which these manuscripts were wrapped before being placed in the jars, although the radiocarbon test involves too large a margin of deviation to be helpful when precise dating within decades is required.) A close connection between the occupants of the building and the manuscripts in the caves is cogently indicated; the community described in the "community documents" and the community which manifestly occupied Khirbet Qumran must have been one and the same community; at least, it would require specially conclusive arguments to make it probable that they were two separate communities.

xxv RAMAT HA-GOLAN. Archaeological and geographical explorations of Erez Israel in the late 19th and early 20th centuries almost completely overlooked the Golan. In 1884–86 the German engineer G. Schumacher prepared the first map of the Golan under the auspices of the Palestine Exploration Fund. During his cartographic work, he visited hundreds of sites and recorded all the 175 surface finds, thus carrying out the first archaeological survey of the Golan. He discovered about a dozen sites containing typical Jewish symbols, such as the seven-branched *menorah* and other motifs, which he attributed to remains of ancient synagogues. These sites include Fīq, Umm al-Qanāṭir, Khan-Bandaq, Lawiyya, al-Dikkī (Dikke), al-Rafīd, al-Aḥmadiyya, al-Burayka, etc.—most of them in southwestern Golan near the shores of Lake Kinneret. In the village of Fīq (apparently Aphek, mentioned in I Kings 20:26), a basalt column was found engraved with a seven-branched *menorah* and under it an Aramaic inscription: "I, Judah, the cantor."

In 1885 L. Oliphant discovered the remains of a synagogue at Khirbat Kānif and a lintel with an incomplete Aramaic inscription: ". . . remembered be for good Yose son of Ḥalfu son of Ḥana[n]." In excavations at Ḥammat Gader in 1932, E. L. Sukenik found the remains of a synagogue. The main hall was paved with mosaics and contained four Aramaic inscriptions in honor of Jewish donors from Susita, Kefar Akavyah (on the northeastern shore of Lake Kinneret), Kefar Naḥum, and Arbel. Israel surveys, begun in July

Remains of a synagogue at Khirbat Kanif, with the original corner and entrance intact. Courtesy M. Neistadt.

1967, have explored more than 100 sites and uncovered carved stones from the talmudic period with Jewish motifs typical of the Golan (and of the Bashan in general). Some 100 inscriptions, the majority in Greek and containing Hebrew names, were also found. The large amount of objects surviving in the Golan is due to the durability of basalt stone, which is characteristic of the area. In addition to the seven-branched *menorah,* the typical Jewish ornamental motifs include bunches of grapes, vine leaves, palm and pine branches, fish, doves, and eagles. Walls and stone courses of buildings have also been well preserved thanks to the basalt stone.

In 1970 a site was discovered on the ridge of Wadi al-Dāliya, near the village of Deir Krūḥ which the surveyors have identified with the village of Gamala, mentioned by Josephus. At the village of Dabbūra in the western Golan above the Ḥuleh Valley, a wealth of objects were discovered, including a Hebrew lintel inscription that attests to the existence of a *bet midrash* in the settlement. On either side of the inscription stands a bird, either a dove or an eagle, which grasps in its beak the end of a wreath that encircles the inscription: "This is the *bet midrash* of the rabbi." To the right and left of the wreath are the words "Eleazar ha-Kappar." This personage belonged to the fifth generation of *tannaim,* i.e., the second century. In addition, five Aramaic inscriptions found there can be related to the existence of a *bet midrash* or synagogue during the talmudic period. Dabbūra should perhaps be identified with the biblical city of refuge "Golan in Bashan" (Deut. 4:43). A seven-branched *menorah* and other stones carved in relief found at al-Yahūdiyya undoubtedly belonged to a synagogue not yet uncovered. It has been proposed to identify al-Yahūdiyya with Sogane, which was fortified by Josephus before the Jewish War (66–70/73). A Jewish community lived at Yahūdiyya up to the 13th century and Jewish travelers of the Middle Ages used to visit the local synagogue.

Stones engraved with Jewish symbols have also been found in the villages of ʿAyyūn, Kafr Ḥārib (Kefar Ḥaruba in the Mishnah), Khasfīn (Ḥasfiyah), and Nāb (Nob) in the southwestern Golan. The names of these four villages are included among the nine villages in the territory of Susita, which are considered as lying within the boundaries of Erez Israel (TJ, Dem. 1:2, 22d). Scores of stone houses from the talmudic period have survived almost intact at al-Rafīd, al-Ruthmāniyya, and Furayj. These houses have been used as dwellings up to the present. Some lack ceilings, but most of them are preserved together with walls, ceilings, doorsills, and partitions, just as they were built in the fourth to fifth centuries.

The discoveries in the Golan clearly attest the existence of a dense Jewish population in the talmudic period, which, despite changes of fortune, survived for more than 600 years from its inception in the time of Herod, who established Jewish settlement in northern Transjordan, up to the Arab conquest. Important Christian remains in the Golan were excavated in 1970 at Kursī, on the eastern shore of Lake Kinneret at the mouth of Wadi al-Samak. This was the site of the city of Gerasa sacred to Christians as the place that Jesus performed the miracle of driving devils out of a man and sending them into a herd of swine (Mark 5:1; Luke 8:26). Inside an enclosure fortified by a wall 492 x 426 ft. (150 x 130 m.) were the ruins of a large church from the fifth to sixth century. Nearby were remains of a chapel with mosaic pavement, pulpit, fragmentary chancel screen with a cross carved on it, and a Greek inscription that mentions the name of the bishop. A series of rooms belonging to the church complex were paved with a colored mosaic floor.

In 1967 when the Israel Archeological Survey Society organized a survey in the Golan it discovered in Qaṣrayn the remnants of

Portal and remains of the north wall of the synagogue at Qaṣrayn. Stone relief decoration on the lintel includes a wreath and pomegranates. Courtesy D. Urman, Israel Archaeological Survey.

a large synagogue dating from the talmudic period, and near it a massive doorpost on which were reliefs of a *menorah* and a peacock. During excavations organized in 1971 part of a synagogue was uncovered. Its area measured 59 ft. (18 m.)×50 ft. (15.4m.) in a north–south direction. Along the length of its walls was a bench about 1 ft. 4 in. (40 cm.) high made of smoothed basalt blocks. In the northern wall, constructed from large hewn basalt stones, a gate which was 1.90 m. (6 ft.) wide was uncovered, adorned with the traditional embellishments of a synagogue of the talmudic period. North of this wall was laid bare a large square built in a later era. On one of the capitals an engraved depiction of a three-branched *menorah* was uncovered. Below the square two additional levels of paved streets were discovered belonging evidently to the earlier stages of the synagogue. Around the synagogue extending over a large area many old buildings were found that testify to the existence in early times of a large community in the place.

xxvi RAMAT RAḤEL. Ramat Raḥel is an ancient tell (Khirbat Ṣāliḥ) situated on the lands of a kibbutz by the same name in the southern outskirts of Jerusalem. The tell contains remains from the First Temple period to the early Arab period. The Hebrew University and the University of Rome conducted five seasons of excavations there (1954–62) under the direction of Y. Aharoni. The finds include especially important discoveries concerning the Judean kingdom and post-Exilic periods and indicate that the site should probably be identified with ancient Beth-Cherem. Seven periods of occupation were uncovered during the excavations: (1) The site was first settled at the time of the kings of Judah in the ninth or eighth century B.C.E. (Stratum VB), when a royal fortress was apparently built, as evidenced by fragments of walls of ashlar stones and a large number of handles of storage jars stamped with royal seal impressions found in this stratum. This fortress was possibly a house located in the king's vineyards (hence the name Beth-Cher-

179

Ashlar masonry of the inner casemate wall of the palace built by one of the last kings of Judah, c. 600 B.C.E. Stratum VA of the Ramat Raḥel excavations. Courtesy Y. Aharoni, Tel Aviv University.

em, "House of the Vineyard"); private dwellings, perhaps belonging to tenant farmers, were built around it. In one of these houses were found seal impressions of "Shebnah [son of] Shaḥar," which have also been discovered at Lachish and Mizpeh. (2) In the following stratum (VA) one of the last kings of Judah erected an imposing palace surrounded by a lower citadel extending over an area of about 20 dunams. This is the first palace of a Judean king found thus far in archaeological excavations, and judging from its late date it was probably built by Jehoiakim son of Josiah (608–598 B.C.E.), whose palace is described by Jeremiah (22:13–19). The palace walls were constructed of ashlar blocks, similar to Ahab's palace at Samaria, and it was decorated with proto-Aeolic capitals, found here for the first time in Judah. Among the other main finds were window balustrades of the palace (cf. Jer. 22:14), a painted potsherd depicting a king seated on his throne (or chariot?), and a seal impression of "Eliakim, steward of Yokhan," also known from Beth-Shemesh and Tell Beit Mirsim and attributed to an official of Jehoiachin (Yokhan) son of Jehoiakim. (3) In the next settlement (Stratum IVB), dating to the post-Exilic period, a new citadel was erected. The many seal impressions found from the Persian period indicate that the site then served as an administrative center and also strengthen its identification with Beth-Cherem, which is mentioned in the Bible as a district capital in the time of Nehemiah (3:14). In addition to the numerous seal impressions inscribed "Yehud" and "Jerusalem," others were stamped with the names of two royal officials,

Brick with the stamp of the Tenth Roman Legion EG(10) X FRE(TENSIS), found in Stratum III of the Ramat aḥel excavations. Courtesy Y. Aharoni, Tel Aviv University.

Jehoezer and Ahzai, who were apparently Jewish governors previously unknown. (4) After the destruction of this citadel in about the third century B.C.E. an unwalled settlement (Stratum IVA) took its place and continued to exist until the end of the Second Temple period. Tomb caves dating to this period contained ossuaries with Jewish names written in Aramaic and Greek. (5) After the fall of the Second Temple, buildings were erected on the hill for the Tenth Roman Legion (Stratum III), as evidenced by bricks stamped LXFR *(Legio X Fretensis).* A Roman-style house and well-built bathhouse were also found. (6) In the fifth century a Christian church was built on the tell with an attached monastery complex (Stratum II). This is the church of the "Kathisma" ("the Seat") often mentioned in Byzantine sources on the way from Jerusalem to Bethlehem. According to Christian tradition, Mary, mother of Jesus, rested there during her journey to Bethlehem where she gave birth. (7) In the early Arab period (Stratum I), the settlement consisted of poorly built structures (seventh century C.E.). This was the last occupation of the tell.

xxvii SAMARIA. Samaria was the capital of the kingdom of Israel in the ninth—eighth centuries B.C.E. The ancient city was founded by Omri, king of Israel, in c. 880 B.C.E. on the hill belonging to one Shemer (I Kings 16:24); hence its Hebrew name Shomron. Its history as known from ancient sources has been supplemented by excavations carried out by an expedition of Harvard University, directed by G. Reisner, C.S. Fisher, and D. G. Lyon in 1908 and 1910–11, and by the British School of Archaeology in Jerusalem and the Palestine Exploration Fund under the direction of J.W. Crowfoot, with the assistance of G. M Crowfoot, E. L. Sukenik (on behalf of the Hebrew University), and K. Kenyon in 1931–35. A few traces o

Early Bronze Age and early Iron Age settlements were uncovered. Omri paid two talents of silver for the site and proceeded to clear the summit to bedrock, quarrying the latter for the foundation walls of an acropolis, which is rectangular in shape and measures c. 290 ft. (90 m.) from north to south and c. 585 ft. (180 m.) from west to east. It was originally enclosed by a wall of fine ashlar masonry, and at a later period was enlarged to the north and west by a casemate wall, which served both as a fortification and as a retaining wall for the palace and storerooms. A lower town protected by a massive wall of ashlar stones surrounded the acropolis. The acropolis contained the palace of Omri and Ahab. In its ruins were found ivories of Phoenician workmanship in style that was a mixture of Mesopotamian and Egyptian motifs; this was probably the "ivory house" Ahab had built for Jezebel, his consort. In the western part were the storehouses, in which 63 ostraca

Excavations at Samaria: 1. Roman theater from the first century B.C.E., 2. Hellenistic tower from the third century B.C.E., 3. remains of the Israelite lower wall. Photo Richard Cleave, Jerusalem.

were found, bearing inscriptions concerning the delivery of wine and oil. Their exact date is disputed, but most scholars tend to date them in the reign of Jeroboam II (c. 785–749 B.C.E.).

The fortunes of Samaria varied with those of the Israelite kingdom, reaching apogees in the reign of Omri and Ahab and again in the time of Jeroboam II. In 722/21 B.C.E., the city, then the capital of a much smaller kingdom, was taken by Sargon II of Assyria and its inhabitants deported. Colonists from Babylon, Cutha, and Hamath replaced the deportees and with an Israelite remnant, they formed the nucleus of the Samaritan population. The city remained the seat of an Assyrian governor. In the Persian period, its rulers, of whom the family of Sanballat was the most famous, were in constant conflict with Nehemiah and his successors. In the time of Alexander, the Samaritans revolted and a colony of 6,000 Macedonians was settled there as punishment, thus transforming Samaria into a Greek town. A round tower of that period has been found. In 107 B.C.E. this town was captured after a long siege by the Hasmonean John Hyrcanus I; the date of its fall was recorded as a day of rejoicing (Marḥeshvan 25). Traces of the destruction wrought by Hyrcanus were found by the excavators, but latest researches show that the town was apparently already resettled under Yannai. Pompey reestablished the Greek town; Herod rebuilt it in 25 B.C.E., erecting a temple dedicated to Augustus on the acropolis, building a colonnaded street, a theater, and a stadium, and surrounding the city with a wall $2\frac{1}{2}$ mi. (4 km.) long, with imposing towers and gateways in the west and north. He named it Sebaste in honor of Augustus (Gr. Sebastos-Augustus). In the second century C.E. the city declined; it was revived by Septimius Severus, who established it as a colony (Lucia Septimia Severa Sebaste, c. 193/4 C.E.). Temples (including those of Kore-Persephone and of Augustus) and a new basilica were erected.

Early Christians associated Samaria with John the Baptist, whose body was believed to be buried there. In th early fourth century the town was made the center of a bishopric. A church and a monastery were built below the acropolis in the fifth century. In 614 Samaria was destroyed by the Persians. At the time of the Crusades a bishopric was reestablished there and a church (now near the eastern end of the village) was built. In 1330 the church was again in ruins, perhaps the result of an earthquake. Apart from the remains of the ancient city, there is now an Arab village on the site .

Remains of the forum built in Samaria by Herod, c. 30 B.C.E.
Photo Richard Cleave, Jerusalem.

xxviii SHECHEM. This ancient Canaanite and Israelite city is situated between Mt. Ebal and Mt. Gerizim in a fertile and well-watered valley in the heart of the central hill country of Erez Israel. Shechem has been identified with the ancient mound known as Tell al-Balāṭa, 1 mi. (2 km.) east of modern Nablus, also called Shechem in modern Hebrew parlance. The site has been excavated by an Austrian expedition (1913–14), German expeditions (1926–32), and an American expedition from 1957 onward. In the Bible, Shechem is first mentioned in connection with Abraham's arrival in Canaan; he sanctified the place and built an altar there at "Elon [the terebinth] of Moreh" (Gen. 12:6). After leaving Succoth Jacob returned to Shechem where he bought land and his sons Simeon and Levi destroyed the city following the rape of their sister Dinah (*ibid.*, 33:18ff.). Joseph was later buried in the plot of land purchased by Jacob (Josh. 24:32). Excavations at Shechem have revealed that the town existed already in the Middle Bronze Age II (Patriarchal period). Remains uncovered from this period include a defensive wall, a large beaten-earth platform, and a cylinder seal impression from the time of the Egyptian 12th Dynasty. The first mention of the town in Egyptian documents (in the tomb inscription of Khu-Sebek from the time of Sesostris III, 1878–1843 B.C.E., and in the later Execration Texts) belongs to the same period. The town flourished in the Hyksos period (c. 1750–1650 B.C.E.), when it was strongly fortified by a double defensive wall; another wall enclosed the acropolis and a large building, 66×98 ft. (20 ×30 m.), probably a temple, was also built. In the late Hyksos period (1650–155? B.C.E.) a great temple was erected, 108 ×92 ft. (33×28 m.) with massive walls 18 ft. (5½ m.) thick. It contained a beaten-earth altar and an entrance flanked by a pair of *maṣṣevot* ("pillars"). The city gates were of the triple type made of pairs of parallel limestone blocks. After the

Egyptian conquest of Canaan (18th Dynasty) Shechem suffered a decline; the temple was reconstructed on a lesser scale with much weaker walls; a huge *maṣṣevah* stood in front of its entrance. Shechem at this time, however, was still politically important; it was ruled by Labayu known from the Tell el-Amarna letters as an ally of the Habiru and a rebel against Pharaoh. Shechem is not mentioned among the cities conquered by the Israelites under Joshua but it was the scene of the great covenant for which Joshua assembled the tribes (Josh. 24) and it has thus been suggested that Shechem was peacefully absorbed by the invading tribes. The archaeological evidence furnishes no proof of a violent destruction of the city as noted at other

...he eastern city gate in the Shechem fortifications, with stairs ...ading down to the city. First constructed in the late Hyksos ...riod (1650–1550 B.C.E.), the structure was rebuilt within a ...ntury, with eight orthostats flanking the entrance. Courtesy ... E. Wright. From J. B. Pritchard, *Ancient Near Eastern Texts* ...upp. ed.), Princeton, N.J.

Canaanite sites and its transition from the Late Bronze to the Early Iron period was apparently peaceful. In the period of the Judges, Shechem was the center of the kingdom of Abimelech son of Gideon (Jerubbaal) who was "made king by the terebinth of the pillar that was in Shechem," after being supplied with money from the "house of Baal-Berith" ("Lord of the Covenant," Judg. 9). Later, however, the people of Shechem rebelled against Abimelech who conquered the city and razed its walls. The various localities in the city mentioned in this narrative have been tentatively identified by the excavators: the "Beth-Millo" ("house of Millo") with the above-mentioned Hyksos temple built on a platform (Judg. 9:20); the "terebinth of the pillar" is taken to refer to a sacred tree near the *massevah* of the Late Bronze Age temple (*ibid.*, 9:6); the city gate with the East Gate, the only one in use from the Late Bronze Age onward (*ibid.*, 9:35, 40, 44). The filling of pits beneath the temple with charcoal and early 12th-century B.C.E. pottery may represent evidence of Abimelech's destruction of Shechem. After Solomon's death his son Rehoboam was repudiated as king by the ten tribes at Shechem (I Kings 12). Jeroboam, crowned king in his place, established his first capital at Shechem (*ibid.*, 12:25). Some archaeological evidence was found for his rebuilding of the East Gate (c. 922 B.C.E.). In the period of the Divided Monarchy Shechem comprised some well-built quarters with two-storied houses, and poor sections; its other buildings include large granaries which recall the role of Shechem reflected in the Samaria ostraca as a center for the collection of taxes in kind. In about 724 B.C.E. the richer quarters of the city were apparently destroyed by the Assyrians. These houses were rebuilt and the new stratum contains a quantity of Assyrian pottery. Further destructions of the city seem to have been connected with Assyrian punitive expeditions in 673 and about 640 B.C.E. Shechem was resettled as a poor town and this settlement disappeared in the fifth century B.C.E. In the Hellenistic period the town revived as an extensive and powerful city. I resettlement has been connected with the expulsion of the Samaritans from Samaria itself after their revolt against Alexander the Great; they established their settlement near Mt. Gerizim on which their sanctuary stood. The Hellenistic city was destroyed in 129 B.C.E. by John Hyrcanus; great amounts of earth were spread over the remains and the mound was leveled off. The site later contained an insignificant village. Eusebius (Onom. 150:1ff.) and the author of the Madaba Map still distinguish between the site of Shechem and the city of Nablus (Neapolis) established in 72 B.C.E. but most later writers erroneously equate the two.

xxix SHILOH. Shiloh was an important biblical city and capital of Israel in the time of the Judges, situated north of Beth-El, east of the Beth-El Shechem highway and south of Lebonah (Judg. 21:19), in the mountains of the territory of Ephraim. Archaeological excavations have shown that the place was already settled in about the 19th–18th centuries B.C.E. (Middle Bronze Age II A); however, it is not mentioned in any pre-biblical source. The site was abandoned and resettled at the beginning of the Israelite period. Under Joshua, the tabernacle was erected at Shiloh (Josh. 18:1). Here lots were cast for the various tribal areas (Josh. 18) and for the levitical cities (Josh. 21:2) and here Israel assembled to settle its dispute with the tribes beyond the Jordan (Josh. 22:9, 12). Shiloh was the center of Israelite worship. During one religious celebration, the daughters of the city danced in the vineyards, an occasion used by the Benjamites, who could not get wives in any way except by abducting them (Judg. 21). Elkanah and his wife Hannah came there to worship and Hannah vowed her child Samuel to the Lord, whom he served as a servant of the sanctuary at Shiloh (I Sam. 1–2). In this sanctuary, the sons of Eli the priest sinned and the Lord revealed Himself to Samuel (I Sam. 3). When the Ark was taken from the city on its fateful journey to Eben-Ezer, never to return to Shiloh, a Benjamite brought news of the disaster to Eli, causing his death there (I Sam. 4). Excavations have revealed that the place was utterly destroyed in that period, a fact alluded to in later times (Jer. 7:12, 14; 26:6, 9; Ps. 78:60). However, its priestly family retained its importance for some time after moving to Nob (I Sam. 21:1–9). Ahijah the son of Ahitub, a priest from Shiloh, appeared with the ephod in the camp of Saul before the battle of Michmas (I Sam. 14:3). The priestly family of the city was finally deposed by Solomon (I Kings 2:27). Ahijah the Shilonite prophesied the future kingship of Jeroboam the son of Nebat (I Kings 11:29–31; 12:15; 15:29; II Chron. 9:29). It was apparently in Shiloh that Jeroboam's wife consulted the prophet and heard the doom of the dynasty (I Kings 14:2–16). Jeremiah refers several times to the destruction of the city as a warning (7:12, 14; Ps. 78:60); his comparison of the fate of Shiloh with that foreseen for the Temple led to his being accused of blasphemy (Jer. 26:6–9). After the destruction of the Temple, the people of Shiloh were among the Ephraimites who came to sacrifice at Jerusalem (Jer. 41:5).

Shiloh is identified with Tell Seilun, 30 mi. (48 km.) north of Jerusalem, south of the ascent of Lebonah. Archaeological excavations there were undertaken by a Danish expedition directed by H. Kjaer (1926, 1929), A. Schmidt (1932), and S. Holm-Neilson and B. Otzen (1963). In general, the excavation results confirm the biblical data. The city enjoyed an era of prosperity in the period of the Judges (12th–10th centuries B.C.E.), when it was fortified. It perished in a violent conflagration, probably a result of the Philistine conquest. It revived in the latter part of the Israelite period, and reached a high point of development under the Romans. From the latter period, a villa with a bath and a city wall were uncovered. In the fifth century (the Byzantine period), a mosaic-paved basilica, measuring 25×12 m., was erected south of the tell; further north was a smaller chapel.

Shiloh is also known from later sources. Eusebius places it in the toparchy of Acraba, which in his time belonged to Neapolis (Onom. 156:28ff.). Jerome found an altar there (Epistula 108; PG, vol. 25, p. 1953). On the Madaba Map, it appears west of Gilgal, following the tradition recorded by Josephus (Ant., 5:68), with the addition of a historical note: "there once the Ark." The site of Shiloh was well known to talmudic sages: R. Joshua b. Korḥa recorded the saying of an elder who visited the place and still inhaled the odor of incense between its walls (Yoma 39b). Jews continued to visit Shiloh to pray at the Masjad al-Sukayma, the Māʿida ("Stone of the Table") and the tomb of Eli until the 14th century, as is recorded by Estori ha-Parḥi[24]. At the wali ("Marabout") known as al-Sittīn or al-Arabʿīn, a lintel, perhaps of a synagogue, is still extant and shows an amphora between two rosettes flanked by two jars. In the last century an ancient sarcophagus, supposedly that of Eli the priest, was being shown there.

The identification of biblical Shiloh with Saylūn was established by E. Robinson and is generally accepted; the topographical position, the remains on the mound, and the name all support this identification. However, the position of the sanctuary within the ancient site is a subject of dispute. Conder and Kitchener in the *Survey of Western Palestine* (1881–83) suggested the terrace north of the mound, a position unsupported by other evidence. The area south of the mound, with its ancient road leading to Turmus Aiya, the sanctuaries of Wali Yetim and Wali Sittīn, seems a much more likely spot for an open-air sanctuary around a tabernacle; a pre-Christian sanctuary can be assumed to have been located in a valley in which there are now a number of Muslim holy places and which, in Byzantine times, contained several churches. Nonetheless, it is not impossible that the sanctuary stood inside the city proper.

[24] First topographer of Ereẓ Israel (1280–1355?)

3   OTHER SITES

ACHZIB. Achzib was an ancient Canaanite harbor town north of Acre near the road called "the ladder of Tyre." North of the village is a tell in which potsherds dating from and after the Early Bronze Age have been found. According to Joshua 19:29 and Judges 1:31, Achzib belonged to the tribe of Asher, but it did not come under the effective control of the Israelites, as the Canaanites continued to occupy it. A large number of tombs from the period of the Israelite monarchy have been discovered south and east of the tell. Sennacherib captured Achzib from the king of Tyre in 701 B.C.E. In the period of the Second Temple, Achzib is mentioned (in the Greek form Ekdippa) as a road station, 9 Roman miles north of Ptolemais (Acre) (Jos., Wars, 1:257; Pliny, 19). A Roman milestone has been found on the site, on the Acre–Antioch road, in addition to many Roman tombs. In the mishnaic period, Achzib, then called also Kheziv (Gesiv in the Palestinian Talmud), was considered a part of Erez Israel and its inhabitants were bound by all the biblical laws pertaining to the sabbatical and jubilee years, priestly dues, and tithes (Shev. 6:1; 4:6; Ḥal. 4:8; 2:6; Tosef. Oho. 18:14). Achzib occupied an important position as a base-camp for the Crusader armies and was known as Casal Imbert after the knight who held it. The site is identified with the Arab village of al-Zīb, 9 mi. (15 km.) north of Acre.

In archaeological excavations conducted in 1941–44 and

A view of present-day Achzib, from the sea.

1959-64, fortifications and occupational levels were discovered beginning with the Middle Bronze Age II (first half of the second millennium B.C.E.) to the Roman period and also from the Crusader period and Middle Ages. Most of the tombs investigated were Phoenician (tenth to seventh centuries B.C.E.); others were from the Persian and Roman periods. The tombs were rock-hewn and also contained pottery, figurines, scarabs, and bronze and silver jewelry. Four tombstones were especially significant, being engraved with the name of the deceased; and in one instance, with his occupation (metal worker). A Phoenician inscription on the shoulder of a jar mentions Adonimelekh.

AI, or **HA-AI.** Ai was an ancient Canaanite city in Erez Israel. It is mentioned together with Beth-El as near the site where Abraham pitched his tent (Gen. 12:8; 13:3). In Joshua 7:2, it is located beside Beth-Aven, east of Beth-El. Ai was the second Canaanite city which Joshua attacked (Josh. 7–8). After the first attempt to capture the city had miscarried because of the sin of Achan, 193 the king of Ai and his army were defeated in an ambush and the city was left in ruins (see also Josh. 12:9). Although the old site of Ai remained abandoned, an Israelite city with a similar name arose nearby. Isaiah mentioned Aiath (עַיָּת—Isa. 10:28) as the first of the cities occupied by the Assyrians in their march on Jerusalem, before Michmas and Geba. In the post-Exilic period, returnees from Ai are mentioned together with people from Beth-El (Ezra 2:28; Neh. 7:32) and Aijah (עַיָּה) appears as a city of Benjamin (Neh. 11:31). Most scholars identify the ancient city with et-Tell near Deir Dibwan, c. 1 mi. (2 km.) southwest of Beth-El. Excavations at the site carried out in 1933–35 by Judith Marquet-Krause were renewed in 1964 by J. A. Callaway. The city was found to have been inhabited in the Early Bronze Age from c. 3000 B.C.E. Several massive stone walls were discovered as well as a sanctuary containing sacrificial objects and a palace with a large hall, the roof of which was supported by wooden pillars on stone bases. The city was destroyed not later than in the 24th century B.C.E. and remained in ruins until the 13th or 12th century B.C.E. when a small short-lived Israelite village was established there. This discovery indicates that in the time of Joshua, the site was a waste (also implied by the name Ai, literally, "ruin"). Scholars explain the discrepancy in various ways. Some consider the narrative of the conquest of Ai contained in the book of Joshua an etiological story which developed in order to explain the ancient ruins of the city and its fortifications. Others assume that the story of Ai was confused with that of nearby Beth-El which evidently was captured during the 13th century. Others dispute the identification without, however, being able to propose another suitable site. Khirbet Ḥaiyan, c. 1 mi. (2 km.) south of et-Tell, has been suggested as the site of the later city; the only pottery found there, however, dates from the Roman and later periods.

ATHLIT. Athlit was an ancient port on the Mediterranean coast of Ereẓ Israel, 19 mi. (31 km.) south of Cape Carmel; now site of a Jewish village. It has been identified with Kartha, a city of Zebulun, mentioned in some Greek versions of Joshua 21:34. The road station Certha was still mentioned in its vicinity in 333 C.E. Excavations have shown that the site was inhabited in the Iron Age, probably by Phoenicians. A colony of Greek mercenaries with Egyptian and native wives

North tower and moat entrance of the Crusader castle at Athlit   195

settled at Athlit in Persian-Hellenistic times. In 1217, Crusader pilgrims built a castle there called the Château des Pèlerins (Castrum Peregrinorum); it was held by Templar knights. This served through most of the Crusader period as a kind of immigrants' hostel and absorption and clearing station for newly arrived knights of the Cross who were sent from here to their posts. It successfully resisted an attack by Sultan Baybars in 1274–65. Evacuated in 1291, a few months later than Acre, the fall of Athlit marked the final end of the Crusades. The castle was built on a promontory, jutting out into a bay which served it as a harbor. It was defended by a flooded fosse, a low outer wall, and an inner wall with two towers, 98 ft. high, one of which is still standing. Inside are vaulted store rooms, the foundations of an octagonal church, a vaulted refectory, and other ruins. A town with its own wall, church, and fort in the southeastern corner was attached to the castle; it contained a bath, and large smithies and stables. Near Athlit was a rock-cut passage (*Bāb al-Hawā;* in Latin: *Petra incisa* or *Districtum;* now *Khirbat Duṣṭrī*) near which Baldwin I was attacked and wounded in 1103. The ruins of Athlit served as a quarry for the construction of Acre.

AZOR. Azor is a place southeast of Tel Aviv-Jaffa on the road to Jerusalem. Although the city Azor is not mentioned in the masoretic text of the Bible, the Septuagint adds the name to the list of cities in Danite territory together with Jehud, Bene-Berak, and Gath-Rimmon (Josh. 19:45). It also appears in the Annals of Sennacherib as one of the cities he conquered on his march south against Egypt together with Beth-Dagon, Jaffa, and Bene-Berak. The name has been preserved at Yāzūr where remains from the Canaanite and Israelite periods have been discovered.

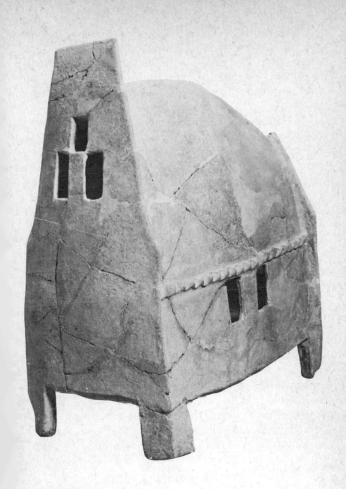

Clay ossuary from collective tomb at Azor, fourth century B.C.E.

A collective burial tomb from the Late Chalcolithic period (c. 3500–3100 B.C.E.) was accidentally discovered at Azor in 1957. The tomb consisted of an egg-shaped chamber 36 ft. (11 m.) long and 26 ft. (8 m.) wide cut deeply into the hard sandstone layers; access was through a circular shaft on the side. Inside, clay ossuaries had been deposited containing the desiccated bones of the dead in a secondary type of burial. The Azor ossuaries belong to a culture remains of which were found at Teleilat Ghassul, in the Jordan Valley, and at Beersheba.

Four groups of ossuaries were distinguished: (1) simple chests; (2) jar-shaped ossuaries, with rounded tops and openings on the shoulders; (3) clay chests in the shape of animals (sheep or dogs) or monsters; (4) house-shaped receptacles, the most prevalent type. The normal type of this group is a box-like clay chest, approximately 2 ft. (60 cm.) long, 1 ft. (30 cm.) wide, and 2 ft. (60 cm.) high, with a rounded top and projecting front and back walls at each end. A square opening in the upper part of the facade, sometimes closed by a door, served to introduce the skull. Above this entrance is often found a schematic human or owl-like figure, which could have had some prophylactic purpose. Some of the ossuaries resemble models of houses, with gabled roofs, walls pierced by windows, and imitations of protruding wooden beams used in a decorative way. Some of the "houses" are mounted on an imitation of piles. The painted ornamentation on the walls and roofs utilizes motifs (palms, lattices) which recall vegetal materials used in buildings. In the Crusader period Richard Coeur-de-Lion built at Azor (Yāzūr) a small fort, Casal des Plains (1191), which served as a meeting place with Muslim representatives. The remains of this tower are still visible inside the old village.

BAB AL-DHRÁ'. A site which is east of the Dead Sea and whose ancient name is unknown. Excavations at the site were carried out in 1965–67 and the main remains are a walled city and a large cemetery. The graves are dated from 3150 B.C.E. to 2300 B.C.E.

DAN. Dan was a biblical city in the Ḥuleh Valley near the sources of the Jordan. It was originally called Laish and was dominated by Phoenicians of Sidon (Judg. 18:7, 27ff.). Laish is mentioned in the Egyptian Execration Texts of the early 18th century B.C.E. and in the list of cities conquered by Thutmose III (c. 1469 B.C.E.). Leshem is a variant spelling of Laish (Josh. 19:47). When the tribe of Dan, under pressure from the Amorites, left their original territory and moved northward, they captured the city of Laish in a surprise raid and renamed it Dan. At the same time a sanctuary was established there with Micah's idol and descendants of Moses acting as priests (Josh. 19:47; Judg. 1:34; 18:2ff.).

Archaeological excavations in progress at Tell Dan, northern Galilee. These excavations, begun in 1966, verified the biblical identification of the city of Dan with Laish (Leshem). Government Press Office, Tel Aviv.

The sanctuary continued to function until Tiglath-Pileser III's conquest in 733 B.C.E. and his exile of the inhabitants to Assyria (II Kings 15:29, where Dan, however, is not explicitly mentioned). The Bible anachronistically calls the city Dan already in the account of Abraham's pursuit of the four kings (Gen. 14:14) and when Moses before his death was shown "all the land, even Gilead as far as Dan" (Deut. 34:1). From the time of the Judges onward, Dan was regarded as the extreme northern point of Erez Israel with Beersheba as the southern (Judg. 20:1, etc.). Jeroboam erected a temple and set up a golden calf at Dan, and a second one at Beth-El (I Kings 12:29ff.); these rivals to Jerusalem were vehemently criticized by the prophets (Amos 8:14). During the reign of his successor Baasa, the city was sacked by Ben-Hadad, king of Aram-Damascus (I Kings 15:20). Dan was the gateway for all northern invasions of Erez Israel (Jer. 4:15; 8:16). In the Hellenistic period it was apparently called Antioch; it marked the northernmost point of Alexander Yannai's conquests (Jos., Ant., 13:394; Wars, 1:105). The city subsequently failed to recover and remained a village called Kefar Dan in the Talmud (TJ, Dem. 2:1, 22c). Dan is identified with Tell al-Qāḍī (now Tell Dan) on one of the main sources of the Jordan. Excavations begun in 1966 and directed by Avraham Biran have uncovered strong fortifications and building remains from the Early Bronze Age to the latter part of the Iron Age—in particular a monumental city gate connected to a paved street, both dating to the time of Jeroboam I of Israel (10th century B.C.E.). The Middle Bronze Age was represented by an immense rampart of earth. Whole pottery vessels and bronze implements indicate that the sloping stone core is to be dated to the Middle Bronze Age II A. while the earthern rampart is of a later date, in the Middle Bronze Age II B. It appears that the Late Bronze Age population of Laish dwelt within the ramparts relying on the earlier fortifications (Judges 18:7). The evidence of the destruction of the Late Bronze Age city confirms archaeologically the biblical story of the conquest of Dan.

DOTHAN. Dothan was a city in the northern part of the territory of Manasseh at the southern extremity of the Jezreel Valley. It was situated on an important trade route and was near extensive pastures. Jacob's sons brought their father's flock to graze there and there they sold Joseph to the passing Ishmaelites-Midianites whose caravan was on its way from Gilead in Transjordan to Egypt (Gen. 37:17ff.). According to II Kings 6:13ff., it was a walled city and the residence of the prophet Elisha. It is mentioned again in the apocryphal book of Judith (4:6; 7:3) among the cities in the Jezreel Valley near Holofernes' camp. Eusebius places it 12 mi. (20 km.) north of Samaria-Sebaste (Onom. 76:13). It is generally identified with Tell Dothan, 3 mi. (5 km.) south of Jenin and 13½ mi. (22 km.) northwest of Shechem at the head of the valley of the same name. Excavations conducted there by J. P. Free between 1953 and 1960 uncovered remains from the Bronze and Iron Ages (Canaanite and Israelite periods)—walls, administrative buildings, private houses, as well as tombs, rich in finds.

EZION-GEBER. The place Ezion-Geber is first mentioned in the Bible as one of the camping sites of the Israelite tribes on their way to Canaan (Num. 33:35–36). As such, it is mentioned next to Elath in Deuteronomy 2:8. From the biblical narrative of the Exodus (Num. 21:4), it may be deduced that Ezion-Geber was somewhere on the Gulf of Elath. Its location on the Gulf of Elath and function as a port and shipyard during the reign of Solomon is clearly stated in I Kings 9:26. II Chronicles 8:17 indicates that it was not Solomon who founded Ezion-Geber and Elath. 201

According to archaeological evidence it was most probably the Edomites or Midianites as early as the end of the Late Bronze Age (see Timna). The port and shipyard of Ezion-Geber are again mentioned in connection with the unsuccessful attempt by Jehoshaphat in the ninth century B.C.E. to renew the gold route to Ophir (I Kings 22:49). After this, it disappears from the biblical annals, and in the eighth century B.C.E., there is mention only of the struggle between the kings of Judah and Edom for the possession of the city of Elath.

In 1934 F. Frank discovered Tell al-Khalayfa, a low mound approximately 1/3 mi. (c. 0.6 km.) north of the shores of the Gulf of Elath, between modern Eilat and Akaba, and he identified it with Ezion-Geber. N. Glueck subsequently excavated the site (1938–40) and identified it with Ezion-Geber and Elath, assuming a change of the former name to Elath in the days of the kings of Judah. According the him, the site was not only the Solomonic port, but also an important industrial center for the manufacture of copper and iron tools, which served as export goods for the trading ventures of Solomon. Recent excavations in the Arabah and the discovery of an early Iron Age I port installation in the bay and on the island Jazīrat Farʿūn, 7½ mi. (12 km.) south of modern Eilat have suggested a reconsideration of the date and character of the ruins of Tell al-Khalayfa, and consequently of the location of Ezion-Geber. It has become clear that the site was fortified, perhaps serving as a caravanserai, and not a copper smelting plant, and an identification with the ancient city of Elath has been suggested. It has been proposed that the port and shipyard of Ezion-Geber should be identified with the island of Jazīrat Farʿūn, the only natural anchorage in the Gulf of Elath. Extensive casemate walls and a well-built port testify to its maritime use in early biblical days. From archaeological discoveries in the southern Arabah (1969), it can be deduced that long before Solomon's ships were assembled at Ezion-Geber–Jazīrat Farʿūn, Egyptian mining expedi

tions on their way to the Arabah copper mines used
Ezion-Geber as their harbor.

GIBEON. Gibeon was a levitical city in
the territory of the tribe of Benjamin
(Josh. 18:25; 21:17) and was the capital
of a league of cities northwest of Jerusalem ("Gibeon, and Chephirah, and
Beeroth, and Kiriath-jearim") in the period of the Israelite conquest (*ibid.* 9:17).
Joshua's great battle with the Canaanite
kings, headed by Adoni-Zedek, king of
Jerusalem, was fought nearby; during this
event the miracle commanded by Joshua
took place: "Sun, stand thou still upon
Gibeon; and thou, Moon, in the valley of Aijalon" (*ibid.*
ch. 10). Gibeon also figures in accounts of events during the
time of David. It was the scene of the clash between the
armies of David and Ish-Bosheth, commanded by Joab and
Abner, and of David's victory over the Philistines (II Sam.
2:12ff.; I Chron. 14:16). In the description of the former
battle, the Bible mentions several topographical features of
the surroundings including a pool beside which David's
men prevailed over Ish–Bosheth's followers. At the
beginning of the monarchy the "great high place" was
located at Gibeon; there Solomon offered sacrifices and had
his famous vision (I Kings 3:4–15). According to other biblical references this "great high place" was connected with the
"tabernacle of the Lord" which was also located at Gibeon
at that time (I Chron. 16:39; 21:29; II Chron. 1:3, 13, etc.).
In the same period the Bible calls the "wilderness of Gibeon"
the eastern slopes of the hills of Benjamin from Gibeon to
the plains of Jordan (II Sam. 2:24). Gibeonites were among
the returning Babylonian exiles: they resettled the city and
took part in building the walls of Jerusalem (Neh. 3:7, 7:25)
Josephus locates Gibeon about 40 or 50 stadia (4½–5½ mi.)
from Jerusalem (Ant., 7:283; Wars, 2:516). The city is
identified with al-Jīb, a small Muslim Arab village situated 203

on an oval-shaped hill about 3½ mi. (6 km.) northwest of Jerusalem's northernmost suburbs. The place al-Jib is already mentioned in early sources by the 13th-century Arab geographer Yakut. In excavations conducted at the site by J. P. Pritchard (1956–62), parts of the city wall were uncovered in the western and northeastern section of the city. Near the wall the above-mentioned round pool was discovered, measuring 37 ft. (11.3 m.) in diameter and 35 ft. (10.8 m.) deep, with a spiral staircase going down to a tunnel 148 ft. (45 m.) long with 93 steps leading outside the city wall to a cistern which was connected by another tunnel 112 ft. (34 m.) long with the main spring of the city. Debris filling the round pool contained numerous jar handles inscribed with the name Gibeon, Gdn (or Gdd) Gibeon, and names of persons such as Damlah, Shebuel, Azariah, Hananiah, Amariah, etc. Wine cellers, containing sherds of storage jars, silos, seals, and weights, were discovered near the pool. The excavations also uncovered remains dating from the Early, Middle, and Late Canaanite periods, but the earliest wall found was built sometime in the 12th century B.C.E. The city flourished in the Israelite period and was destroyed during the Babylonian invasion. There was also evidence of a small settlement in the Persian and Hellenistic periods and of a thriving city, not defended by a wall, from Hasmonean to Roman times.

HAMMATH. A city in the territory of Naphtali mentioned in the Bible together with Rakkath and Chinnereth (Josh. 19:35). Its name indicates the presence of hot springs. Most scholars identify Hammath with Hammath-Dor, a city of refuge and a levitical city (Josh. 21:32), which is generally located at Hammath Tiberias, south of Tiberias. No remains from the biblical period, however, have thus far been uncovered there, and the site of the ancient town should probably be identified with the early remains within the confines of Roman Tiberias. Hammath was famous for its hot baths in the Second Temple period (Jos., Wars 4:11; Jos., Ant. 18:36); when Tiberias rose to prominence in talmudic times, Hammath, one mile away and joined to Tiberias for halakhic purposes, also became well known (Meg. 2b; Tosef., Er. 7:2; TJ, Er. 6 (5); 13). After the destruction of the Second Temple, priests of the Maaziah course settled there (*Baraita of Twenty-Four Mishmarot*,[25] 24); the Emmaus mentioned in the Mishnah *Arakhin* 2:4 may refer to the place. R. Meir was one of the many talmudic scholars who lived there. A Jewish community is attested there up to the time of the Cairo *Genizah*[26].

During the excavation of the foundations of bathhouses, two synagogues were discovered; the first was excavated by N. Slouschz in 1920 and the other by M. Dothan in 1961–63. The first, belonging to the transitional type of synagogue, consisted of a basilica-shaped hall without an apse. The facade oriented to Jerusalem contained four small marble columns which apparently supported a marble lintel above the Ark of the Law. The synagogue was paved with mosaics; fragments of the "seat of Moses" (see p. 17) were found there, as well as a stone seven-branched *menorah*, carved in relief and decorated with a "button and leaf" pattern in the form of pomegranates. In the second synagogue four building phases were distinguished. (1) The earliest structure consisted of a public building (probably not a synagogue) with rooms surrounding a central courtyard. (2) A synagogue from the third century C.E. (3) Directly above this synagogue and using its columns was another synagogue built in the form of a basilica with an outstanding mosaic pavement which contained (from north to south): a dedicatory inscription flanked by two lions; a zodiac of a high artistic standard with the sun god Helios on his chariot in the center and representations of the four seasons in the corners; the Ark of the Law with *menorot* and other ritual articles. Inscriptions in Greek and one in Aramaic commemorate several builders, especially a certain

---

[25] A baraita dealing with the priestly divisions in the Temple
[26] Depository of sacred books and documents discovered in the synagogue of Fostat (old Cairo)

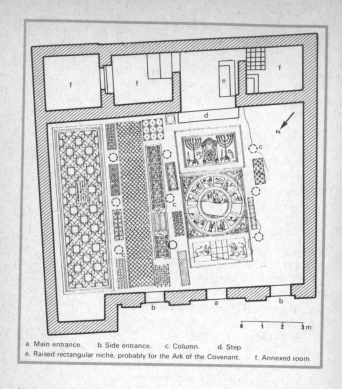

a. Main entrance.　b. Side entrance.　c. Column.　d. Step.
e. Raised rectangular niche, probably for the Ark of the Covenant.　f. Annexed room.

Plan of the synagogue of Severus at Hammath, first half of the
fourth century, C.E. Courtesy M. Dothan, Israel Department of
Antiquities, Jerusalem.

Greek inscription on the floor mosaic in the synagogue of Severus
at Hammath, listing the names of Severus and other builders, first
half of fourth century C.E. Courtesy M. Dothan, Israel Department
of Antiquities, Jerusalem.

→

The mosaic floor of the Hammath synagogue near Tiberias shows that Jewish figurative art was highly developed in the fourth century C.E.

"Severus, the pupil of the most illustrious patriarchs." The building, 47 ½ ft. (14 ½ m.) wide, contains a nave with two aisles east of it and to the west of it, an aisle, and a hall (women's gallery?). The synagogue is attributed to the beginning of the fourth century C.E.; in a later period a stationary *bamah* ("platform") was installed and the entrance was moved from the southern to the northern side. (4) Above the site of this synagogue another one was built in the sixth century with a slightly different orientation. It was basilica in shape, 62 x 49 ft. (19 x 15 m.) with an apse and a mosaic pavement with geometric designs.

HERODIUM. Judean fortress built during the Second Temple period, located 60 stadia (c. 7 mi.) S. of Jerusalem near Tekoa. It was built by Herod at the spot where he had routed his pursuers during his flight from Jerusalem to Masada in 40 B.C.E. It was also his burial place and he was interred there with great pomp (Jos., Ant., 17:199; Wars, 1:673). Josephus relates that the fortress was erected on a natural hill which was further heightened by debris heaped on it. A staircase, with 200 marble steps, led to the fortress wall which was a circular structure defended by round towers; within the wall were several palaces. At the foot of the mountain a settlement was established, the water supply for which was brought from Solomon's Pools by means of an aqueduct passing through Naḥal Taḥuna (Ant., 14:360; 15:323–5; Wars, 1:265, 419ff.; 4:518). A large terrace, that probably served as a hippodrome, remains of a large pool and imposing palaces (probably Herodian), were found there in 1972.

Herodium is identified with Jebel Fureidis, an artificial hill 2½ mi. (4 km.) southeast of Bethlehem which looks like a truncated cone from afar. The site was partly excavated by V. Corbo on behalf of the Custodia di Terra Santa in 1962–67. The fortress was found to consist of a double

The fortress of Herodium, south of Jerusalem. Courtesy Government Press Office, Tel Aviv.

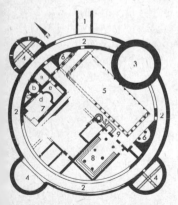

1. Remains of staircase which led to the fortress.
2. Double circular curtain wall.
3. Round tower.
4. Semicircular towers.
5. Colonnaded portico.
6. Exedrae (semicircular benches).
7. Bath house.
    a. Entrance.
    b. *Tepidarium* (lukewarm room).
    c. *Frigidarium* (cold room).
    d. *Caldarium* (hot room).
    e. *Apodyterium* (wardrobe).
8. Herodian hall with post-Herodian benches, probably from the Jewish War (66–70/73 C.E.)
9. Mikveh (?).

Plan of the fortress of Herodium. Courtesy Ministry of Defense, Publishing Section, Tel Aviv.

circular curtain wall with four towers (three semicircular and one round). Within the wall was a colonnaded portico with two exedrae, a bath, and a hall with four pillars. Traces of pre-Herodian and post-Herodian occupation were found; the latter included remains from the time of the Jewish War (66–70/73), the Bar Kokhba War (132–35), a Roman garrison, and a Byzantine monastery. Air photos show the steps and the buildings which stood at the foot of the fortress, as described by Josephus. Herodium also served as the capital of a toparchy (Wars, 3:55; Pliny, *Natural History*, 5:15). During the Jewish War it was one of the last strongholds remaining in Zealot hands and was captured by the Romans (by the governor Lucius Bassus) a short time after the fall of Jerusalem (Wars, 4:555; 7:163). According to documents found in the Murabba'at Cave in the Judean Desert, it served as one of Bar Kokhba's district headquarters during his war. In Byzantine times a monastery was erected there. Clearance of the site was continued by G. Foerster in 1968–69.

MAMPSIS. A city in the Negev. According to Eusebius it was situated between Hebron and Elath, one day's march from Thamara (Onom. 8:8). The Madaba Map shows it between Beersheba and Thamara and calls it Maps. Ptolemy also refers to it as Maps. It appears in the episcopal lists of Palaestina tertia. Mampsis is identified with Kurnub where excavations were begun by A. Negev in 1966. The town, which is surrounded by a wall, consists of three hillocks. On the western side of the town are the remains of a palace including a guard room, audience hall, records room, and stairs leading to an upper story with balconies; nearby is a tower with office rooms. A complex of residential buildings extending over 1,900 sq. yds. (1,600 sq. m.) on the eastern hill included stables with mangers. Some of the rooms were decorated with frescoes; a hoard of 10,400 Roman tetra-drachms was discovered there. Mampsis was apparently settled in about 50 C.E. and continued into Byzantine times; its ruins include two churches. A Nabatean and Roman military cemetery were found nearby. The remains of several dams were found in the vicinity.

MARESHAH. Mareshah was a biblical city in Judah connected with the families of Shelah and Caleb (I Chron. 2:42; 4:21). It was in the fourth district of the territory of the tribe of Judah (Josh. 15:44). Mareshah was one of the cities fortified by Rehoboam (II Chron. 11:8-9). It was the home town of the prophet Eliezer the son of Dodavahu (II Chron. 20:37) and possibly also of the prophet Micah (Micah 1:1; Jer. 26:18). In Persian or Hellenistic times, a Sidonian colony settled there and it served as an administrative center and a market for slave trading. Its population, however, was mostly Edomite, and as such, Mareshah served as a base for the Seleucid armies at war with Judah Maccabee, who ravaged its territory (I Macc. 5:66; II Macc. 12:35). John Hyrcanus conquered it with the rest of Idumea and it remained in Hasmonean possession until Pompey. In 40 B.C.E., shortly after its "liberation" by Pompey, the Parthians completely destroyed it (Jos., Ant., 12:353; 14:75, 364; Wars, 1:269). After the destruction of the city, Bet Guvrin became the center of the region. Robinson identified it with Tell Sandaḥanna, south of Bet Guvrin. Bliss and Macalister, excavating there in 1900, uncovered the Hellenistic stratum, which contained a city wall nearly square in plan (measurements, at its widest points: 520 ft. (156 m.) wide from east to west; 500 ft. (150 m.) wide from north to south). Inside, the town was laid out in the so-called Hippodamic plan, with streets intersecting at right angles. This plan was slightly distorted at a later

211

Painting from one of the Hellenistic tombs found near Mareshah, third century B.C.E. Courtesy Hebrew University, Department of Archaeology, Jerusalem.

stage of the town's existence. In the eastern part of the town were a marketplace and a temple. Ptolemaic inscriptions, pottery, and execration texts on limestone tablets were the main finds. In 1902, Hellenistic tombs with paintings and inscriptions were found near Mareshah. The principal tomb is decorated with representations of real and mythological animals; the inscriptions are of one Apollophanes, head of the Sidonians at Mareshah, and his family. The tomb was used from the second to the first century B.C.E. and the inscriptions indicate a gradual assimilation of the Sidonians into the Idumean and Jewish populations there. Other tombs of similar character were found in 1925 and 1962.

NAHARIYYAH. Tell Nahariyyah, near the city of Nahariyyah is about ½ mi. (700 m.) north of the Ga'aton stream. The excavations conducted in 1947 and 1954-56 revealed a temple, cultic installations, a court for burning incense and female figurines. The temple served from the Hyksos period (18th–17th centuries B.C.E.) to the 15th cent. B.C.E. On the top of the tell were found potsherds from the 20th cent. B.C.E. to the Persian period (587 B.C.E.).

SHIVTAH. Shivtah or Sobata is a former city in the Negev, 35 mi. (56 km.) southwest of Beersheba, near the Nessana highway. It was founded in the first century B.C.E. by the Nabateans, but it flourished principally in the Byzantine period. The city is mentioned in the story of St. Nilus and in the Nessana papyri. The buildings were made of local limestone, without any particular planning; the city is unwalled, the outer walls of the houses at its limits forming a defensive line. (1,200–1,300 rooms have been counted in its total area of 115 dunams (c. 29 acres); its population could hardly have numbered more than 5,000. The southern and older

North Byzantine Church at Shivtah, c. sixth century C.E. Courtesy Government Press Office, Tel Aviv.

part of Shivtah is centered on two large pools. The nearby southern church was built after the other buildings. The northern part, covering 40 dunams (10 acres) with 340 rooms, contained a church with a tower, perhaps a public building, at its southern end and a large church dedicated to St. George at its northern extremity. This church consists of an open court, a narthex, a mosaic-paved side chapel, and a baptistry; the main church (66×37 ft.) has a nave and two aisles separated by six columns. It has three apses and its walls were once covered with white marble. Near the church was a large square surrounded by 36 shops and workshops (for potters, dyers, etc.).

The inhabitants of Shivtah cultivated an extensive area in the Lavan Valley, amounting to 4,945 dunams (over 1,270 acres); rainwater from a drainage area of 77 sq. mi. (197½ sq. km.) was carried by means of a series of complicated channels into their fields. In the city itself, water was scanty (4 liters a head per day) and the cleaning of the reservoirs was a duty to be performed by every citizen; each house was also provided with one to two cisterns. The city was inhabited until Arab times (a mosque was built near the southern church) and was abandoned in the time of the Crusaders.

TAANACH. Taanach is a Canaanite city-state, identified with Tell Ti'innik, about 5 mi. (8 km.) S.E. of Megiddo. The earliest city flourished during the 27th–25th centuries B.C.E. (end of Early Bronze Age II to the first half of Early Bronze Age III). Relations with Egypt may have been established at an early date, as is evidenced by a possible imitation of Egyptian tomb construction of the third dynasty. The city was abandoned in about 2500 B.C.E. and was only reoccupied in the second millennium (Middle Bronze Age II). In the Late Bronze Age, Taanach came under Egyptian domination. A palace, rebuilt several times in this period, attests the continuing prosperity of the city. Taanach appears in the list of cities subject to Thutmose III (no. 42) and on a contemporary papyrus listing the envoys of the Canaanite kings (Ermitage papyrus 1115/6). Forty cuneiform tablets, dating to the 15th–14th century B.C.E., were uncovered in the excavations. In them an Egyptian governor named Amenhotep (the pharaoh?) orders the king of Taanach to supply men and materials to Megiddo and Gaza. The city appears again in connection with Megiddo in the Tell el-Amarna letter no. 248 (as Tahnuka).

The king of Taanach is listed among the Canaanite kings defeated by Joshua (Josh. 12:21). While the city appears among those supposedly held by Manasseh in the territory of Issachar (Josh. 17:11; I Chron. 7:29), it follows from Judges 1:27 that the Israelites did not capture the city at the time of the conquest. The city played an important role in the war of Deborah. From the description in Judges 5:19—"Taanach by the waters of Megiddo"—Albright has concluded that during an eclipse of the latter city, Taanach was predominant in the Jezreel Valley. Others doubt this interpretation, especially as the latest excavations indicate that the city was destroyed in about 1125 B.C.E. and lay in ruins for most of the 11th century. The city revived in the period of the United Monarchy, when David established it as one of the levitical cities (Josh. 21:25), which served as administrative centers. Solomon included it in his fifth district, administered by Baana the son of Ahilud (I Kings 4:12). To this period possibly belongs the pillared building similar to those found at Megiddo and Hazor, which some have regarded as a stable. Taanach was conquered by Shishak and it appears in his list of conquered cities between Shunem and Megiddo (no. 14).

The city's existence in later times is attested by Eusebius, who variously locates it 3 and 4 mi. (5 and 6 km.) from Legio (Onom. 98:12; 100:7ff.). In the crusader period, it was a *casal* (village) known as Tannoc, which was dependent on Legio and was a subject of dispute between

215

the bishop and abbey of Nazareth. The present-day village of Ti'innik is located near the ancient site.

Tell Ti'innik was excavated by E. Sellin on behalf of the Vienna Academy (1902–04) and by an American expedition under the direction of P.W. Lapp (1963–68). Among the finds of the recent excavations are a cuneiform tablet in Ugaritic script and an early Israelite high place.

TELL ABU HUWWAM. Tell Abu Huwwam is a small mound on the coastal plain situated at the foot of Mount Carmel. It was excavated in 1932–33, in 1952, and in 1963. The earliest occupation dates to the 15th cent. B.C.E., and lasted without any long break until the end of the 10th cent. B.C.E. After a long interval it was reoccupied from the 6th cent. until the beginning of the 4th cent. B.C.E.

TELL AL-'AJJŪL. Tell al-'Ajjūl is located about 4½ mi. (7 km.) southwest of Gaza, and was excavated from 1929 to 1931 by Sir Flinders Petrie (who identified it with ancient Gaza). The remains at Tell al-'Ajjūl date mainly from the Middle and Late Bronze Ages and include Hyksos fortifications and graves, and the palace of an Egyptian governor. Rich finds of gold, silver and jewelry were discovered in the tombs. Tell al-'Ajjūl is most probably Bet Aglaim, a place mentioned by Eusebius (Onom. 48:19).

TELL AL-FARI'A. Tell al-Fari'a is located about 7 mi. (11 km.) northeast of Shechem and was identified with Tirzah the capital of Omri before he moved to Samaria (I Kings 16:23–24). Excavations directed by R. de Vaux in 1946–60 revealed remains from the Chalcolithic period and an important Early Bronze Age town with a sanctuary, city-wall, and fortified gate. After a gap of several centuries later occupation was resumed in the Middle Bronze Age. The town of the Late Bronze Age is poorer. The city was rebuilt in the Israelite period, and in a later phase, a palace was constructed which apparently remained unfinished: this may be due to the removal of the capital to Samaria. The later Israelite level is characterized by large private houses which are in sharp contrast to those of the poor, from which they are separated by a wall. This level was destroyed by the Assyrians in c. 723 B.C.E., after which settlement continued, but on a smaller scale. The site was eventually abandoned in c. 600 B.C.E.

TELL AL-FŪL. Tell al-Fūl is located 3 mi. (5 km.) north of Jerusalem, at a height of about 2,755 ft. (840 m.) on the road from Jerusalem to Shechem, which was the highroad leading from the territories of Judah to Ephraim during the period of the Judges (Judg. 19:11–13). It was identified by E. Robinson with Gibeah (Gibeath-Benjamin, Gibeath-Shaul), the center of the territory of the tribe of Benjamin (Josh. 18:24; Judg. 19:14) and Saul's royal city (Judg. 15:34).

It was excavated by W. F. Albright in 1922–23 and 1933 and by P. W. Lapp in 1964. According to biblical and archaeological evidence, the site passed through four main phases: (1) The earliest settlement belongs to the Early Iron Age and was in existence until about the middle of the 12th century B.C.E. Its destruction can be connected with the biblical tradition of the war waged by the tribes against Benjamin because of its crime against the levite's concubine (Judg. 19–20). (2) The city was rebuilt in the latter part of the 11th century B.C.E. Excavations have uncovered a rectangular citadel; its wall, made of undressed blocks, and a square tower in the excavated corner. The latest investigations have refuted the 217 view that this fortress was built by the Philistine garrison at Geba (I Sam. 10:5; 13:3), which was routed by Saul's son Jonathan (I Sam. 13–14). It was thus apparently built by Saul, served as his royal residence and was henceforth named after him (*ibid.* 11:4; 15:34; II Sam. 21:6). Gibeah's importance ended with the fall of Saul's monarchy, and the fortress was perhaps destroyed by the Philistines after the battle of Gilboa, but its repair and reconstruction probably date from the days of David. One of David's warriors came from Gibeah (II Sam. 23:29). (3) Gibeah was rebuilt a third time in the latter part of the monarchy, when it was surrounded by a feeble casemate fortification. This is the city mentioned by Isaiah on the northern approach of Jerusalem (Isa. 10:29), probably along the route taken by part of Sennacherib's army. It was destroyed by the Chaldeans. (4) A new fortress, built in the late fourth century B.C.E., survived until the second century B.C.E. Josephus (Wars 5:51) mentions Gibeah as a settlement situated 30 ris (3½ mi.) north of Jerusalem. Titus camped there on his march to Jerusalem, and his troops demolished it. Excavations indicate that an impoverished settlement existed there down to the period of the Bar Kokhba war (132–135 C.E.). By Eusebius' time (early fourth century), the site was already forgotten.

TELL AL-HASI. A site on the south bank of Wadi Hasi about 15½ mi. (25 km.) southeast of Gaza. It was excavated by Sir Flinders Petrie in 1890 and continued by F. J. Bliss in 1892. At this site Petrie made the first beginnings of stratigraphical excavations in Palestine and pioneered the linking of strata with pottery. Petrie's identification of the site with Lachish is not now accepted, while other scholars identify it with Eglon (Josh. 10:3). In the excavations 8 levels and 3 sub-levels were uncovered, extending from 2600 B.C.E. to the First Temple period.

TELL AL-NASBEH. An ancient site about 8 mi. (13 km.) north of Jerusalem, which is identified with Mizpah or Mispah, a city belonging to the tribe of Benjamin (Josh. 18:26). The Israelites gathered there to punish the tribe of Benjamin after the outrage committed by the men of Gibeah (Judg. 20–21). Samuel assembled the people to fight against the Philistines and judged them in Mizpah (Sam. 7:5ff.; 10:17). Asa of Judah fortified the place (I Kings 15:22; II Chron. 16:6). Gedaliah, the son of Ahikam, established the capital of Judah in Mizpah after the fall of Jerusalem and was later assassinated there (II Kings 25:22ff.; Jer. 40–41). It was a district capital in the time of Nehemiah (Neh. 3:7, 15, 19).

The ancient site was excavated from 1926 to 1936 by W. F. Badè on behalf of the Pacific Institute of Religion in Berkeley. The first settlement there dates to the Early Bronze Age. Its main period of occupation, however, belongs to the Iron Age. The excavations uncovered the main part of the city, which contained many four-room houses typical of the period, some unusually large and built with pillars. Outstanding is a ninth-century wall and gate, evidently built by Rehoboam, which had been preceded by a tenth-century casemate wall. The mound was occupied until the Hellenistic period. A number of tombs uncovered there date from the Canaanite to the Hellenistic periods and were very rich in finds.

Hebrew seals and seal impressions were particularly abundant on the site. A seal with the inscription "Jaazaniah servant of the king" is ascribed by some to the Jezaniah who met with Gedaliah at Mizpah (Jer. 40:8; 42:1). A special seal from the Persian period reading *mṣh* (Mozah?) is interpreted by various scholars as an abbreviation of Mizpeh *(mṣ[p]h)*.

TELL AL-SAFI. A tell 5 mi. (8 km.) northwest of Bet

Guvrin. Its identification with Gath of the Philistines has been suggested. Excavations conducted there between 1898 and 1900 uncovered remains extending from the Early Bronze Age to the time of the Seleucids (312 B.C.E.). In the upper level of the tell, remains of the Crusader fortress Blanchegarde were found.

TELL AL-SAMAK. A tell south of Haifa · identified with the town Shikmonah which was a Jewish city in the Second Temple and Talmud periods (Dem. 1:1). Excavations at the tell begun in 1963 revealed remains from the 10th and 9th centuries B.C.E., and from the Persian, Hellenistic, Roman, and Byzantine periods.

TELL BEIT MIRSIM. Tell Beit Mirsim is an important mound about 15 mi. (25 km.) southwest of Hebron. It is identified by W.F. Albright with Debir, a Canaanite royal city (Josh. 11:21). Debir is also called Kiriath-Sepher and Kiriath-Sannah (*ibid.* 15:15, 49). Albright excavated the tell from 1926 to 1932, uncovering a series of strata dating from the late third millennium to the end of the monarchy. The city was strongly fortified in the Hyksos period and after a gap in occupation was resettled in the Late Bronze Age, suffering total destruction sometime in the latter part of the 13th century B.C.E. It was again occupied in the period of the Judges and provided with a casemate wall in the 10th century. Numerous dyeing plants for a textile industry were found in the city belonging to the period of the monarchy. The sequence of Bronze and Iron Age pottery found there still serves as the basis of the ceramic study of these periods. Some scholars reject Debir's identification with Tell Beit Mirsim arguing that this tell is actually located in the Shephelah ("lowland") whereas the Bible places Debir in the hill region of Judah, south of Hebron.

TELL DEIR 'ALLĀ. A tell in Transjordan northeast of the fall of the Jabbok river into the Jordan river. Most scholars are of the opinion that the site is the town Succoth (Gen. 33:37). From excavations carried out at the tell in 1960–62 it seems that the site was the center of the valley of Succoth (Ps. 60:8). The site was occupied in the Chalcolithic period, Late Bronze Age, and Iron Age I, II.

TELL QASILA. A small tell in north Tel Aviv on the eastern bank of the Yarkon river. Excavations conducted there by B. Mazar in the years 1948–49 uncovered 12 levels of occupation extending from the second half of the 12th cent. B.C.E. to the Arab–Mamluk period (15th cent. C.E.). The findings show evidence of agricultural (baking ovens, granaries, oil and wine presses) and industrial (smelting furnace and dyeing utensils) activities. Remains of fortification from the 12th cent. B.C.E. and of walls from the 10th cent. B.C.E. were found, as well as two Hebrew ostraca. In the renewed excavations (1972) a Philistine temple with a courtyard surrounding it, and numerous cult objects near the altar, were revealed. 221

TELL SHARUHEN (TELL AL-FARA/SOUTH). A site located about 14 miles (22 km.) south of Gaza, which was excavated between 1928 and 1929 by Sir Flinders Petrie. The remains date from Middle Bronze Age II down to Iron Age. Petrie identified the site with Beth-Pelet (Josh. 15:27), but the identification of the site by Albright with Sharuhen (Josh. 19:6) is more accepted.

TELL SHEIKH AL-'ARYANI. A mound which is situated 5 mi. (8 km.) northwest of Lachish. At first the mound was identified with Libnah (Josh. 10:29–30), on account of the white color of the calcareous hills around the mound (Heb. *lavan*, "white"). Later it was identified with Gath of the Philistines (I Sam. 5:8), but all this was disproved by the excavations carried out there by S. Yeivin from 1956 to 1961. The excavations revealed a cult place from the third millennium B.C.E., Egyptian pottery dating from the 8th and 7th centuries B.C.E., and buildings and graves from the Persian and Hellenistic periods. Its identification remains uncertain.

TELL ZEROR. A tell east of Ḥaderah which was excavated between 1964 and 1966 by a Japanese archaeological mission. The findings revealed occupation extending from the 20th to the 9th centuries B.C.E. In the upper levels remains of the Persian, Hellenistic and Roman periods were found. It seems that the small town, the name of which is unknown, controlled part of the Via Maris, an international highway connecting Egypt with Babylon.

TIMNA. Timna is the site of intensive ancient copper mining and smelting activities. The Timna Valley (Ar. Wadi Manāʿiyya) is located 12½–18¾ mi. (20–30 km.) north of Eilat, and three wadis run through it into the Arabah: Naḥal Mangan, Naḥal Timna, and Naḥal Neḥushtan. Explorations on the site were carried out by F. Frank and N. Glueck in 1932–34, and by B. Rothenberg from 1959. The ancient mines are situated in the western part of the Timna Valley, and malachite and chalcocite ores can still be found there in white sandstone formations. The mines and mining camps are spread over an area of approximately 4 sq. mi. (c. 10 sq. km.). The ancient smelting camps, where crude copper was produced, are located in the center of the valley, west of Mt. Timna.

During the Chalcolithic period (fourth millennium B.C.E.), tribes of shepherds and hunters with a good knowledge of copper metallurgy settled around Timna, collecting copper ore nodules and smelting them in well-built bowl furnaces. The Chalcolithic copper smelting furnace excavated on the fringes of the Arabah, east of the modern Timna copper mines, is the earliest smelting installation so far found. The next industrial installations for the smelting and casting of copper date to the Late Bronze and Early Iron I periods. These large installations include workshops, storehouses, cisterns, furnaces, and slagheaps. The date of this complex, called "King Solomon's Mines" by N. Glueck, was for some time much disputed. The discovery of numerous hieroglyphic inscriptions in Timna dating to the 14th–12th centuries B.C.E. now indicate that the copper industry of Timna, and probably of most of the other copper-producing sites in the Arabah, was developed by Egyptian mining expeditions during the 19th and 20th dynasties. The inscriptions were found inside an Egyptian temple dedicated to the Egyptian goddess Hathor 223 and located at the foot of "Solomon's Pillars" in the center of the milling and smelting area, it was probably the central sanctuary of Timna. This temple was built in the reign of Seti I at the end of the 14th century B.C.E. Gifts were also sent to it by Ramses II, Merneptah, and Seti II. It was destroyed in 1216–1210 B.C.E. and was restored only during the reign of Ramses III (1198–1166 B.C.E.). The second temple was short-lived and came to an end with Ramses V (1160–1156 B.C.E.).

Timna, and perhaps also the other copper plants in the eastern Arabah, not yet explored, can now be identified with "Atika, the great copper mines, " described in the Papyrus Harris I dating to the time of Ramses III. According to this source, Egyptian copper mining expeditions traveled to Timna from Egypt by way of the sea and by overland caravans. The bay of Jazīrat Farʿūn, the only natural anchorage in the Gulf of Eilat, can be identified as the Egyptian mining port before it beame the shipyard of King Solomon (see also Ezion-Geber).

Numerous temple gifts, including a partly gilded copper snake, a *neḥushtan* of Midianite origin, and finds in the smelting camp indicate that the Egyptians operated the copper industry of Timna together with the Midianites, Kenites, and, probably, the Amalekites from the central Negev, i.e., the indigenous inhabitants of the area, possessing metallurgical traditions going back to prehistoric times, as reflected in Genesis 4:22. The Egyptian-Midianite temple and copper industry, built in the Arabah at a time close to the Exodus, and the numerous objects found in the excavations contribute materially to understanding of the cultural and social relations between the tribes of Israel at the time of Moses and the Midianites and Kenites, through the Midianite priest Jethro, father-in-law and adviser to Moses.

The mines of Timna were not operated after the 12th century B.C.E., except during the second to fourth centuries C.E., apparently by soldiers of the Third Roman Legion (of Cyrenaica). At this time copper ore was transported from

Timna to the large copper furnace at Be'er Orah (Ar. Bīr Hindis), south of Timna, the site of which was excavated in 1969.

TULAYLAT AL-GHASSUL. A few small mounds which are located about 1¦ mi. (2 km.) northeast of the Dead Sea. Excavations were carried out in 1929–38, 1960, and 1967–68, and it was ascertained that the whole range of occupation appeared to lie within the Chalcolithic period (2nd half of the 4th millennium B.C.E.), and its economy was based on agriculture. Of special interest are the local geometric paintings in black, white, red and brown, and the pottery. The Ghassulian Culture is named after it.

ARCHAEOLOGISTS

AHARONI, YOHANAN (1919–), Israel archaeologist.
Aharoni conducted an archaeological survey in Upper
Galilee, excavated at Kadesh, Tell Ḥarasim, Ramat Raḥel,
and Tell Arad. He participated in the exploration of the
Judean Desert Caves, investigated the temple at Lachish,
and commenced (1969) the excavation of the biblical
Beersheba.

ALBRIGHT, WILLIAM FOXWELL (1891–1971), U.S.
biblical archaeologist and Semitic scholar. His excavations in Ereẓ Israel include Tell al-Fūl, Beth-El, Petra,
and Tell Beit Mirsim. He also excavated in Moab
(Transjordan) and Arabia.

AMIRAN, RUTH (1914–), Israel archaeologist. She
was a staff member of the Hazor expedition, and excavated
at Tell Arad, Tell Nagila, and Jerusalem.

AVIGAD, NAHMAN (1905–), Israel archaeologist.
He excavated at Bet Alfa, Ḥammat Gader, tombs near
Jerusalem, Bet She'arim, and in the Old City of Jerusalem.
He participated in the survey of Masada, and excavations
at the Judean Desert Caves, Samaria, Afulah, Tell
Kudadi, Tell Garisha.

AVI-YONAH, MICHAEL (1904–), Israel archaeologist.
He excavated at Ḥusifa, Beth-Shean, Nahariyyah,
Bet Yeraḥ, Caesarea, and other sites. He was also a mem-
ber of the Masada survey.

BADE, WILLIAM FREDERIC (1871–1936), U.S.
biblical archaeologist. He excavated at Tell al-Nasbeh.

BAR-ADON, PINḤAS (1907–), Israel archaeologist.
He excavated at Bet Yeraḥ, Kevutzat Kinneret, and
participated in the survey of the Judean Desert Caves.

BIRAN, AVRAHAM (1909–). Israel archaeologist. He excavated at Tell Dan, and participated in the excavations at Marwa (Transjordan) and Ein-Gev.

BLISS, FREDERICK JONES (1859–1937), British archaeologist. He excavated at Tell al-Hasi, Jerusalem, and at various mounds in the Shephelah.

CLERMONT-GANNEAU, CHARLES (1846–1923), French orientalist. He discovered the Moabite Stone, an inscription from Herod's Temple, and identified Gezer.

CONDER, CLAUDE REGNIER (1848–1910), British army officer. He discovered Kadesh, and began a survey of Transjordan.

CROWFOOT, JOHN WINTER (1873–1959), British orientalist. He excavated in Jerusalem, Gerasa in Transjordan, and at Samaria where his wife Grace Mary Crowfoot (1878–1958) also participated.

DEVER, WILLIAM GWINN (1933–), U.S. archaeologist. He excavated with others at Gezer from 1964, at Jabal qa'aqir, west of Hebron, and at Shechem.

DOTHAN, MOSHE (1919–), Israel archaeologist. He excavated at Nahariyyah, Tell Mor, Afulah, Hammath Tiberias, and Ashdod.

GARSTANG, JOHN (1876–1956). British archaeologist. He excavated at Ashkelon, Jericho, Dor, and identified Hazor.

GLUECK, NELSON (1900–1971), U.S. archaeologist. He excavated at Gerasa and Jebel el-Tannur in Transjordan, Tell-el-Kheleifeh near Akaba, and surveyed ancient sites in the Negev.

GUY, PHILIP LANGSTAFFE ORD (1885–1952), British archaeologist. He directed excavations at Megiddo, Bet Yerah, Jaffa, and Ayyelet ha-Shaḥar.

KAPLAN, YAACOV (1908), Israel archaeologist. He excavated at Yavneh and Jaffa.

KENYON, KATHLEEN MARY (1906–), British archaeologist. She excavated at Samaria, Jericho, and Jerusalem.

APP, PAUL (1930–1970), U.S. archaeologist. He   227

directed excavations at Taanach (1963). Tell al-Fūl (1964), and Iraq al-Amir (1961–62).

MACALISTER, ROBERT ALEXANDER STEWART (1870–1951), Irish archaeologist. He participated in the excavation of mounds in the Shephelah, and directed the excavation of Gezer and Jerusalem.

MARQUET-KRAUSE, JUDITH (1907–1936), Israel archaeologist. She excavated at Ai.

MAYER, LEO ARY (1895–1959), Israel orientalist. Mayer participated in the excavations of the Third Wall in Jerusalem, the synagogue at Eshtemoa, and Khirbat Susiyye.

MAZAR, BENJAMIN (1906–), Israel archaeologist and historian. He directed excavations at Ramat Raḥel, Bet She'arim, Tell Qasila, En-Gedi, and Jerusalem.

NEGEV, AVRAHAM (1923–), Israel archaeologist. He excavated at Avedat, Kurnub, Beth-Shean, and Caesarea.

PALMER, EDWARD HENRY (1840–1882), English orientalist. Palmer traveled in Sinai and the deserts of Edom and Moab, and described the discovery of Kurnub.

PERROT, JEAN (1920–), French prehistorian. He excavated at Tell Abu Matar (Beersheba), Einan, Neve Ur, Munḥata and Azor, and participated in the excavations at Tell al-Fari'a, Hazor, and Khirbat Minim.

PETRIE, SIR WILLIAM MATTHEW FLINDERS (1853–1942), British Egyptologist. He excavated in southern Palestine at Tell Jamma, Tell Sharuhen, and Tell al-'Ajjūl.

ROBINSON, EDWARD (1794–1863), U.S. orientalist. Robinson identified hundreds of forgotten biblical locations in Erez Israel, discovered the remains of the Third Wall in Jerusalem, discovered five ruined cities in the Negev, and identified Masada.

SAULCY, LOUIS FÉLICIEN DE JOSEPH CAIGNART (1807–1880), French numismatist, orientalist, and archaeologist. He cleared the Tombs of the Kings in Jerusalem.

SCHUMACHER, GOTTLIEB (1857–1924), architect, cartographer, and archaeologist. He was born in the U.S. Schumacher surveyed the Hauran, northern Transjordan, and excavated at Megiddo, Baalbek and Samaria.

SELLIN, ERNST (1876–1946), German Bible scholar and archaeologist. He conducted excavations at Tell-Ta'annek, Jericho, and Shechem.

SLOUSCHZ, NAHUM (1871–1966), scholar and writer, archaeologist, historian, traveler and translator. He conducted excavations at Tiberias, cleared Absalom's Tomb in Jerusalem, and excavated in Transjordan.

STARKEY, JOHN LLEWELYN (1895–1938), British archaeologist. Starkey participated in the excavations at Tell Jamma, Tell Sharuhen, and Tell al-'Ajjūl in southern Palestine, and directed the excavation of Lachish.

SUKENIK, ELIEZER LIPA (1889–1953), Israel archaeologist. He directed excavations at Bet Alfa and Hammath-Gader, participated in the excavations of the Third Wall in Jerusalem and at Samaria, and also excavated synagogues and tombs all over the country. He was instrumental in acquiring some of the Dead Sea Scrolls (1947).

VAUX, ROLAND DE (1903–1971), biblical scholar and archaeologist. He excavated at Ma'in, Abu-Ghosh, Tell al-Faria, Qumran, Ein Fashhah, Murabba'at, and Jerusalem.

VINCENT, LOUIS HUGUES (1872–1960), French Dominican monk and archaeologist. He dug in the tunnels of the Gihon (Jerusalem), wrote on the remains of Jerusalem, and studied the antiquities of Bethlehem, Hebron and Emmaus.

VOGÜÉ, CHARLES EUGENE MELCHIOR, COMTE DE (1829–1916), French architect and archaeologist. Vogüé discovered many ruined cities in the Hauran and Northern Syria. He published sketches of the Temple enclosure including a restoration of the Second Temple.

WARREN, SIR CHARLES (1840–1927), British army officer and archaeologist. Warren made a survey of western Palestine and southern Transjordan, excavated the outer wall of the Temple enclosure, and discovered the wall of the Ophel.

WATZINGER, CARL (1877–1948), German archaeologist. He participated in excavations at Jericho and in clearing ancient synagogues in Galilee.

WEILL, RAYMOND (1874–1950), French Egyptologist and historian. He directed excavations in Egypt, the Sinai Peninsula, and the hill of Ophel in Jerusalem.

WILSON, SIR CHARLES WILLIAM (1836–1905), English army officer and topographer. He directed the survey of Jerusalem and Sinai.

WRIGHT, GEORGE ERNEST (1909–), U.S. archaeologist. He participated in the excavations of Be Shemesh and Gezer, and directed excavations at Shechem (1956–66).

YADIN, YIGAEL (1917–), Israel archaeologist an second chief of staff of the Israel Defense Forces. H excavated at Hazor, Masada, Megiddo and th Judean Desert Caves, and interpreted some of the Dea Sea Scrolls and also the Judean Desert Scrolls.

YEIVIN, SHEMUEL (1896–), Israel archaeologis He excavated at Luxor (Egypt), Beth-Shean, and Ira He participated in the excavation of Ai, and excavate at Tell Sheikh al-'Aryani.

GLOSSARY

Amora (pl. **Amoraim**), title given in the third to sixth centuries to Jewish scholars in Erez Israel and Babylonia.

Anastasi Papyrus, an Egyptian papyrus from the 2nd half of the 13th cent. B.C.E.

Arabah, rift valley between the Dead Sea and the Gulf of Elath.

Bamah, "high place", name of the legitimate altars prior to, and of the illegitimate after the establishment of a central sanctuary at (Shiloh) and the Temple of Jerusalem.

Baraita, statement of tanna (rabbinic teacher of mishnaic period) not found in Mishnah.

Bet ha-Midrash, school for higher learning; often attached to or serving as a synagogue.

Bimah, platform in the synagogue on which stands the desk from which the Torah is read.

Devir, Holy of Holies.

Essenes, a religious communalistic Jewish sect or brotherhood in the latter part of the Second Temple period.

Etrog, citron; one of the "four species" used on Sukkot.

Habiru, an element of society in the Fertile Crescent during the greater part of the second millennium B.C.E.

Hakham, sage.

Hasmoneans (= Maccabees), name of priestly family and dynasty in the Second Temple period (2nd–first centuries B.C.E.)

Heikhal, Shrine.

Hospitaler Order, also known as Knights of St. John, an order of knights bound by religious vows founded at Jerusalem c. 1070 to help Christian pilgrims to the Holy Land.

Hyksos, an Asiatic dynasty who exercised political control over Egypt between approximately 1655 and 1570 B.C.E.

Lulav, palm branch; one of the "four species" used on Sukkot.

Madaba Map, a 6th cent. mosaic map of the biblical Holy Land and neighboring regions found at Madaba in Transjordan.

Mari, one of the principal centers of Mesopotamia during the 231 third and early second millennia B.C.E. The archaeological and epigraphical discoveries are *inter alia* important for Bible research and formative stages of Israelite history.

Masorete, scholar who deals with the body of traditions regarding the correct spelling, writing and reading of the Hebrew Bible.

Menorah, candelabrum; seven-branched oil lamp used in the Tabernacle and Temple.

Nabateans, a Semitic people who established a kingdom in the ancient territory of Edom and Transjordan between 4th cent. B.C.E. and the 1st cent. C.E.

Naḥal, dry stream.

Negev, the southern, mostly arid, area of Israel.

Nessana Papyri, papyri discovered in 1936 at Nessana (Nizzanah) a ruined town in the Negev.

Nuzi, ancient city in N.E. Iraq, near modern city of Kirkuk. The many tablets found there shed light on the lives and customs of the Hurrians, and are of importance for biblical studies, particularly for the patriarchal period.

Ostraca, ancient inscribed potsherds.

PICA (The Palestine Jewish Colonization Association), society for Jewish settlement in Palestine, founded 1923 by Baron Edmond de Rothschild.

Sanhedrin, the assembly of ordained scholars which functioned in Palestine, both as a supreme court and as a legislature from before the destruction of the Second Temple until 425 C.E.

Shephelah, southern part of the coastal plain of Erez Israel.

Shofar, horn of the ram or any other ritually clean animal excepting the cow; blown on the High Holidays and other occasions.

Tanna (pl. **Tannaim**), rabbinic teacher of mishnaic period.

Tell, ancient mound in the Middle East composed of remains successive settlements.

Tell el-Amarna, the site of the Egyptian capital, Akhetato around the middle of the 14th cent. B.C.E. (about 190 m (340 km.) south of Cairo) where a collection of cuneiform tablets, many originating from Canaan, were found.

Ugarit, ancient city near Latakia, northern Syria, which existed from the 6th or 5th millennium to 12 cent. B.C.E. discovery had a profound effect on biblical studies in the field of religion, literature and language.

Wadi, the bed or valley of a stream in arid regions.

232 **Yaḥad** (Heb. "union" or "unity"), term used in the D

Sea Scrolls in the sense of "community" with special reference to the Qumran community.

Yarmukian Culture, a culture in the Neolithic period (New Stone Age) named after the findings near the Yarmuk River, a confluent of the Jordan river on its east side.

Zealots, group of Jewish resistance fighters in Jewish War, 66–73 C.E.

Zeno Papyri, archives of a Greek called Zeno (3rd cent. B.C.E.) who was an Egyptian government official. Discovered in 1915 in Egypt.

ABBREVIATIONS

AASOR	*Annual of the American School of Oriental Research* (1919ff.).
Abel, Géog	F.-M. Abel, *Géographie de la Palestine*, 2 vols. (1933–38).
Acts	Acts of the Apostles (New Testament).
Aharoni, Land	Y. Aharoni, *Land of the Bible* (1966).
AJA	*American Journal of Archaeology* (1885).
AJSLL	*American Journal of Semitic Languages and Literature* (1884–95 under the title *Hebraica*, since 1942 JNES).
Albright, Arch	W. F. Albright, *Archaeology of Palestine* (rev. ed., 1960).
Albright, Arch Bib	W. F. Albright, *Archaeology of Palestine and the Bible* (1935³).
Avi-Yonah, Geog	M. Avi-Yonah, *Ge'ografyah Historit shel Erez Yisrael* (1962³).
Avi-Yonah, Land	M. Avi-Yonah, *The Holy Land from the Persian to the Arab Conquest (536 B·C· to A.D. 640)* (1966)
Av. Zar.	*Avodah Zarah* (talmudic tractate).
BA	*Biblical Archaeologist* (1938ff.).
Barthélemy-Milik	D. Barthélemy and J. T. Milik, *Dead Sea Scrolls: Discoveries in the Judean Desert*, vol. 1. *Qumran Cave I* (1955).
BASOR	*Bulletin of the American School of Oriental Research*.
Ber.	*Berakhot* (talmudic tractate).
BIES	Bulletin of the Israel Exploration Society, see below BJPES.
BJPES	Bulletin of the Jewish Palestine Exploration Society—English name of the Hebrew periodical known as:
	1. *Yedi'ot ha-Ḥevrah ha-Ivrit la-Ḥakirat* 235

Ere<u>z</u> Yisrael va-Attikoteha (1933–1954);
   2. Yedi'ot ha-Ḥevrah la-Ḥakirat Ere<u>z</u> Yisrael va-Attikoteha (1954–1962);
   3. Yedi'ot ba-Ḥakirat Ere<u>z</u> Yisrael va-Attikoteha (1962ff.).

BRF	*Bulletin of the Rabinowitz Fund for the Exploration of Ancient Synagogues* (1949ff.).
Bright, Hist	J. Bright, *A History of Israel* (1959).
I (or II) Chron.	Chronicles, Books I and II (Bible).
Clermont-Ganneau, Arch	
	Ch. Clermont-Ganneau, *Archaeological Researches in Palestine,* 2 vols. (1896–99).
Dem.	*Demai* (talmudic tractate).
Deut.	Deuteronomy (Bible).
Eccles R.	*Ecclesiastes Rabbah.*
Ecclus.	Ecclesiasticus or Wisdom of Ben Sira (or Sirach; Apocrypha).
EḤA	*En<u>z</u>iklopedyah la-Ḥafirot Arkheologiyyo be-Ere<u>z</u> Yisrael,* 2 vols. (1970).
EM	*En<u>z</u>iklopedyah Mikra'it* (1950ff.).
Er.	*Eruvin* (talmudic tractate).
Ex.	Exodus (Bible).
Ezra	Ezra (Bible).
Frey, Corpus	J.-B. Frey, *Corpus Inscriptionum Iudaicarum* 2 vols. (1936–52).
Gen.	Genesis (Bible).
Goodenough, Symbols	
	E. R. Goodenough, *Jewish Symbols in tʰ Greco-Roman Period,* 13 vols. (1953–68
Ḥal.	*Ḥallah* (talmudic tractate).
IEJ	*Israel Exploration Journal* (1950ff.).
Isa.	Isaiah (Bible).
JBL	*Journal of Biblical Literature* (1881ff.).
Jer.	Jeremiah (Bible).
JNES	*Journal of Near Eastern Studies* (continu tion of AJSLL) (1942ff.).
John	Gospel according to John (New Testamen
Jos., Ant.	Josephus, *Jewish Antiquities* (Lᶜ Classics ed.).
Jos., Life	Josephus, *Life* (Loeb Classics ed.).
Jos., Wars	Josephus, *The Jewish Wars* (Loeb Class ed.).

Josh.	Joshua (Bible).
JPESJ	Jewish Palestine Exploration Society Journal—Eng. title of the Hebrew periodical *Kovez ha-Ḥevrah ha-Ivrit la-Ḥakirat Erez Yisrael va-Attikoteha*.
JPOS	*Journal of the Palestine Oriental Society* (1920–48).
JQR	*Jewish Quarterly Review* (1889ff.).
Judg.	Judges (Bible).
Kaufmann Y., Religion	
	Y. Kaufmann, *The Religion of Israel* (1960), abridged tr. of his *Toledot*.
Ket.	*Ketubbot* (talmudic tractate).
LA	Studium Biblicum Franciscanum, *Liber Annuus* (1951ff.).
Lam.	Lamentations (Bible).
Lam. R.	*Lamentations Rabbah*.
Luke	Gospel according to Luke (New Testament).
I, II, III, and IV Macc.	
	Maccabees, I, II, III (Apocrypha), IV (Pseudepigrapha).
Mark	Gospel according to Mark (New Testament).
Matt.	Gospel according to Matthew (New Testament).
Mayer, Art	L. A. Mayer, *Bibliography of Jewish Art* (1967).
Meg.	*Megillah* (talmudic tractate).
MK	*Mo'ed Katan* (talmudic tractate).
Neh.	Nehemiah (Bible).
Nid.	*Niddah* (talmudic tractate).
Num.	Numbers (Bible).
Oho.	*Oholot* (mishnaic tractate)
Onom.	Eusebius, *Onomasticon*.
PAAJR	*Proceedings of the American Academy of Jewish Research* (1930ff.).
PdRE	*Pirkei de-R. Eliezer* (Eng. tr. 1916, 1965[2]).
Pe'ah	*Pe'ah* (talmudic tractate).
PEFQS	*Palestine Exploration Fund Quarterly Statement* (1869–1937; since 1938–PEQ).
PJB	*Palaestinajahrbuch des deutschen evangelischen Institutes fuer Altertumswissenschaft*. Jerusalem (1905–1933).

Prawer, Ẓalbanim	J. Prawer, *Toledot Mamlekhet ha-Ẓalbanim be Ereẓ Israel,* 2 vols. (1963).
Press, Ereẓ	I. Press, *Ereẓ-Yisrael, Enẓiklopedyah Topographit-Historit,* 4 vols. (1951–55).
QDAP	*Quarterly of the Department of Antiquities in Palestine* (1932–).
RB	*Revue biblique* (1892ff.).
RH	*Rosh Ha-Shanah* (talmudic tractate).
RHJE	*Revue de l'histoire juive en Egypte* (1947ff.).
Roth, Art	C. Roth, *Jewish Art* (1961).
I and II Sam.	Samuel, books I and II (Bible).
Schuerer, Gesch.	E. Schuerer, *Geschichte des juedischen Volkes im Zeitalter Jesu Christi,* 3 vols. and index vol. (1901–11[4]).
Shab.	*Shabbat* (talmudic tractate).
Shev.	*Shevi'it* (talmudic tractate).
Sot.	*Sotah* (talmudic tractate).
Ta'an	*Ta'anit* (talmudic tractate).
TB	Babylonian Talmud or Talmud Bavli.
Ter.	*Terumah* (talmudic tractate).
TJ	Jerusalem Talmud or Talmud Yerushalmi
Tosef	Tosefta.
VT	*Vetus Testamentum* (1951ff.).
Yaari, Sheluḥei	A. Yaari, *Sheluḥei Ereẓ Yisrael* (1951).
YMHEY	See BJPES
Yoma	*Yoma* (talmudic tractate).
ZAW	*Zeitschrift fuer die alttestamentliche Wissenschaft und die Kunde des nachbiblischen Judentums* (1881ff.).
ZDPV	*Zeitschrift des Deutschen Palaestina-Vereins (1878–1949; from 1949–BBLA).*

BIBLIOGRAPHY

General: A. Negev, *Mavo le-Archaeologyah shel Erez Yisrael* (1967); L. Hennequin, *Dictionnaire de la Bible.* Supplement (1933), s.v. *Fouilles*; M. Burrows, *What Mean These Stones* (1941); K. Watzinger, *Denkmaeler Palaestinas,* 2 vols. (1933–35); G.A. Barrois, *Manuel d'archéologie biblique* (1939, 1953); Goodenough, *Symbols,* 13 vols. (1953–68); W. F. Albright, *Archaeology of Palestine* (1960⁴); K. Kenyon, *Archaeology in the Holy Land* (1965⁷); J.B. Pritchard (ed.), *Archaeological Discoveries in the Holy Land* (1967); G.E. Wright, *Biblical Archaeology* (1963); J. Finegan, *Light from the Ancient Past: the Archaeological Background of Judaism and Christianity* (1959); D.W. Thomas (ed.), *Archaeology and Old Testament Study* (1967); M. Avi-Yonah and S. Yeivin, *Kadmoniyyot Arzenu,* 1 (1955); B.D. Mazur, *Studies on Jewry in Greece* (1935); Mayer, *Art,* index, s.v. *Synagogues; Enziklopedyah la-Ḥafirot Arkhe'ologiyyot be-Erez Yisrael,* 2 vols. (1970).

Part 1: Arad: Abel, *Geog.* 2 (1938), 248f.; N. Glueck, *Rivers in the Desert* (1959), 50–53, 114f.; Aharoni and Amiran, in: IEJ, 14 (1964), 131–47; idem, in: *Archaeology,* 17 (1964), 43–54; Mazar, in: JNES, 24 (1965), 297–303; Aharoni, in: IEJ, 17 (1967), 233–49; idem, in: *Fourth World Congress of Jewish Studies, Papers,* 1 (1967), 11–13; idem, in: BASOR, 184 (1966), 14–16; idem, in: BA, 31 (1968), 2ff.; idem, in: D. N. Freedman and J.C. Greenfield (eds.), *New Directions in Biblical Archeology* (1969), 25–39 (incl. bibl.); Naor, in: PAAJR, 36 (1968), 95–105; idem, in: *Eretz Israel,* 9 (1969), 10–21; idem, in: *Ariel,* no. 24 (1969), 21–36.

Ashdod: Schuerer, *Gesch,* 2 (1907⁴), 96ff.; Beyer, in: ZDPV, 56 (1933), 248; Dothan, in: IEJ, 4 (1954), 229–32; 13 (1963), 340–2; 14 (1964), 79–95; 15 (1965), 258–60; Dothan and Freedman, in: *Atiqot,* 7 (Eng., 1967); Dothan, in: D. N. Freedman and J.C. Greenfeld (eds.), *New Directions in Biblical Archeology* (1969), 15–24 (incl. bibl.).

Avedat: N. Glueck, *Deities and Dolphins* (1965), index; A. Negev, *Arim ba-Midbar* (1966); idem, in: IEJ, 11 (1961), 127–38; 13 (1963), 113–24; idem, in: *Sefer Eilat* (1963), 118–48; idem, *Avedat* (Heb., 1962); idem, in: *Archaeology*, 14 (1961), 122–36; Palmer, in: PEFQS (1871), 1–80; A. Musil, *Arabia Petraea*, 2 (Ger., 1908), 106–51; Janssen et al., in: RB, 13 (1904), 404–24; 14 (1905), 74–89, 235–44; Woolley and Lawrence, in: *Palestine Exploration Fund, Annual*, 3 (1914–15), 93–107.

Beersheba: G. Dalman, *Sacred Sites and Ways* (1935), index; S. Klein (ed.,) *Sefer ha-Yishuv*, 1 (1939) s.v.; Albright, in: JPOS, 4 (1924), 152; Alt, *ibid.*, 15 (1935), 320; L. Woolley and T. E. Lawrence, *Wilderness of Zin* (1915), 45ff., 107 ff.; Perrot, in: IEJ, 5 (1955), 17, 73, 167; Contenson, *ibid.*, 6 (1956), 163, 226; Dothan, in: *Atiqot*, 2 (Eng., 1959), 1ff.; EM, 2 (1965), 6–8 (incl. bibl.); Press, Erez, 1 (1951), 62–63.

Bet Alfa: E. L. Sukenik, *Ancient Synagogue of Beth Alpha* (1932); N. Avigad, *Bikat Beit She'an* (1964), 63–70; E. R. Goodenough, Symbols, 1 (1953), 241–53; Roth, Art, 209–13.

Bet(h)-El: Y. Kaufmann, Religion, index; N. H. Tur-Sinai, *Ha-Lashon ve-ha-Sefer*, 2 (1950), 307; Alt, in: PJB, 21 (1925), 28ff.; Noth, *ibid.*, 31 (1935), 7–29; Albright, in: BASOR, 55 (1934), 23–25; 56 (1934), 2–5; 57 (1935), 27–30; 74 (1939), 15–17; U. Cassuto, *La Questione della Genesi* (1934), 284–6, 291–7; Galling, in: ZDPV, 66 (1943), 140–55; 67 (1944), 21–43; H. H. Rowley, *From Joseph to Joshua* (1950), 19, 111, 138; Kelso, in: BASOR, 137 (1955), 5–10; 151 (1958), 3–8; 164 (1961), 5–19; Bright, Hist, index; Aharoni, Land, index.

Bet(h)-Shean: A. Rowe and G. M. Fitzgerald, *Four Canaanite Temples of Beth-Shan*, 2 vols. (1930–40); *Publication of the Palestine Section of the Museum of the University of Pennsylvania*, vols. 1–4 (1930–40); A. Rowe, *Topography and History of Beth-Shan* (1930); G. M. Fitzgerald, *Beth-Shan Excavations 1921–1923* (1931); idem, *A Sixth Century Monastery at Beth-Shan* (1939); J. Braslavi (Braslavsky), *Ha-Yadata et ha-Arez*, 1 (1940); 5 (1960); 6 (1964), indexes; Israel Exploration Society, *Bikat Bei She'an* (1962); Aharoni, Land, index; Z. Vilnay, *Guide to Israel* (1966⁹), 398–406; H. Z. Hirschberg (ed.), *Naftali* (1967), 61 Albright, in: AASOR, 6 (1926), 32–38; Wright, in: AJA, 44 (1941 484–5; B. Maisler, in: BIES, 16 (1951–52), 14–19; N. Zori, in: IE 16 (1966), 123–34; idem, in: *Eretz Israel*, 8 (1967), 149–67.

Bet She'arim: B. Mazar, *Bet She'arim . . . 1936-40,* 1 (Heb., 1957²); Avigad, in: IEJ, 4 (1954), 88–107; 5 (1955), 205–39; 7 (1957), 73–92, 239–55; 9 (1959), 205–20; Mazar, *ibid.,* 10 (1960), 264; Brill, *ibid.,* 15 (1965), 261f.; Avi-Yonah, in: *Eretz Yisrael,* 8 (1967), 143–8; Frey, Corpus, 2 (1952), 177–212; M. Schwabe and B. Lifschitz, *Bet She'arim,* 2 (Heb., 1967).

Bet(h)-Shemesh: Press, Erez, 1 (1951), 104–5; EM, 2 (1965), 110–8 (includes bibliography).   Y. Aharoni, *Hitnaḥalut Shivtei Yisrael ba-Galil ha-Elyon* (1957), 52, 74–5.   Abel, Geog, 2 (1938), 282–3; Aharoni, Land, index.   EM, 1 (1965), 147; 2 (1965), 119.

Bet Yeraḥ: Maisler et al., in: IEJ, 2 (1952), 165–73, 218–29; P. Bar-Adon, in: *Eretz Israel,* 4 (1956), 50–55; Albright, in: AASOR, 6 (1926), 27ff.; idem, in: JPOS 15 (1935), 200; Sukenik, *ibid.,* 2 (1922), 101ff.; P. Delougaz and R.C. Haines, *Byzantine Church at Khirbat al-Karak* (1960).

Caesarea: S. Klein (ed.), *Sefer ha-Yishuv,* 1 (1939), s.v.; L. Haefeli, *Caesarea am Meer* (1923); Reifenberg, in: IEJ, 1 (1950), 20–32; L. Kadman, *The Coins of Caesarea Maritima* (1957); A. Frova, *Scavi di Caesarea Maritima* (1966); Avi-Yonah, in: BRF, 3 (1960), 44–48; Prawer, Ẓalbanim, index (Heb.).

Capernaum: H. Kohl and C. Watzinger, *Antike Synagogen in Galilaea* (1916), 4ff.; G. Orfali, *Capharnaum et ses ruines* (1922); Goodenough, Symbols, 1 (1953), 181–92.

En Gedi: B. Mazar et al., *En-Gedi, Ḥafirot . . .* (1963); B. Mazar, in: BIES, 30 (1966), 183ff.; idem, in: *Archaeology,* 16 (1963), 99ff.; idem, in: *Archaeology and Old Testament Study,* ed. by D. Winton Thomas (1967), 223ff.; idem, in: IEJ, 14 (1964), 121–30; 17 (1967), 133–43; Y. Aharoni, in: *Atiqot,* 5 (1961–62), En-Gedi, *ibid.,* 3 (1961), 148–62; idem, in: IEJ, 12 (1962), 186–99. B. Mazar, S. Lieberman and E. E. Urbach, in: *Tarbiz,* 40 (Oct. 1970), 18–30.

Gezer: Clermont-Ganneau, Arch, 2 (1899), 224ff.; R. A. S. Macalister, *Excavation of Gezer,* 3 vols. (1912); Abel, in: RB, 35 (1926), 513ff.; Rowe, in: PEFQS, 67 (1935), 19ff.; EM, 2 (1965), 465–71; A. Malamat (ed.), in: *Bi-Ymei Bayit Rishon* (1961), 35ff.; Yadin, *ibid.,* 66ff.; idem, in: IEJ, 8 (1958), 80ff.; W. G. Dever, in: *Jerusalem Through the Ages* (1968), 26–32); idem, in: *Qadmoniot,* 3 (1970), 57–62; idem, in: *The Biblical Archaeologist,* 30 (1967), 47–62; H. Lance, *ibid.,* 34–47; J. Ross, *ibid.,* 62–71.

Hazor: Y. Yadin et al., *Hazor*, 4 vols. (Eng., 1959–64); Y. Yadin, in: D. W. Thomas (ed.), *Archaeology and Old Testament Study* (1967), 245ff. (includes bibl.); Y. Yadin, in: *The Biblical Archaeologist*, vol. 32 no. 3, 50ff.

Hebron: O. Avisar (ed.), *Sefer Hevron* (1970); I. S. Horowitz, *Erez-Yisrael u-Shekhenoteha* (1923), 248–63; Z. Vilnay, *Mazzevot ha-Kodesh be-Erez-Yisrael* (1963), 71–98; A. M. Luncz (ed.), *Yerushalayim*, 10 (1914), 304–10; I. Kaplan, *Ir ha-Avot* (1924); J. Braslavsky, in: *Eretz Israel*, 5 (1958), 221–3; idem, in: YMHEY, 10 (1943), 66–70; idem, *Le-Heker Arzenu* (1954), index; J. Pinkerfeld, in: YMHEY, 6 (1939), 61–65; *Sefer ha-Yishuv*, 1 (1939), 40–42; 2 (1944), 6–9; N. H. Torczyner, in: E. L. Sukenik and I. Press (eds.), *Yerushalayim: . . . Le-Zekher Avraham Moshe Luncz* (1928), 109–10; Press, Erez, 2 (1948), 244–6; Prawer, Zalbanim, 2 (1963), index; B. Meisler, in: *Sefer Dinaburg* (1949), 310–25; L. H. Vincent, E. J. H. Mackay and F. M. Abel, *Hebron Le Haram el-Khalil* (1923); Abel, Geog, 2 (1938), 345–7; G. L. Strange, *Palestine under the Moslems* (1890), 309ff.

Machpelah: I. S. Horowitz, *Erez Yisrael u-Shekhenoteha* (1923), 248–63; L. H. Vincent, E. J. H. Mackay and F. M. Abel, *Hébron, Le Haran El-Khalil, Sépulture des patriarches* (1923); Braslavi, in: *Eretz Israel*, 5 (1958), 220–3; idem, in: *Beit Mikra*, 14 (1969), I, 50–56; Luria, *ibid.*, 13 (1968), iii, 10–11; M. Ha-Kohen, *Me'arat ha-Makhpelah ba-Mekorot u-va-Masorot* (1965); O. Avisar (ed.), *Sefer Hevron* (1970).

Eshtemoa: Mayer and Reifenberg, in: BJPES, 9 (1941–42), 41–44; 10 (1942–43), 10–11; idem, in: JPOS, 19 (1939), 314–26.

Bet Zur: O. R. Sellers, *Citadel of Beth Zur* (1933); Lapp, in: BASOR, 151 (1958), 16–27; Aharoni, Land, index; Avi-Yonah, Geog, index.

Jaffa: S. Tolkowsky, *Gateway of Palestine: A History of Jaffa* (1924); Brauer, in: ZAW, 48 (1930), 75; Noth, in: ZDPV, 61 (1938), 47; Ginzberg, in: AJSLL, 57 (1940), 71–74; Abel, in: JPOS, 20 (1943), 6–28; Mazar, in: *Eretz Israel*, 1 (1951), 46; 2 (1953), 46; J. Kaplan, *Ha-Arkheologyah ve-ha-Historyah shel Tel Aviv-Yafo* (1953); Yeivin, in: *Eretz Israel*, 3 (1954), 35; idem, in: AJA, 59 (1955), 163; Ben-Zvi, *Eretz-Yisrael*, index; Kaplan, in: BJES, 20 (1956), 192–4; 24 (1960), 133–5.

Jericho: E. Sellin and C. Watzinger, *Jericho* (1913); J

Garstang, *The Story of Jericho* (1948); Kelso and Baramki, in: AASOR, 19–30 (1955); Pritchard, *ibid.,* 32–33 (1958); H. H. Rowley, *From Joseph to Joshua* (1958); K. M. Kenyon et al., *Jericho,* 2 vols. (1960–65); Aharoni, Land, index; EM, 3 (1965), 839–60; Press, Erez (1952), 459–62; EHA, 1 (1970), 243, 259

Jerusalem: C. W. Wilson, *Recovery of Jerusalem* (1871); C. Warren, *Underground Jerusalem* (1876); G. Saint Clair, *The Buried City of Jerusalem* (1887); F. J. Bliss, *Excavations at Jerusalem 1894–1897* (1898); L. H. Vincent, *Jérusalem; recherches de topographie, d'archéologie et d'histoire,* 2 vols. (1912–26); Z. Vilnay, *Mazzevot Kodesh be-Erez Yisrael* (1963), index; K. M. Kenyon, *Jerusalem: Excavating 3000 Years of History* (1967), incl. bibl.; idem, *Royal Cities of the Old Testament* (1971); *Enziklopedyah la-Hafirot Arkhe'ologiyyot be-Erez Yisrael,* 1 (1970), 207–42; B. Mazar, in: *Ariel* (Autumn, 1970), 11–19 (Eng.); *Qadmoniot,* nos. 1–2 (1968); nos. 19–20 (1972); J. Simons, *Jerusalem in the Old Testament* (1952).

Judean Desert Caves: Avigad et al., in: IEJ, 11 (1961), 1ff.; 12 (1962), 176ff.; Y. Yadin, *The Finds from the Bar Kokhba Period in the Cave of Letters* (1963); Aharoni et al., in: *Atiqot,* 3 (1961), 148ff.

Lachish: H. Torczyner, et al., *Lachish,* 1 (1938); idem, *Te'udot Lakhish* (1940); F. M. Cross, Jr. and D. N. Freedman, *Early Hebrew Orthography* (1952), 51–57 (incl. bibl.); O. Tufnell et al., *Lachish,* 2 (1940); 3 (1953); 4 (1958); O. Tufnell, in: *Enziklopedyah la-Hafirot Arkhe'ologiyyot be-Erez Yisrael,* 1 (1970), 290–8; Aharoni, in: IEJ, 16 (1966), 280–1; 18 (1968), 157–69; 254–5; idem, in: BIES, 31 (1967), 80ff.; Elath, *ibid.,* 140ff.

Masada: Y. Yadin, *Masada, Herod's Fortress and the Zealot's Last Stand* (1966), incl. bibl.; Livneh, in: *Ha-Teva ve-ha-Arez,* 10 (1954), 507ff., Alon and Avi-Yeftah in: *Mi-Bifnim,* 16 (1953), 468–76; Kadman, in: IEJ, 7 (1957), 61–65; Y. Aharoni, *Mezadah* (1957); M. Livneh and Z. Meshel, *Mezadah* (1966).

Megiddo: P. L. O. Guy and M. Engberg, *Megiddo Tombs* 1938); H. May, *Material Remains of the Megiddo Cult* (1935); R. S. Lamon, *The Megiddo Water System* (1935); R. S. Lamon and M. Shipton, *Megiddo,* 1 (1939), 2 (1942); Y. Yadin, in: *Bi-Ymei Bayit Rishon,* ed. by A. Malamat (1961), 66ff.; Aharoni, Land, index; EM, s.v. (incl. bibl.).

Qumran: Barthélemy-Milik (1955–): R. de Vaux, *L'Archéologie et les manuscrits de la mer morte* (1961); J. van der Ploeg, *The Excavations at Qumran* (1958); J.T. Milik, *Ten Years of Discovery in the Wilderness of Judaea* (1959); Zeuner, in: PEFQS, 92 (1960), 27ff.; E. L. Sukenik, *Dead Sea Scrolls of the Hebrew University* (1955); D. Barthélemy et al., *Discoveries in the Judaean Desert,* 5 vols. (1955–68). A. M. Habermann, *Megillot Midbar Yehudah* (1959); J. M. Allegro, *Dead Sea Scrolls* (1956); M. Burrows, *Dead Sea Scrolls* (1956); idem, *More Light on the Dead Sea Scrolls* (1958); C. Rabin and Y. Yadin (eds.), *Aspects of the Dead Sea Scrolls* (in: *Scripta Hierosolymitana,* 4 (1958); K. G. Kuhn et al., *Konkordanz zu den Qumrantexten* (1960); R. de Vaux, *L'archéologie et les manuscrits de la Mer Morte* (1961); M. Black, *The Scrolls and Christian Origins* (1961); M. Mansoor, *Dead Sea Scrolls* (1964); G. R. Driver, *Judaean Scrolls* (1965); C. Roth, *Dead Sea Scrolls; A New Historical Approach* (1965); A. Dupont-Sommer, *The Jewish Sect of Qumran and the Essenes* (1954); C. T. Fritsch, *Qumran Community* (1956); J. Licht, *Kat Midbar Yehudah u-Khetaveha* (1957); J. P. M. van der Ploeg, *Excavations at Qumran; a survey of the Judaean Brotherhood and its ideas* (1959); H. A. Butler, *Man and Society in the Qumran Community* (1959); J. M. Allegro, *People of the Dead Sea Scrolls* (1959); K. Schubert, *Dead Sea Community; Its Origins and Teaching* (1959).

Ramat Raḥel: Y. Aharoni, *Excavations at Ramat-Rahel,* 2 vols. (1962–64); idem, in: *Eretz Israel,* 6 (1960), 56–60; idem, in: BIES, 19 (1955), 147–74; 20 (1956), 44–48; 24 (1960), 73–119; B. Maisler and M. Stekelis, in: *Mazie Jubilee Volume* (1934–35), 4–40 (Heb.).

Samaria: G. A. Reisner, et al., *Harvard Excavations at Samaria,* 2 vols. (1924); J. W. Crowfoot, et al., *Samaria-Sebaste,* 3 vols. (1942–57); R. W. Hamilton, *Guide to the Historical Site of Sebastieh* (1936); Abel, Geog, 2 (1938), 443ff.; Aharoni, Land index; Avi-Yonah, Land, index; A. Parrot, *Samaria . . .* (1958) Ackroyd, in: *Archaeology and Old Testament Study,* ed. by D. W. Thomas (1967), 343ff.

Shechem: F. M. T. Boehl, *De opgraving van Sichem* (1927) E. Sellin, in: ZDPV, 49 (1926), 229–36, 304–27; 50 (1927), 265–74 H. Steckeweh, *ibid.,* 64 (1941), 1–20; G. E. Wright, in: BASOR 144 (1956), 9–20; 148 (1957), 11–28, 161 (1961), 11–54; 167 (1962) 5–13; E. F. Campbell and J. F. Ross, in: BA, 26 (1963), 2–27; G. E

Wright, *Shechem; The Biography of a Biblical City* (1965); idem, in: D. W. Thomas (ed.), *Archaeology and Old Testament Study* (1967), 355ff.; H. Raviv, in: *Tarbiz,* 33 (1963/64), 1–7; *Enziklopedyah la-Ḥafirot Arkheologiyyot be-Erez Yisrael,* 2 (1970), 539–49.

Shiloh: Albright, in: BASOR, 9 (1923), 10–11; Kjau, in: PEFQS, 60 (1927), 202–13; 64 (1931), 71–88; Eissfeldt, in: VT *Supplement,* 4 (1957), 138ff.; Aharoni, Land, index; M. Buhl and S. Holm-Nielsen, *Shiloh: the Pre-Hellenistic Remains* (1969).

Part II: Achzib: Saarisalo, in: JPOS, 9 (1929), 38ff.; Abel, Geog, 2 (1938), 237; Prawer, Zalbanim, index; EM s.v.; Press, Erez, 1 (1946), 18; Prausnitz, in: IEJ, 15 (1965), 256–8; Saarisalo, in: JPOS, 11 (1931), 98; Elliger, in: ZDPV, 57 (1934), 121–4.

Ai: J. Marquet-Krause, *Les fouilles de 'Ay (et-Tell)* (1949); Vincent, in: RB, 46 (1937), 231ff.; Albright, in: AASOR, 4 (1924), 141–9; idem, in: BASOR 74 (1939), 15ff.; Abel, Geog, 2 (1938), 239–40; Aharoni, Land index; U. Cassuto, *Commentary on the Book of Genesis,* 2 (1964), 331–2; M. Noth, in: PJB, 31 (1935), 7–29; J. M. Grintz, in: *Sinai,* 21 (1947), 219ff.; J. A. Callaway, in: BASOR, 178 (1965), 13–40; J. A. Callaway and H. B. Nicol, *ibid.,* 183 (1966), 12–19.

Athlit: Johns, in: QDAP, 1–6 (1932–38), excavation reports; S. Runciman, *History of the Crusades* (1965²), index; Prawer, Zalbanim, index.

Azor: Aharoni, Land, index; Abel, Geog, 2 (1938), 258; Perrot, in *Atiqot,* 3 (1961), 1–83.

Dan: J. Braslavski, *Ha-Yadata et ha-Arez,* 1 (1955⁶), 176ff.; Avi-Yonah, in: BJPES, 10 (1943), 19–20; Dothan, in: *Eretz Israel,* 2 (1953), 166ff.; Aharoni, Land, index; Press, Erez, s.v.; Albright, in: AASOR, 6 (1926), 16ff.; Biran, in: IEJ 16 (1966), 144–5; 19 (1969), 121–3.

Dothan: EM, 2 (1954), 772–3; Press, Erez, s.v.; Aharoni, Land, index; Free, in: BASOR, 143 (1956), 11ff.; 152 (1958), 10ff.; 156 (1959), 22ff.; 160 (1960), 6ff.

Ezion-Geber: F. Frank, in: ZDPV, 57 (1934), 191–280, esp. 244; N. Glueck, *The Other Side of the Jordan* (1940), 89–113; idem, *Rivers in the Desert* (1959), index; idem, in: BA, 28 (1965), 70–87, incl. bibl.; B. Rothenberg, in: PEQ, 94 (1962), 5–71; 101 (1969),

57–59; idem, *Zefunot Negev* (1967), 189–213; idem, in: *Illustrated London News,* 255 (Nov. 15, 1969), 32–33; 255 (Nov. 29, 1969), 28–29.

Gibeon: B. Maisler, *Toledot Erez Yisrael* (1938), 224–5; R. Amiran, in: *Eretz Israel,* 1 (1951), 136 n. 12 (Heb.); Dalman, in: PJB, 8 (1912), 12; Albright, in: AASOR, 4 (1924), 10ff.; idem, in: BASOR, 35 (1929), 4; idem, in: JQR, 22 (1931–32), 415ff.; idem, in: JBL, 58 (1939), 179; Jirku, in: JPOS, 8 (1928), 178ff.; C. C. McCown, *Tell-en-Nasbeh* (Eng. 1947), 40ff.; S. Yeivin, in: RHJE, 1 (1947), 143ff.; J. B. Pritchard, *Gibeon* (1962); idem, in: *Enziklopedyah la-Ḥafirot Arkhe'ologiyyot be-Erez Yisrael,* 1 (1970), 107–9; Reed, in: D. W. Thomas (ed.), *Archaeology and Old Testament Study* (1967), 231ff.

Hammath: Slouschz, in: JPESJ, 1 (1921), 5–39, 49–52; W. F. Albright, in: BASOR, 19 (1925), 10; M. Dothan, in: IEJ, 12 (1962), 153–4; idem, in: *Qadmoniot,* 1 (1968), 116–23; idem, in: *Enziklopedyah la-Ḥafirot Arkhe'ologiyyot be Erez Yisrael,* 1 (1970), 196–200; A. Saarisalo, *Boundary between Issachar and Naphtali* (1927), 128 n. 1; M. Noth, *Das Buch Josua* (1938), 90–91; D. W. Thomas, in: PEFQS, 65 (1933), 205; 66 (1934), 147–8.

Herodium: Schick, in: ZDPV, 3 (1880), 88ff.; Alt, in: PJB, 24 (1928), 18; P. Benoît et al., *Les Grottes de Murabba'at* (1961), 122 no. 24; Yadin, in: IEJ, 11 (1961), 51–52; V. Corbo, in: LA, 13 (1962–63), 219–77 (It.); 17 (1967), 65–121 (It.); idem, in: *Yerushalayim le-Doroteha* (1968), 42–47 (It.).

Mampsis: C. L. Woolley and T. E. Lawrence, *The Wilderness of Zin* (1915), 121ff.; Kirk, in: PEFQS, 70 (1938), 218ff.; A. Reifenberg, *Milḥemet ha-Mizra ve-ha-Yeshimon* (1950), 62, 130; Applebaum, in: BIES, 30 (1956), 224ff.; Negev, in: IEJ, 16 (1966), 145ff.; 17 (1967), 48ff.; idem, in: *Zeitschrift fuer Kunstgeschichte und Archeologie,* 7 (1967), 67–86.

Mareshah: F. J. Bliss and R. A. S. Macalister, *Excavations in Palestine* (1902), 52ff; 204ff.; J. P. Peters and H. Thiersch, *Painted Tombs in the Necropolis of Marissa* (1905); Abel, in: RB, 34 (1925), 267–75; E. Oren, in: *Archaeology,* 18 (1965), 218–24.

Shivtah: C. L. Woolley and T. E. Lawrence, *The Wilderness of Zin* (1915), 72ff.; Baly, in: PEFQS (1935), 171ff,; Kedar, in: IEJ, 7 (1957), 178ff.

Taanach: E. Sellin, *Tell Ta'annek* (Ger., 1904); idem, *Eine Nachlese auf dem Tell Ta'annek in Palaestina* (1905); Albright, in: JPOS, 4 (1924), 140; idem, in: BASOR, 94 (1944), 12–27; idem, in: JNES, 5 (1946), 9; Mazar, in: *Sefer Klausner* (1937), 44ff.; Lapp, in: BA, 30 (1967), 1ff.; idem, in: BASOR, 173 (1964), 45–50; 185 (1967), 2–39; Aharoni, Land, index.

Tell Al-Fari'a: de Vaux, in: RB, 54 (1947), 394–433, 573ff.; 69 (1962), 212ff.; idem, in: PEFQS, 88 (1956), 125ff.; idem, in: D. W. Thomas (ed.), *Archaeology and Old Testament Study* (1967), 371ff.; idem, in: *Enziklopedyah la-Ḥafirot Arkhe'ologiyyot be-Erez Yisrael*, 2 (1970), 602–7; Jochims, in: ZDPV, 76 (1960), 73–96.

Tell Al-Fūl: Albright, in: BJPES, 1 (1925), 53; idem, in: AASOR, 4 (1924), 1–160; idem, in: BASOR, 52 (1933), 6; Sinclair, in: AASOR, 34–35 (1960), 1–52; idem, in: *Enziklopedyah la-Ḥafirot Arkhe'ologiyyot be-Erez Yisrael*, 1 (1970), 109–11; Lapp, in: BA, 28 (1965), 2–10; Aharoni, Land, index.

Tell Al Nasbeh: C. C. McCown et al., *Tell en Nasbeh*, 1 (1947); J. C. Wampler, *Tell en Nasbeh*, 2 (1947); Avigad, in: IEJ, 8 (1958), 113ff.; Albright, in: AASOR, 4 (1924), 90ff.; Abel, Geog, 2 (1938), 340ff.; Aharoni, Land, index; Diringer, in: D. W. Thomas (ed.), *Archaeology and Old Testament Study* (1967), 329ff.; EM, s.v. incl. bibl.

Tell Beit Mirsim: Albright, Arch Bib, 77ff.; Albright, Arch, index s.v. *Tell Beit Mirsim;* idem, in: AASOR, 12 (1932), 13 (1933); 17 (1938); 21–22 (1943), 155ff.; Abel, Geog, 2 (1938), 303–4; EM, 2(1965), 588–90; Galling, in: ZDPV, 70 (1954), 135–41; Aharoni, Land, index.

Timna: J. H. Breasted, *Ancient Records of Egypt*, 4 (1927), 204; F. Frank, in: ZDPV, 57 (1934), 191–280; N. Glueck, *Rivers in the Desert* (1959), 36; B. Rothenberg, in: PEQ, 94 (1962), 5–71; idem, *Zefunot Negev* (1967), index; idem, in: *Museum Haaretz. Bulletin*, 8 (1966), 86–93 (Eng. section); B. Rothenberg and A. Lupu, *ibid.*, 9 (1967), 53–70 (Eng. section); B. Rothenberg and E. Cohen, *ibid.*, 10 (1968), 25–35 (Eng. section); B. Rothenberg, *ibid.*, 11 (1969), 22–38 (Eng. section); *ibid.*, 12 (1970); PEQ, 101 (1969). 57–59; idem, in: *Illustrated London News*, 255 (Nov. 15, 1969), 32–33; 255 (Nov. 29, 1969), 28–29.

INDEX

248

249

252

253

256

259

Tyre, 92, 110, 173, 192

Ugarit(ic), 5, 32, 66, 216
Umayyad, 19, 136, 140, 141
Umm al-Qanātir, 176
United Monarchy, 47, 102, 215
University of Rome, 179
Ussishkin, D., 130
Uzziah, 10, 32, 36, 170

Vaux, R. de, 169, 216
Vespasian, 17, 34, 49, 74, 106, 112, 173
Via Maris, 92, 222
Vienna Academy, 216
Vincent, L. H., 124, 126, 130, 134, 140

Warren, Charles, 21, 122, 123, 130–1, 139, 153
Warren's shaft, 127
Watzinger, C., 81, 114
Weill, R., 124, 130, 139
W. F. Albright Institute of Archaeological Research, 134
Wilson, Charles, 122, 130, 139
"Wilson's Arch", 130–1, 142

Wolcott, S. W., 153
Wright, G. E., 66, 91

Yabniilu of Lachish, 145
Yadin, Y., 93, 144, 154, 164, 168
Yakut, 204
Yannai, Alexander, 13, 37, 54, 69, 73, 86, 108, 152, 154, 172, 184, 200
Ya'ush, 148
Yavneh-Yam, 9, 11
Yāzūr, 196, 198
Yeivin, S., 106, 222
Yeno'am, 88
YHD coins, 12

Zealots, 16, 17, 102, 150, 152, 153, 158, 160–3, 210
Zebulun, 195
Zeno, 73
Zeno papyri, 110
Zikron Ya'akov, 75
Zinabri, 68
Zoan, 100
Zoilus, 73
Zorah, 88